SAILING INTO SUNSHINE

Peter Hancock has also written:

Sailing Out of Silence: 30,000 miles in a Small Boat
(Waterline Books, 1995)

and is Associate Editor of Nigel Calder's

The Cruising Guide to the Northwest Caribbean
(International Marine Publishing, 1991).

SAILING INTO SUNSHINE

5,000 miles through the Caribbean and Gulf of Mexico

PETER HANCOCK

Drawings by David Wright

WATERLINE

First published in the UK in 1997
by Waterline Books, an imprint of Airlife Publishing Ltd

British Library Cataloguing in Publication Data
A catalogue record for this book
is available from the British Library

ISBN 1 85310 833 2

Typeset by Hewer Text Composition Services, Edinburgh
Printed in England by Livesey Ltd., Shrewsbury

Waterline Books
an imprint of Airlife Publishing Ltd
101 Longden Road, Shrewsbury SY3 9EB England

Notice to Mariners

What follows is an account of a 5000-mile journey in a sailing boat from Antigua to Guatemala by way of the USA, Mexico and Belize. The journey forms part of a longer voyage of 55,000 miles which began in 1985 and ended in 1992. Earlier parts of the voyage are described in *Sailing Out of Silence*; the book you are now looking into is therefore its sequel.

Mariners thinking of buying this book are cautioned that its contents may not be what they expect.

Initially I planned to set down information of a wholly nautical kind, focusing on the methodology of working a small boat unaided and alone. The plan failed. Most of the journey was indeed made single-handedly, but while I was setting down the ins and outs of how I got from A to B, piloted through coral, shortened sail, heaved-to and all the rest of it, certain persons began to pluck insistently at my sleeve and pull faces. I thought to get rid of them by promising to mention their names in the footnotes. This was an error. No sooner did I insert the names than their owners began to elbow aside my text and demand living room. I fought them off as best I could, but their determination and vigour were no easier to resist in manuscript than they had been in real life. They rampaged through the pages, scattering my finely worked nauticalia, and soon everything was in such a mess that I had to go back and start again. The book has therefore not come out at all as I intended, though here and there I have managed to retain some early paragraphs of exclusively maritime relevance. But only here and there. The armchair sailor may still glean a number of recondite facts about ships and the sea from these pages but not perhaps as many as he is hoping for.

Intending purchasers who are seeking the addresses of marinas and comfy digs in the area would do better to spend their money on stamps and send off for leaflets.

Peter Hancock
Southwold

Contents

Appendices

Charts

To
Karen, Sarah and Esther,
my pilots in all weathers.

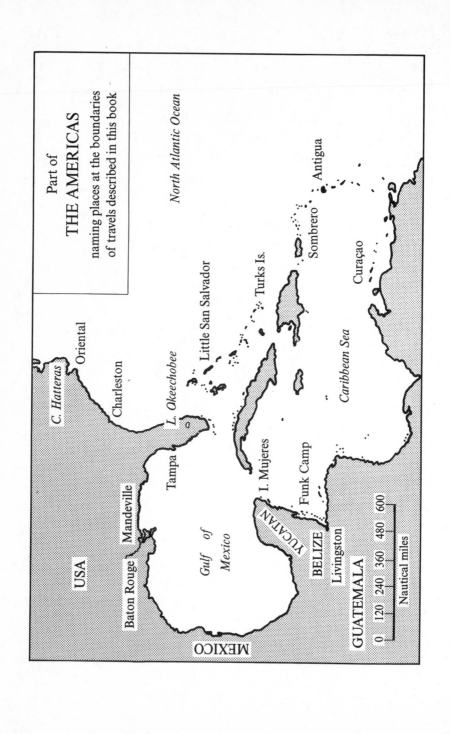

Part of
THE AMERICAS
naming places at the boundaries
of travels described in this book

North Atlantic Ocean

Sombrero   Antigua

Curaçao

Little San Salvador

Turks Is.

Caribbean Sea

Oriental

Charleston

L. Okeechobee

C. Hatteras

USA

Baton Rouge Mandeville

Tampa

Gulf of
Mexico

I. Mujeres

YUCATAN

Funk Camp

BELIZE

Livingston

GUATEMALA

MEXICO

0 120 240 360 480 600

Nautical miles

At sea there is always a catch somewhere,
as Columbus bitterly remarked on sighting America.

Peter Fleming *One's Company*

1

Cack-handed Coming In

With sunshine warming my shoulders, trade wind fanning my neck and the green hills of Antigua rising ahead, I unlatched the wind-vane self-steering gear and took hold of the tiller. At last *Kylie* was leaving the Atlantic and entering the Sea of the Caribbees. This was my first ocean-crossing in a sailing boat. To me it was an achievement, one which had been many years a-coming, and now that it had come I was feeling the need to exult. One way to exult would have been to throw my headgear high into the air but in the trade wind this was impractical because what I was wearing was a flimsy cap made in China, yours for 99 pence but no refunds, uncatchable after being hurled aloft in any wind anywhere, including Beijing.

As it was, I celebrated the event by raising high my rum toddy to a black man in a flowery shirt who was inspecting me from Barclay Point. By way of reply he gave a smile and woggled a can of cola. The smile was the shape of a nine-day moon and was just as welcome. I swallowed the toddy and pointed *Kylie*'s bows towards English Harbour.

From a mile distant the harbour entrance had looked easy but in the lee of Shirley Heights it became somewhat less so because the sheet of the foresail fell slack and for the first time since leaving the Canary Islands the mainsail, too, started running short of wind. Though her sails were becoming limp and her engine had long been useless, *Kylie* carried her way across a hundred yards of English Harbour, drawing abreast of other boats anchored in Freeman's Bay. Their nautical ensigns looked brand-new but they hung utterly lifeless. Owing to the fact that she was still moving, however, *Kylie*'s old Red Duster was still flapping.

The rum was strong, the sun was hot and by now I was tired, and so for a moment my memory slipped its cogs. Had I been at sea only three weeks or had it been centuries? The name English Harbour and the persistence of my elderly British bunting suggested that *Kylie* was

Kylie off the Yucatán coast

arriving at an outpost of our old Empire. If I had brushed this delusion from my mind as quickly as my hand had then brushed an insect from my face I would have saved myself a spot of bother later. Unluckily, at this moment a uniformed gentleman aboard one of the anchored boats consolidated my whimsy by dancing on its coachroof and yelling 'Death to the French!'

Now, I had been somewhat deaf since birth and Bonaparte had been dead for well over a century but this battle-cry was stirringly familiar, having sprung from the lips of our West Indian colonists whenever Horatio Hornblower's frigate had hove into view – an event which happened often in the novels of the late C.S. Forester – to defend them from the appalling horrors of rape, pillage and the Metric System.

'God be praised!' – or something rather like it – shrieked the officer, dashing what I might have called a pious tear from his eye if I had been as diligent a reader of Captain Marryat's sea stories in the nineteenth century as I had been of Forester's in the twentieth, 'Methought ye'd never come!'

This bloke is taking his idolatry a bit far, I thought, turning my back on his antics to splash more rum into my plastic beaker. Such carry-ons wouldn't do. By fixing my gaze on the genoa luff I tried to insinuate that an officer and gentleman ought not to be so open with his passions: one's shipboard discipline might slip. A chap's boat might end up woozing its lind or – if he was uttering his words more accurately than I was presently uttering mine – losing its wind. Besides, his cries were over-exciting the lower orders of colonial society, numbers of whom appeared to be roistering on the quayside of Nelson's Dockyard, which was now creeping into view ahead.

But my studied nonchalance only sent the officer more ecstatic. He redoubled his disgraceful clamour, and suddenly another official joined in, vibrating his half-clenched fists in the air as if showing me how to shake Napoleonic boarders out of my rigging.

It really was too much. Whether it is scripted or spontaneous, adulation makes my toes curl. Crossing the Atlantic by oneself was meant to be a private pleasure, not an excuse for public revelry. What on earth would the silly beggars do next? Mice the splainbrace? Fire a nine-gun salute?

My knuckles whitened – just like Hornblower's would have done – on the tiller. *Kylie* was keeping to the centre of the channel alright, but some authorities had let on that it was not exactly a nice place to be. Hartley Coleridge, son of the poet who wrote *The Ancient Mariner*, had written that the way into English Harbour was so narrow in 1825 that . . . *every preparation was made to moor the ship in the event of the wind baffling her.*

I twiddled the jib-sheet, scratched my left ear and wondered again about what the gentlemen in uniform might be shouting. Was it altogether adulation or were the blighters trying to baffle me? Like square-rigged ships and sealing-wax, ancient attitudes could linger on. If Antiguan habits were as odd as King George the Third's, trying to **Baffle:** (bæ, f'1) *To subject* (esp. a perjured knight) *to public disgrace or infamy* might be what the officials were up to. If that were so, they were wasting their time on me; I was way below the knightly crust. Though months of standing in dole queues had never goaded my father to speak ill of the monarchy or eat peas from the wrong side of his fork, he had not been dubbed a knight and so far neither had I. And, apart from pulling faces at other Wolf Cubs who wouldn't share their jelly babies, I had not broken any of the more solemn sorts of oaths. Admittedly, *Kylie* was a Contessa, a *foreign* countess, but her morals were traditional English: she got on with the job, kept her head up and never played fast and loose. So these colonial officials could jolly well try baffling someone else and leave me alone; I needed to get my boat safely into harbour.

I swigged rum and peered ahead again. Neither the harbour entrance nor the wind seemed to have improved themselves since Coleridge had visited. When I looked into his writings later I saw that Captain E. Barnett, compiling his *West India Pilot* in 1859, had gloomed that . . . *no confidence can be placed in the wind, which* . . . (here we went again) . . . *baffles about in all directions.* And a century afterwards, the editor of the 1969 *Pilot*, probably thinking the days of sail had gone for ever but possibly also fearing he might be carried off by the melancholia which seemed to afflict everyone who had so far tried to describe it, had made no mention of the wind at all.

Not to acknowledge even in general terms the existence of wind – let alone its local vagaries – was to take the art of understatement a bit far. If the wind departed now, I would have to anchor three cables short of the spot which I had chosen on the chart. Cutting 600 yards from a voyage which if I could reach Ordnance Bay ahead would be exactly 2738 sea-miles in length seemed a measly thing to do, though it was top of the list of seamanlike activities prescribed by Captain Barnett, who at this point in his *Pilot* was going on about gales rushing down the local valleys before advising – rather ungrammatically it seemed to me – that not one but two anchors . . . *will most probably be required to bring up with.* My boat was carrying five anchors, but I did not intend to have her brought up, with, on, or by any single one of them just then.

The wind ignored the Admiralty and lent me a hand. Abreast of Freeman Point a small breeze came eddying down the hillside to the west of Shirley Heights. As the mast canted sideways I wedged my rum toddy in the leeward corner of the cockpit and eased the sheets. Doing two knots, *Kylie* glided past Nelson's Dockyard. The officials were still calling to me from astern but the colonial red-necks were too busy throwing their women into the water to give me even a glance.

In Ordnance Bay I rounded up into the breeze and struggled to prise the swollen plug out of the navel pipe. From the shallows a black face smiled at my cack-handed impatience.

'Take it easy, man. You got all the time in the world here.'

I smiled back and relaxed, for I had seen what he had said. Unlike the receding faces of the officials, his was clearly visible and so his words were clear too. Seconds later the plug came out and I was able to let go the anchor. I backed the foresail and waited for the anchor warp to draw tight. The onlooker grinned and the sweat stopped dripping from my chin. With the bewilderment of Freeman's Bay behind me, Antigua was now seeming like a good place for my defective ears to get to, for I had read his wide West Indian lips at twenty yards.

2

Rummaged

This was my first visit to Antigua but I had been to the Caribbean before, during the post-war 1940s, aboard tankers trading to the oil terminals on the Dutch islands of Aruba and Curaçao. With their refinery chimneys rising above the horizon like ships' funnels and their silver-grey oil tanks squatting like gun turrets, the islands had bustled into my telescope with the bravura of battle-cruisers looking for a scrap.

These seaborne hints of violence had flared our young nostrils as powerfully as did the stench of crude oil, and so we had swaggered ashore wearing clothes suitable for the scuffles which took place in or near the Hotel Curaçao, where we joined the other tanker crews to booze ourselves into silliness, sentimentality or stupor.

It was 'B'-movie stuff and the scripts were corny, but we acted our parts with conviction, helped out by a residential cast who could have outplayed most of Hollywood. Wide-shouldered fixers offered to supply whatever your fancy ran to in exchange for your wrist-watch, and beachcombers with crumpled faces informed us of how their lives had gone awry. A one-eyed bartender poured pale rum into thick glasses, while a girl called Paloma slid red flowers into her hair and stroked your thigh beneath a table. When you ducked behind it later, the up-ended table proved thick enough to stop a small bullet fired by a big Venezuelan donkeyman in the belief he was shooting a gringo who had seduced his sister in Caracas. Though you managed to stagger out of the hotel unscathed, on the way back to the ship some of your mates began a friendly scrap which ended with two policemen belabouring everyone with rubber truncheons and so you finished up with a torn shirt and bruises just as you thought you might.

I would not have missed these earlier voyages to the Caribbees for anything, but though they added to my knowledge of what my parents gravely called life, they told me next to nothing about the West Indies.

Nor could they have been expected to; ships made voyages to profit

'. . . *in the belief he was shooting a gringo who had seduced his sister in Caracas.*'

their owners not to teach human and regional geography to their crews. We shuttled between the European and West Indian oil ports at a steady 11 ½ knots, chugging past the beauties of the Antilles without stopping, taking compass bearings of headlands on which we could never set foot and avoiding by miles beautiful coral-island beaches we stood no chance of enjoying unless someone lit a ciggy while he was cleaning the petroleum tanks and thereby gave us an excuse to take to the lifeboats.

Now I was in the Caribbees again and my circumstances were different. The vessel I was sitting in was not much bigger than one of those 1940 lifeboats, but it was my own. In it I could anchor off all those colourful beaches and explore them at leisure. As the man had just said, I'd now got the time.

I spread the cockpit awning and reclined beneath it, drinking tea and shuffling my thoughts. Strictly speaking, *Kylie* had not yet arrived in Antigua and would do so only when I had displayed my passport and ship's papers to the customs and immigration inspectors, who presumably had an office in English Harbour. But if the words of the man who had welcomed me to the anchorage were anything to go by, Antiguan bureaucrats wouldn't mind waiting awhile. I sipped tea and looked around.

On the chart, Antigua was the shape of a jigsaw which had lost its border pieces. English Harbour was the space left by a small but very knobbly piece which had disappeared from the jigsaw's lower right-hand edge and Ordnance Bay was the area vacated by one of the missing knobbles.

This is without exception the prettiest little harbour I ever saw, wrote Coleridge, who scatters his superlatives as generously as greengrocers sprinkle their apostrophes. In this case, however, he was probably telling the truth.

You could not expect to find elephants, giant sequoias or another Niagara Falls near English Harbour. The beauty of the place lay in the smallish scale of what you saw and the ways in which the hills, clouds and bays harmonized and echoed in their curves and forms. Nothing was so great in size or quantity as to daunt the timid, oppress the weak or offend the stinking rich. In whichever direction I looked from *Kylie*'s cockpit, the tallest hill, the largest cloud or the widest bay could be spanned by my extended hand held at arm's length. After an early squall which had speared the harbour with rain, the scud had gone and all was now open and sunny. Trade-wind clouds with skirts of white tulle glided like formation dancers across a cobalt sky. The scene was very Vera Lynn-ish: the white cliffs of Dover and English Harbour could have been painted from the same palette. Half-way through my mug of tea I noted down that Nature around English Harbour looked manicured, middle-class and well managed. The surroundings were altogether agreeable to my senses, and I re-read the comment several times, wondering whether repeating the m's made it sound false. In the end I kept the wording unaltered because it was as honest a judgement as I could make and it was intended as a compliment. I shut my notebook and rowed ashore to look for the officials.

But Customs and Immigration were in no mood to bandy compliments. Tapping his desk with a nifty ballpoint pen provided by Alpha Company Formations Limited, segments of whose embossed telephone-number kept eluding me behind his fingers, a sergeant declared that an incoming vessel from abroad was required to anchor in Freeman's Bay, not Ordnance Bay where I was. Furthermore, nobody was allowed to set foot ashore until customs had visited the vessel and granted clearance. Also, failing to call him by radio before entering harbour was bad enough, but ignoring the verbal and visual commands of his colleagues had been a whole lot worse. In fact, my actions had been criminal. So, having broken every regulation in the book, what did I have to say before he passed sentence? He laid down the ballpoint, crossed his arms and waited.

At last the whole pen was in view but as well as being upside down the phone number was now back to front and so I still could not read it.

I yo-yoed between petulance and hope. Did he expect me to stand on my head? Was he getting his own back because some of my ancestors might have transported some of his ancestors here in a slave ship? On the other hand, and more encouragingly, whatever his motives for foxing me with the ballpoint were, it was decent of him to invite me to give him a reply. When a similar imbroglio had happened in the Dardanelles, his Turkish counterpart had not let me get a word in edgeways before awarding me my punishment.

Withdrawing my cupped hand from behind my right ear, I took my gaze from his lips and looked him in the eye.

'I'm sorry, but I'm a bit deaf and so I couldn't make out what your colleagues were calling to me when I passed them. I have a walkie-talkie radio but its battery is flat and also my engine's no good. I appreciate that regulations are regulations and I'm sorry to have

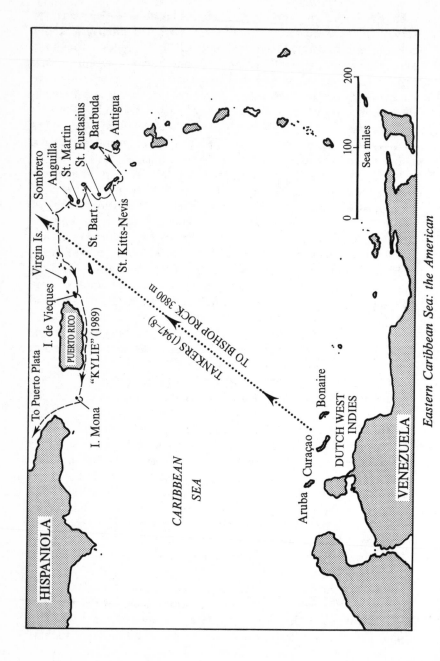

Eastern Caribbean Sea: the American

broken them but my pilot book doesn't say that Freeman's Bay is a quarantine anchorage and so I've anchored where there's enough room for my boat to swing and where there's also enough wind for her to get way on after getting under way . . .'

He was beginning to look puzzled, so I didn't press on to the end. Adding information like '. . . when I weigh the anchor which she is now brought . . . up . . . with . . . on' would've sounded so vintage Barnett that he might have thought I was taking the mickey. Even without the ending, though, my statement was the truth. The only possible untruth was the bit about the walkie-talkie battery being flat. Perhaps it was or perhaps it wasn't. I hadn't used the radio for months because I hated having to ask people to say it again when I couldn't hear whatever it was they were trying to tell me. I could have blamed static for any mis-hearings, but I would've felt uneasy about telling a lie. Also, manuals of radio procedures imply that expressions of courtesy are superfluous, which stops me apologising for my deafness, something which I always want to do even though the deafness is not my fault.

All in all, the walkie-talkie had been more of a worry than a help; I would have done better with carrier pigeons.

The officer rolled the pen between his fingers and pronounced sentence: instead of hanging her skipper from the nearest gibbet he decreed that *Kylie* herself should suffer the humiliation of being rummaged before my very eyes.

They hustled me back aboard and started work. After lugging thirty-two tins of corned beef and seven Spams from under the port-hand berth and finding nothing suspicious, the officers began ferreting into the starboard lockers. They extracted thirty-seven tins, all with their labels removed and mostly coded 'TOMSP' in black laundry-marker.

Even to me, the acronym still sounded like the name of a railway station in Siberia.

'Tomsp? What on earth dat?'

'Er . . . tomato soup.'

He held a tinful to his ear, shook it and looked sceptical. I hoped he would not order me to open it. If he did I would have to let out that between removing the labels and coding the tins my helper had got himself stoned and forgotten which tins were which. Of the seven Tomsps I had opened while crossing the Atlantic, four had turned out to be rice puddings and the others mushy peas.

Half an hour later, after having dug up a sickly green choc-bar which had gone missing during a gale in the Bay of Biscay, the officers uncricked their backs and called the rummage off. To show my gratitude I poured each of them a half-beakerful of orange juice which was only four weeks past its sell-by date. They sipped it and made faces. The liquid was at 82° Fahrenheit (28 °C) and I had no ice to put in it but we parted on better terms than those on which we had met. Then, after checking, wiping and re-stowing each of the thirty-seven Tomsps in such a way that they would not clatter around their lockers during the next leg of my travels, I slompsed into the first real sleep I had had for weeks.

3

Happy Hours with Nelson's Heroes

Do cruising boats need engines? It was a question which I could not yet answer because every time I asked it memories of Philippe Fau kept cropping up. Philippe is a very experienced, resolute, intelligent and humorous French sailor with whom I had greatly enjoyed drinking wine, but when I met him in Menorca he had seemed a bit cracked. On the strength of having listed fifty-four reasons against having an engine and only six reasons in favour of it, he was setting off on his second circumnavigation in a sloop which was the same size as *Kylie* but the blighter was doing it without an engine. Not knowing the relative weights of each of the reasons or even what the reasons were, it was impossible for someone who has read as little of Voltaire as I have to judge whether or not he was right, and what with all the wine I drank I never got around to asking him these reasons, which was what I ought to have done. Hearing his vivid description of how he had beat through a narrow reef-pass into the anchorage at Rodriguez, the

Hornblowered bits of my brain had yearned to be cruising without an engine just like he was, but other segments took the view that trying to voyage the world exclusively under sail would be as impractical as trying to sightsee the whole of London on foot without ever once using a bus or taxi. Listening to him in Menorca, it seemed to me that Philippe Fau was either a masochist or a madman, or possibly both.

Since then, though, my attitude to engines had become a bit mixed. The lessons from my Mediterranean travels and Atlantic crossing had been conflicting. On the one hand they had taught me that using only sails I could get around the Mediterranean a bit more speedily than the ancient Greeks did, and could manouevre in harbours safely without using an engine. On the other hand, my experience suggested that without an engine I could not avoid collision dangers in windless weather and that without an engine-driven alternator to charge the battery my navigation light would die long before dawn. For these reasons I therefore thought it would be daft to leave Antigua until the broken engine had been repaired. After tinkering for hours and getting nowhere, I asked Andrew Ball to have a go.

In their cutter *Balize* Andy and Val had crossed the Atlantic some months before I had and now they were working their way round the world. Though only 28 feet in length, their boat was beamy and comfortable, with a table large enough to lounge around. Andy repaired my engine in a day of hard but cheerful labour and in the evening Val fed us with one of the best curries that I had ever tasted. We drank red wine by the light of an oil lamp and swapped thoughts on where to head next.

'We're going to Saint Bart,' said Andy.

'That's not very far.'

'No, but it's where the work is. We've got to earn some lolly before shoving off westward.'

'To the Pacific?'

'Yes,' said Andy, adding, when Val looked down into her glass, 'but not this year though . . . Val needs to go back to England for a while. What about *Kylie*? Have you thought of taking her through Panama?'

'Oh yes, I've *thought* about it . . .'

'Why not?' said Andy, topping up my wine.

'Perhaps I'll do it,' I said.

As things stand in 1996, though, *Balize* has reached New Zealand but I have managed to make westing only as far as the Bay Islands of

Honduras, 600 miles short of the entrance to the Pacific. My slower progress is due partly to timidity but is also the product of circumstance. I returned from *Balize*, my mind filled with visions of cruising the South Seas, and for a few days the Admiralty's *Ocean Passages for the World* displaced Shakespeare as my book at bedtime. It would be pleasant, I thought, to wander through all those agreeably-named Pacific archipelagos. My eyes voyaged through their names on the chart; the Society Islands, the Friendly Islands . . . What could be more inviting?

But then came a letter from England which was not at all friendly. If I deprived England of my presence, it said, for the length of time I would need so as to passage to, say, the Friendly Isles, I would forgo a large slice of my income. This worked out that I would be able to afford only one bottle of rum a fortnight instead of two a week. With the possible exception of marmalade, rum is the last of life's solaces I am prepared to give up, and so I put *Ocean Passages* away, poured two fingers of Lamb's Navy Rum and went back to Shakespeare. For a while at least, I would have to stay out of the Pacific.

The sentiments in another letter were more positive. In it my daughter Sarah implied that, since Antigua was not much farther from Louisiana than the distance which the best batter in the LSU Cougars could hit a baseball, she and Joe thought it would cut down my travelling expenses if they held their wedding reception in an antebellum mansion in Baton Rouge, in a region where it would be easy to park *Kylie* in a bayou.

Baton Rouge lies a couple of hundred miles up-river of the Mississippi South-west Pass sea-buoy. Since the river could be flowing against me at up to four knots, it looked as though my engine would be needing lots of fuel.

'How does that song go?' I asked Andy. 'The one about Bobby McGhee which you sang after supper?'

'*Busted flat in Baton Rouge . . .,*' began Andy.

'Sing it again,' I said, pulling out my notebook. 'I shall need to learn the words.'

Apart from the engine, another item needing repair was an upper right pre-molar. A chunk had fallen out of it south-west of Tenerife when I had bitten too hard on my pipe stem and was now lying three miles deep on the Cape Verde Abyssal Plain or − if it had been intercepted on its way down there − was being ingested by a puzzled squid.

In search of a dentist I bussed to the city of St John's, along with an enormous policewoman and two visitors from Illinois. The police-woman's shirt was stretched so very tightly across her bosom that, while surging down the aisle as we cornered, her frontage lurched sideways like two spinnakers on the gybe. The bus thundered along a narrow road bordered by yellowy houses. Overhung by thick greenery, they resembled ripe pumpkins. The couple from Illinois glanced out of the windows hardly at all. From the way they were holding hands I assumed they were newly wedded or rather keen to be so. If they had troubled to look through the windows they would have seen many opportunities on offer because roadside churches were advertising their services at every bus stop. According to the notices, if the Illinois couple were Anglicans, Lutherans, Primitive Baptists or Ebenezer Methodists they could start into their rites at 7 a.m., but if they happened to be Roman Catholics they would have to practise restraint because the doors did not open till 10.

At All Saints village we got talking just before the bus stopped. They liked Antigua in general but were feeling sore about the behaviour of one of the St John's taxi-drivers, who had charged 25 US dollars to drive them twelve miles to Shirley Heights when the official fare was only 19.

'What was his number?' growled the policewoman, on her way to the exit door.

The woman mumbled a number I didn't catch.

'I knew it! I knew it!' roared the policewoman. 'I tell you, dat man is real bad! Him really, really ba-a-ad!' Shaking her head and chuckling, she disappeared into a thicket of pumpkins.

But the taxi-driver was not the only opportunist around. Walking down Market Street towards the dentist, I was confronted by a man whose smile was as wide as a sliced melon.

'Let us change places!' he cried. 'I smoke your pipe and you smoke my cigarette!'

Matching actions to words, he plucked my London-made briar from my mouth and placed his home-rolled cigarette between my lips. We blew smoke into each other's faces before going our separate ways, both shaking with merriment which lasted in my case till I entered the dentist's.

'I don't want another piece to fall out, so please make the repair a good one,' I said to a pink-cheeked chap who claimed between drillings to have once played cricket for Surrey.

Soon he was angling the chair upright and joking that I could now bite through however many pipe stems I fancied while crossing whatever number of oceans lay ahead. His fee of 150 dollars seemed high, but I smiled with the usable side of my mouth and paid without question, not realizing that he had fitted me with a temporary acrylic crown for which dentists in England were charging their patients damn all.

Barefaced robbery of this sort was no commoner in Antigua than in Ashby-de-la-Zouch, but here it was leavened by the cheerful roguery of the Caribbean. Though I never again met the man who cheekily plucked out my pipe I may have encountered his younger brother when a boy wearing what looked like a two-gallon tea-cosy seated himself at my café table where, between sipping tea to unfreeze my upper jaw, I was addressing picture postcards of rural Antigua. In England I would have taken him for a 14-year-old but here he was certainly older. As though we had been matey for years, he pushed aside my romantic photoviews of his homeland and commanded me to pen him a realistic letter.

His effrontery caused me to misnumber a Glaswegian postcode.

A letter? To whom, and for what reason?

It is from you, mister, to me, Henry, mister, and it is promising me a job, mister, without which written promise I, Henry, am not getting a visa to enter the UK, mister.

Dear land of hope and glory, I thought; what will I be letting myself in for if I write it?

'See here!' I said huffily. 'I'm on a boat in English Harbour. I'll have to think about what to say and how to say it. If you're serious about needing this letter, meet me at the Galley Bar at the Dockyard tomorrow morning at twelve . . . and this is the name of my boat.'

He peered at what I'd written and his lips moved, trying the word before saying it.

' "*Kill-hee*"?'

'No. "*Kai-lee*".'

He walked off, looking at the card and practising the boat name. I was not annoyed that he had not thanked me for my trouble. From what I had so far seen and heard, saying thank-yous was not an Antiguan custom. Words were uttered as gruffly to native friends as to strangers from Illinois or Southwold. I didn't take their brusqueness as being insulting. From what I could discover, 'please' and 'thank you' had not been among the words their ancestors had learned from the English colonists. The nineteenth-century pep-talk given by a West Indian governor to a group of black people whom the British had freed from slavery in New Orleans may have got the people working but it could hardly have taught them politeness:

> 'Silence there!' [had roared the Governor in a voice which must have fluttered the pages of Coleridge's notebook]. 'What for you make all dat dere noise? Me no tand dat, me can tell you . . . You ought to be ashamed; you no longer now slave . . . King George have tak you from America (you know dat dis much better place dan America) he make you free . . . What den? Me tell you all dis . . . (What for you no make quiet your picaninny, you great tall ting dere?) . . . me tell you dis . . . if you free, you no idle; you savey dat? You worky, but you worky for yourselves, and make grow nice yams and plantains . . . den your wives all fat, and your picaninny tall and smooth . . . wel den, you be glad to send dem to school, make dem read, write; savey counting, and able pray to God Almighty in good words . . .'

Not being partial to yams or plantains, back at the Dockyard I went shopping for bread, and was sold what a slim, pretty girl in a chequered apron called 'a white hero'. While wrapping the loaf and sorting out my change, she said that calling a loaf a hero was a tribute to Nelson. During his time on the West Indies station Nelson had commanded that the shore-baked loaves for his crew were to be of a specific size, shape and consistency. As a result of his forceful particularity, long before his victory off Cape Trafalgar the Antiguan bakers had anticipated his later fame by bestowing the name 'hero' on his loaf. I thought her story a nice one. As a way of keeping his fame fresh, daily bread-baking seemed a more warmly personal tribute to Nelson than that of placing his statue on top of a 170-foot column where it could be intimate only with pigeons.

But while buttering a slice of her bread aboard *Kylie*, I wondered if the story was true. To mercantile Antiguans Nelson must have seemed a twit. From English Harbour in 1784 he had set out in HMS *Boreas* to blockade their trade with the traitorous North Americans. Until the stripling Nelson came along, the trade had been doing rather well. Angered by his assault on their profits, the local merchants had come aboard the frigate, cursing him with oaths sharp enough, he wrote later, to penetrate, '. . . .even as the sea-phrase is, "through a nine-inch plank". . . .'. Remembering this incident, I couldn't see many

Antiguans calling him a hero. Given half a chance, it was likelier they would have stuffed him into the oven with the dough.

I finished off the hero for breakfast next morning, helped by a brace of Antiguan finches. By the way they made themselves at home in *Kylie*'s cabin, hopping from the companionway to the grid of the oil stove and from there to my marmalade sandwich, it seemed that the prospector for job-letters and his pipe-snatching brother might have learned their boldness from the local birds.

At half-eleven at the Galley Bar, having been served a Red Stripe beer by someone advertising Antigua Race Week on his tee shirt, I seated myself beneath a lifeless flag, wondering whether the visa-hunter would show up. A lady named Mavis padded by, sporting a white bandanna round her head, carrying a basket on her hip and offering to wash my shirts for 1.75 East Caribbean dollars a go. Converting out at 37 pence a shirt, this was cheaper than a bottle of Red Stripe and therefore rather tempting, but before I could negotiate a bagwash I was attracted by a notice which said that Happy Hour had almost come. Because this was the first time that I had seen or heard the phrase, I spluttered uncontrollably into my beer. Mavis backed away towards the Admiral's Quarters, making faces into her basket. Asked tersely by the bartender what the joke was, I choked that calling any hour a happy hour was implying that the other twenty-three were chronically sad, and was his employer someone named Barnett?

By 12.30 I had given up waiting for the visa-hunter but had discovered that the day was a Saturday and had seen that the flag above me was now lisping to a pleasant breeze. I walked out of English Harbour and into the village of Falmouth. Entering a church on the slopes above the bay, I beheld a group of children rehearsing for the Sunday service. Sobered by their voices, I sank into a pew at the rear and to the tinkle of their recitations bowed my head. After saying words of thanks for a safe Atlantic crossing, I asked that my future journeys be granted protection until at least as far as Baton Rouge. Shutting my eyelids tighter, I then said a prayer for my late wife, who had helped to plan the voyage but had not lived long enough to make it.

Outside again in the churchyard I gazed at Falmouth Bay. Waves were plucking at the beach as steadily as her fingers used to unpick a hem. Couples were swimming in the shallows, their bodies parallel and close, and three palm trees were waving their top-knots in the breeze. Two were tall and one was short . . .

31

'. . . lined up like the children after their bath, waiting for us to towel them,' I murmured.

A cloud shadow crawled across the bay and darkened the churchyard. I looked upward and shook my head.

'It was a rotten hand you dealt her,' I said.

Pip had died young but a kinsman had died younger. The Hon. James Pitt, commander of HMS *Hornet* and brother of the William who became Prime Minister, had departed this life at 20, scarcely half her age. My eye followed the chisellings on his gravestone. The reminders of mortality had been cut deeply but they did not persuade me to agree with Patrick Leigh Fermor. Contemplating the gravestone in the same year as I had been admiring Paloma's hair, he had thought the churchyard dismal and the landscape bleak. To me they both looked lovely.

I returned aboard and re-read my mail. One letter said that Jennie Cooke would be arriving on a flight from Heathrow in three weeks' time and, apart from thick-cut marmalade, a jar of Marmite and as much duty-free tobacco as Patricia could say she intended smoking in her non-existent pipe, what else did I need?

News of their coming was as refreshing as a cold shower. Andy and Val were about to leave for St Bart, and so Jennie and Patricia's company would be invigorating.

But the skipper of a boat which had glided in from Guadeloupe sucked his lips when I told him the news. Did I realise what I was letting myself in for? Piloting women through eighteenth-century graveyards might be tolerable but lodging them aboard *Kylie* would be madness. Having salvaged his own boat from a stormy divorce, he was chewing the fruits of experience. Judging from his expression they appeared to be prunes.

'Two of 'em? In your twenty-six footer? Where'll they sleep? You've only got two berths.'

I shifted uneasily on his cockpit cushion, a wodge of pneumatic leather which made rude noises when it was sat on. Perhaps he had a point. Sleeping Jennie and Patricia aboard wouldn't be the only problem, either, for *Kylie* had no flushing lavatory, only a bucket. His boat was replete with all mod cons, but powered showers and flushing loos hadn't held his marriage together, so what chance was there of my friendship with Jennie and Patricia staying intact when all I could offer them was a bucket?

Talking above intermittent honks from the cushion and phlegmmy gurgles from an engine which was running for two hours every day so as to feed a battalion of batteries, I declared that things wouldn't be as bad as he feared. Jennie and Patricia had acquaintances in St John's with vacant beds. They wouldn't want to sleep in *Kylie*'s cramped cabin when there were sprung mattresses waiting ashore. I sketched an itinerary of short-distance potters to Falmouth Harbour and Indian Creek, interspersed with car tours of the island.

'Coming from Norfolk in winter,' I argued, 'they'll be unused to the heat of the tropics. They'll not want to spend all day in a small boat, with no ice for their drinks and no room to swing their make-up bags.'

He flexed his eyebrows and snorted. 'Don't kid yourself! You never know what women will get up to from one day to the next. My ex came from Norfolk, too. She'd money in sugar beet but then she switched it into shipping. Disastrous. She didn't know a derrick from a davit.'

'They'll be happy to be just day-guests, not permanent crew.'

'You can never tell with Norfolk women,' he said. 'My ex did peculiar things anywhere she was, but in the tropics she was outrageous. In Grenada she unrove all my halyards.'

He rattled tongs among the ice-cubes. 'I can tell you another thing, too.'

'What's that?'

'They'll tangle your sheets when you tack.'

Trimming the wick of *Kylie*'s oil lamp later, I thought such disasters were unlikely. Having sailed to Barbados at 18 aboard a West-Country trader, Jennie would know how to handle *Kylie*'s lines. And Patricia's history was almost as satisfactory: I remembered hearing that she'd ridden a small horse through Glencoe. Keeping its reins from catching on the heather, I thought, would have been about the same level of difficulty as keeping *Kylie*'s lines from snarling on cockpit winches.

Pictures of Patricia whizzing side-saddle down a glen, pursued by ghillies playing bagpipes, were crossing my mind as it sank into sleep.

4

Grit and Geranium

They commanded me to take off my underpants and then they stretched me out face downwards in the shade of a tamarind tree.

'Sage or lemongrass?' asked Patricia, uncorking her bottles of oil.

'Geranium, I think,' said Jennie. 'Geranium with a light efflorage would be best. He's strained his whatsit.'

Between half-closed eyelids I watched the waves breaking on Ffryes Mill beach and *Kylie* nodding to her anchor eighty yards off. The trade wind was filtering down the lush hills of Antigua, through the ruined sugar mill, through the asterisks of the palm trees and the wispy branches of the tamarind. Seed pods were falling on to the beach but from however high they fell the pods made no dents in the sand. At first I found this only mildly surprising but soon I became annoyed by the falling pods because I could not work out why their impact did not disturb the sand. Where had their gravitational energy gone? I ought to know the answer but I did not. Was I still as ignorant as ever of the workings of the universe? It was only a small failure but it was another to add to the list. Having failed to obtain lodgings in Downing Street, having almost wrecked a troopship at Mauritius, and now discovering in middle life that I knew nothing about the fall of the tamarind seed was distinctly unsettling. Even through half-closed eyes my past looked a flop.

'Silly of you, wasn't it, leaping around the deck with those poles? At your age your body isn't up to that sort of thing.'

'Ouch!'

'Shut up and relax,' said Patricia. 'You're not skipper *here*; I'm in charge now.'

'You have been all week,' I said.

She tossed a towel over my head and elbowed my left buttock.

Her assertion was only half true, really. Patricia and Jennie had *both* been in charge . . . And it hadn't been for one week but for almost two . . .

Ffryes Mill beach

At first things had been a bit touch-and-go. It had taken two dinghy trips to ferry them and all their bags to *Kylie*. They had clambered through the lattice-work of backstays, guardrails and awning lanyards to explore the travel-stained interior.

'Lovely!' they'd laughed, squeezing their bags through the keyhole companionway. 'How convenient!' they'd cried, patting the smoky Primus. 'So sensible!' they'd said, smoothing the grubby lee-cloths.

I watched with displeasure as they stowed their bags in the forepeak. If I wasn't careful, soon they would be unzipping them and getting out their nighties. I decided to state the obvious.

'As you see,' I shrugged, 'there is no lavatory aboard; all I've got is a bucket.'

Their smiles did not slip a micron; they just held out their glasses for another lukewarm gin-and-tonic. After we had downed the third there was nothing for it but to get horizontal for the night, they in the bunks and I on the cabin sole. Before I could tilt the chimney and pinch out the flame of the oil lamp, Patricia was squeezing my hand and murmuring something into my worst ear.

'What's that you say?' I said, turning my other ear towards her.

She cleared her throat and tried a louder whisper.

'It's forgetful of me, I know, but . . .'

I did not need to ask what she meant. Even in the dim lamplight I could see that her eyes were moist.

'Where d'you keep the bucket?' she said.

Concealing the bucket beneath her bath robe, the following morning Patricia squatted on the foredeck and gazed at the mangroves.

'If he asks you,' she said, nodding towards my neighbour's boat and lifting the binoculars, 'please inform him that I am studying the egrets.'

While preparing a breakfast of brown heroes, marmalade and paw-paw, Jennie made plain that pottering round the corner to nearby beaches and sleeping on sprung mattresses were two activities which were absolutely not to be thought of. She and Patricia were not only willing to sail more extensively, they *demanded* to do so, and as often as possible. And ideas of motoring were unthinkable: the noises coming from the boat next door was *quite* enough to put one off *that* caper for life, thank you very much. And, though she sympathised with my deafness, did I *have* to have the radio going full blast? They had flown out to Antigua to get away from all that.

36

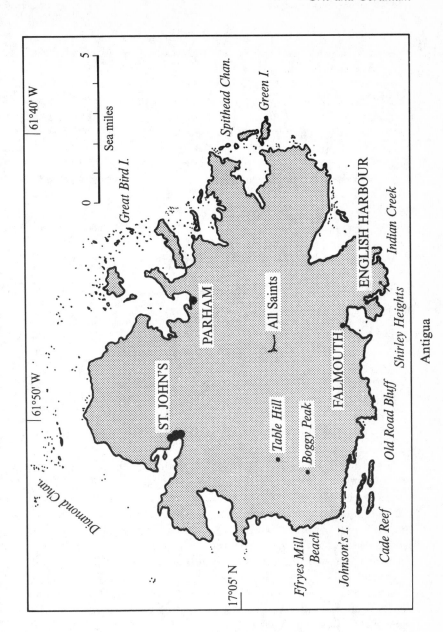

Before I could switch it off, Nicholson's station was saying that today's wind would be 15–20 knots, and wouldn't we like to shake off our cobwebs and come out for a race?

'A *race*!' they cried. 'May we go?'

'Alright, then; but not just yet . . . not straight away. Before anything can happen you'll have to learn about *Kylie* and her gear.' I thought of my neighbour's warning, looked tentatively into Patricia's eyes and took her hands in mine.

'Patricia,' I asked gently, 'do you know how to work the sheets?'

She withdrew her hands quickly, gave me a funny look and turned away.

We weighed anchor under sail. I backed the jib, the main filled and *Kylie* glided forward with Jennie at the helm.

'Coming out to play?' called Patricia as we sidled past our neighbour.

'Work to do,' he snarled, forking through a spaghetti of wires in the cockpit.

Kylie gathered more way, bearing down on boats moored at the Dockyard.

'Port a bit,' I called to Jennie from the foredeck.

'Which way's that?'

'Left,' I said. *Kylie*'s head swung to starboard. I flung out an arm.

'*Other* way!' I shouted, rushing back to the cockpit.

On the serried boats, people were lifting their beers and binoculars. Faintly from a hammock came a cheer.

'It's owing to a childhood trauma,' explained Jennie. 'There's times when I can't tell my left hand from my right . . .'

It was not a beginning filled with promise. If they made a hash of things in harbour, what would they do when it came to the race? Ten minutes of close-quarter work on the starting line might be enough to reduce us all to pop-eyed paralysis.

'Port wine is red,' I said, tying a scrap of scarlet bunting round her left wrist.

After this *aide memoire* Jennie quickly recovered her sailing skills and Patricia learned fast. In floppy hat and baggy shorts, she rattled the winches with gusto while Jennie steered with her backside and tailed the sheets. I leaned vigorously against the chart table and smoked my pipe. At the starting gun *Kylie* was fifth over the line and soon we were heading downwind for a buoy at the far end of Falmouth harbour. Ahead of us, spinnakers were blooming like petunias.

'Where's ours?' cried Patricia, panting slightly.

'Haven't got one.'

She eyed me reproachfully, as though I were an infant with faulty plumbing. 'We cannot *possibly* win like this!'

'All right!' I cried, laying aside my pipe. 'So we'll pole out two headsails instead.'

That was how I came to strain my back. I clung to the mast, groaning. Jennie leapt forward and rammed the poles in place. We hurtled downwind, rolling like a goose trying to get airborne.

'Where's the buoy?' I gasped, unable to bend and peer beneath the headsails. Jennie levered me back into the cockpit, scrambled under the feet of the genoas and perched herself on the pulpit, directing my steering by making shadowy semaphores on the sails. Patricia tended the sheets and cushioned my back while I steered lopsided zig-zags.

Back at the yacht club that evening they gave us a prize for coming fourth out of a fleet of eleven. After that, nothing would satisfy my crew but to sail round Antigua.

They pulled out my charts, including photocopied remnants of Seller's *Atlas Maritimus* of 1675.

'*The Ifland* Antigua . . .,' began Patricia, after swilling salt off her specs, '. . . *on the S.W. fide . . . from the Land lieth a Shoal off into the Sea . . . the land inward is foft and guggy . . . fo that you muft be sure not to be fparing of the Lead when coming hereabouts.*'

'"Not to be sparing of the lead",' said Jennie briskly, 'means that he was telling them to check the depth of water rather often.'

'You don't fay fo?' said Patricia archly.

'Coming as far as Green Island?' they called to our neighbour as they weighed anchor next day.

'Not likely!' he scowled, flapping a Weatherfax. 'There's a trough on the way . . .'

We beat and tacked and tacked and beat through twenty miles of water against wind and current to get to Green Island. In a 20-knot breeze *Kylie* sliced through the steeper swells, white water over the foredeck, spray rattling on the dodger and soaking our vests. At my insistence we were down to a reefed main and small genoa so that the lee rail was not submerged too often; but this rig was not good enough for Patricia.

'The other boat,' she said, wringing out her hat, 'is catching us up.' Abaft our beam a Nicholson 30 was plunging ahead on a parallel course.

'It's a bigger boat,' I explained, peering out from the shelter of the dodger, 'and bigger boats go faster.'

'Do you think,' said Patricia thoughtfully, 'that if we unlaced that sail or something . . .?'

Obediently I eased the main while Jennie shook out the reef points. Although the hat got even wetter, we beat the Nicholson to the anchorage.

'Well done!' beamed Patricia, slapping my thigh. 'Twenty miles in three and a half hours is . . .? . . . is?'

'Five point seven knots,' I said, wondering if the weals would show.

'Oh, *jolly* well done!' they cried, pummelling the unbruised parts of my back.

The following days were a daze of delights. Concerned about my injury, they insisted on doing all the donkey work. In their company I savoured small but delightful adventures which, left to myself, perhaps I would not have bothered to attempt: always weighing anchor under sail, wriggling through the reefs off Bird Island, snorkelling for two-hour stints among the coral and whooshing out to sea through the Spithead Channel under full main and number one genoa in twenty knots of wind. Even on quieter days they were bustling and adventurous, grazing their legs on rocky islets in search of flowers, rowing the dinghy into the mangroves and returning with bucketfuls of shellfish and mosquito-bitten faces.

We completed our circuit of Antigua by beating back to English Harbour, against the current for much of the way. The wind was east at more than 20 knots. Should we go inside Cade Reef, where the water was smoother, or outside where the wind might be slanting more in our favour but the seas would be rougher? I glanced at Patricia, who was humming experimentally in the cockpit.

'What were the words of that song you were singing last night?' she said. 'The rather saucy one about the elephant . . .?'

To the cadence of the trade wind in the rigging and the percussion of waves on the bow, I repeated the words; watching their smiles grow wider with each line:

I wanted to go on the stage,
And now my ambitions I've got 'em!
In pantomime I am the rage,
For I am the elephant's bottom.

'*La-dah-da-da-di-dah!*' chimed in Jennie.

'O, I say!' cried Patricia, rattling a winch. 'What a *saucy* little song! And isn't this all great *fun!*'

I had no doubts which course we must take; outside the reefs we went, bucking the steep seas, drenching ourselves all the way to the Pillars of Hercules.

'Four and a half knots over the ground,' I said, watching Jennie peg out my vest on the guardrail as we glided home past Barclay Point.

'And against the current, too. That's *quite* satisfactory, I think,' said Patricia as they laced up the sail cover.

It seemed to call for yet another lukewarm gin-and-tonic. We invited our neighbour to join us but he was still repairing his engine and so he was unable to come. Aboard his silent boat he was dismantling a water pump. He had been unable to re-charge his batteries and so his fridge now contained soggy food, the air conditioning was off, and his drinks, like ours, lacked ice.

'Haven't you missed the mod cons at all?' I asked them.

'Not a bit,' said Patricia, stowing the bucket in the locker. 'It's been the most marvellous holiday of my life.'

Singing of elephants' bottoms, she then rowed us ashore to celebrate her birthday.

It happened to be her seventy-fifth.

5

Barnacles

'What's nice about West Indian harbours,' I remarked, 'is that my comings and goings aren't at the mercy of the tides.'

It was the last hour of their final day and the cabin was in turmoil. Patricia was searching for her sandals while reciting saucier verses about the elephant's bottom, verses which she wanted to sing to whoever met her at Heathrow or – if nobody turned up – to a ghillie in Glencoe, and Jennie was packing.

'You must be very happy about that,' said Jennie, cramming damp shorts into Patricia's holdall. 'Tides can be a dreadful nuisance. There's nothing like being able to sail in and out of places whenever you please.'

Squeezed minutes later into a taxi which was soon afterwards hurtling us into the airport, she told me of the time she had nearly come to grief off Wells-next-the-Sea, in a 25-knot north-easterly which was blowing against a strong ebb, while navigating three seasick crew members across a sand bar and into a pub. Listening to the details of her nasty experience between screeches coming from an aeroplane which was landing from Toronto made me feel like starting a society to abolish the moon. Before I could draft the first clause of its constitution, however, we were at the departures gate and, with a last wave of their floppy hats, soon afterwards they had gone.

Riding back alone on a bus, lurching past a lopsided church which sported a high-sounding name but held its morning service at the low hour of 6.30, I reminded myself that tides did have some points in their favour. At Southwold the tidal range of between four and seven feet sometimes stopped *Kylie* from entering or leaving harbour for an hour or so at low water, but the rise and fall of the tide did at least let me scrape the weed from her hull and slap on a coat of anti-fouling paint without a lot of bother. All I had to do was lean her against the Walberswick quay at High Water Ordinary Springs, snooze for an hour till the tide started falling, scrub her bottom from the dinghy with my garden broom, slap on the paint at low water and drink beer at the Bell Inn until she floated again. The business took ten hours from start to finish but what with Broadside Ale and snoozes it was a pleasant doddle. Doing the same in English Harbour was unthinkable because here the tide rose only twelve inches. *Kylie*'s hull had last been cleaned in Majorca nine months previously, and though during the first month in Antigua I – and, later, Jennie – had plunged overside every few days in a mask and snorkel to scrub it, in recent weeks I had been resting my strained whatsit and, according to Jennie, her bottom – by which she meant the boat's – had sprouted weed which was as thick as winter wheat is in late April.

Before leaving, Jennie had prophesied that if I did not get rid of the weed or at least stop it growing, soon *Kylie* would be dragging a botanical garden in her wake.

When my whatsit had recuperated I jumped overboard and saw that she had been right. The hull was wearing a green skirt with fronds four inches long. What I needed to keep the growth down, I observed to my neighbour, was a residential manatee, a sort of marinised cow.

My neighbour, who six months after his divorce was suffering withdrawal symptoms, also required the services of a female companion. Before setting out for an assignation with a non-smoking Sagittarian spinster who had replied to his lonelyheart ad from Florida, he stroked his eyebrows and informed me that I would have to have *Kylie* lifted out of the water or else fully careen her. I told him that I did not wish to do either thing. A lift-out would cost more than I could afford and, though Nelson would not have batted an eyelid about lugging the guns and other movables out of his frigate before hauling it down onto its beam ends at the careenage, for me a full-blown careening was out. Whereas Nelson would have had hundreds of stalwart men on capstans performing the operation, I had available only my small self with a tender whatsit, plus a winch with a loose tooth.

Instead, early one fine morning I motored a quarter of a mile to Freeman's Bay. After steering the boat on to a bank of white sand I laid out an anchor from the bow and another from the starboard quarter. Then I lifted two of my five-gallon water breakers into the cockpit, hung them on the end of the main boom and swung out the boom to starboard. The weight of a hundred pounds of water ten feet from the centreline canted the mast ten degrees. By laying out a third anchor and running its warp through a block at the masthead, I was able to drag *Kylie* farther into the shallows and heave the mast down until the sea was lapping the cockpit coaming on one side and the other side was bared to well below the turn of the bilge. Two hours of scraping and brushing got rid of all the weed but did not deplete a colony of goose barnacles.

With the exceptions of cockroaches and maggots, goose barnacles are the most repulsive-looking of creatures. According to the scientist T.H. Huxley, a barnacle is a crustacean . . . *fixed by its head and kicking its food into its mouth with its legs,* which reads like a description of a starving escapologist who has forgotten how to get out of his chains. When I put down the scraper and peered at them, however, I saw that *Kylie*'s barnacles were not kicking. In fact, they did not look like living creatures at all. Brown, soggy, crenellated and bent, they resembled those awful cigarillos which Mexican bandits hang from their lips when they are about to ravish the rancher's daughter while he is elsewhere busting his broncos. Armed with righteous wrath, derring-do, and a hammer from Woolworth's, I bashed their heads in and consigned them to the deep.

When the hull had dried I painted most of the starboard side with red anti-fouling. The sea level fell a couple of inches while I was at it, so that with *Kylie* lying over at an angle of 45 degrees another six inches of hull became bare. All in all I managed to paint almost three feet of her bodywork measured downwards from the waterline. The remaining fifteen inches were unpaintable because they stayed under water but even without the assistance of a grazing manatee I thought that my scrubbings could keep this area free of weeds until I reached the Mississippi and had a proper haul-out. Before twelve o'clock I had re-painted the boot-topping above her waterline and an hour after noon I kedged her into deeper water and re-anchored. The next day I did the same to the other side of the hull and was so bucked by my progress that I began planning the next leg of *Kylie*'s travels.

In the six months still to go before the wedding in Baton Rouge, *Kylie* could well sail 6000 miles: more than enough to carry her south-west to Panama or north-west to the Bahamas before heading for Mississippi. Blowing as they did from between north-east and east-south-east, the trade winds would be not be unhelpful whichever destination I chose. After a think about the pros and cons I stowed Panama charts away but I kept open the charts of the Bahamas. What tipped the balance in favour of heading for the Bahamas and Florida was my fear of being caught in a hurricane while far out in the

Caribbean or the Gulf of Mexico, but also I was curious about the state of the United States. I had last visited that country forty years previously, when the people had been driving cars which were longer than brewers' drays, gasoline had been ten cents a gallon and dollars had been four to the pound. My future son-in-law had told me that things had changed a lot since then, but I wanted to see whether the people had changed too.

Personally, I felt like leaving for the Bahamas straight away but *Kylie* herself was not ready. I spent two hours just checking her standing rigging. Climbing to the masthead with a magnifying glass attached to my wrist by a piece of string, I made a round turn on the mast with the lanyard of the safety harness before clipping it back to its D-ring. Thus secured, thirty-four feet above sea level I looked around. At eight in the morning I was not the only person who was doing jobs. In the bows of *Vår Flicka II*, a handsome cutter in which Sherman and Marilyn Fairbank were voyaging back to the USA from Brazil, Marilyn was rubbing down the varnished capping with a fresh sheet of the 400-grit sandpaper she had used on the previous day to abrade the varnish on the wheel, the cockpit fittings and the skylight. Twenty yards to starboard, Bill Fowler, whom I had only recently met in Antigua although for years we had both been living in Lowestoft, was checking the foresail hanks on his ketch *Xicale*, while his wife Patricia, hidden by a hat which was wider than my Patricia's but was not so floppy, was sitting in the dinghy with her shopping bag, waiting to be ferried ashore.

Sure that there were no cracks in the upper swages and that the halyard sheaves were free, I checked the lower swages, the toggles, the bottlescrews and the chainplates. I looked closely at the chainplate which rooted the starboard forward lower shroud. A year previously a gale in the Malta Channel had wrenched the chainplate apart, and afterwards it had been welded together by a blacksmith who had not been too steady on his feet when I had cajoled him out of his siesta in Sicily. Under the magnifying glass the weld still looked sound but it also looked ugly. Shamed by the sandpapering that was going on aboard *Vår Flicka II*, I decided that from that moment onward appearances would be everything and so the welded chainplate would have to be replaced. By this time the string attaching the magnifying glass to my wrist had become so knotted and twisted that my hand was a throbbing beetroot and I had to do some awkward left-handed knife-sawings before I could restore its circulation and row to the chandler's store.

The foreman at the Antigua Slipway Company found a lovely new chainplate among his bits-and-pieces.

'It's made of best quality 316 stainless,' said he, but he let me have it very cheaply.

His kindness encouraged me greatly. By late afternoon I had replaced the ugly chainplate, re-sewn several stitches in a seam of the mainsail – stitches which, despite the baggy-wrinkle on the shrouds, had chafed themselves adrift – greased the winches and the wind-vane steering gear, and filled the four water breakers almost to their brims. At six o'clock, having swum round the boat to admire the winks of sunshine on the hull, I rowed over to *Vär Flicka II* to drink Bloody Marys with Sherm and Marilyn.

'All set to leave, eh?' said Sherm.

'Not quite,' I said. 'I need your help.'

'Go ahead,' said Sherm, lighting his umpteenth cigarette of the day. 'What's the problem?'

'It's to do with the speech I'm going to make at the wedding,' I said. 'With Sarah being Protestant and Joe's family being Roman Catholic, I don't know what to say.'

'That's no problem,' said Sherm; 'just be ecumenical. Tell them a story about making money; making money is a universal religion. And because America is short of history, give them a bunch of history. And go for the Catholic thing too; they will appreciate that.'

'Money, history and the Church of Rome . . .' I mused. 'Any ideas?'

'He was hoping you'd ask him that, anyways,' Marilyn said happily. 'Go on, Sherm, admit it! Weren't you just hoping he'd say that to you anyways?'

'Well,' said Sherm, looking in the half-light like Orson Welles playing the Cardinal in *A Man for All Seasons* and sounding a bit like him too, 'why not tell them a story about Colonel Sanders and the Pope . . .?'

Still chuckling, at 10.30 next morning I filled the hammock beneath *Kylie*'s deckhead with fruit and vegetables, placing on top of them four heroes which were still warm from the oven. With real-life heroes being rare, you would think that loaves called heroes would cost a packet but they had not. Brown heroes were cheap but white heroes were even cheaper, which was a nice reversal of the usual colour-coded scale of Western values.

'Why don't you stay for Race Week?' called Bill Fowler as I

shortened cable. 'There'll be thousands of boats and lots of parties.'

'No, thanks,' I said. 'I need to get a move on. You know what Nelson said: "Men and ships rot in port".'

'D'you think Nelson really did say that?' said Bill, scratching his head. 'Quotations are often mis-remembered, sometimes with terrible results.'

Feeling another story was about to come out, I made a turn on a cleat, lit my pipe, and settled down to listen to Bill's.

'A friend of mine – well, an acquaintance really – was drafted into the navy in the War, and years later he takes up yachting – well, boating really – but he's been away from the sea for a long time, making pots of money – well, quite a lot, enough to buy a big powerboat anyway . . . So he goes on a cross-Channel booze-'n-cruise in it to Cherbourg . . . and it gets pitch black – well, quite dark really – and he finds himself among hundreds of ships – you know what it's like: illuminated Christmas trees moving in all directions . . . And so there's two lights coming towards him, a red and a green, . . . and he doesn't know what to do. He gets flustered and tries to recollect the rhymes about the right-of-way rules . . . You know how they go . . .?'

I removed my pipe and chanted:

> *Green to green or red to red:*
> *Perfect safety – go ahead.*

'That's the verse he was trying to remember! That's how the quotation *should* have been said! But how d'you suppose he said it?'

'I haven't a clue.'

'Go on . . . Have a guess.'

'Honestly, I haven't the slightest.'

'"*Red to red or green to green* . . .,"' said Bill, looking at me expectantly. 'Come on! You used to be a *poetry* teacher, didn't you? What rhymes with "green"? It's *easy* . . .!'

'"Tureen"?'

'Hard luck! Try again.'

'"Ultramarine"?'

'No! *No*! He mis-remembered it as:

> *Red to red or green to green:*
> *Perfect safety – go BETWEEN!*

'Crikey!'
' 'S a fact.'
'What happened to his boat?'
'Constructive total loss . . . so he went back to playing golf.'

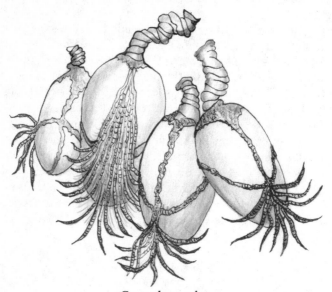

Goose barnacles

6

A Mountain Called Misery

Blowing across Barclay Point at twenty knots, the east-south-easter crackled the burgees and pennants above the Galley Bar. Under working jib and with two reefs in the main, *Kylie* beat past Nelson's Dockyard, tacked abreast of Barclay Point and then I eased her sheets to head westward for Old Road Bluff. Because of a current flowing in the same direction, there were few white florets on the wave-tops and so *Kylie* set about making her own, embroidering the blue sea as she surged along Goat Head Channel between Cade Reef and the shore. English Harbour radio was still urging its listeners to shake away their cobwebs and come out for a race. I switched it off and sank my teeth into a paw-paw.

At twenty-past-one Johnson's Island bore north. Afterwards, in the lee of Antigua the wind fell so light that at half-three I cranked the engine to make into Dickinson Bay. I anchored close inshore in three fathoms and uncorked a nice-looking wine but the first sip made me grimace. The stuff tasted almost as awful as the wine which Coleridge had been offered at Nevis, wine so leanly anorexic that he exhorted the colonists to pour it into the sea and re-stock their bins with London Particular. Fortified with brandy, though, my bottle of wine proved quite drinkable. Between downing two glassfuls of it, I reclined in the cockpit and practised 'Bobby McGhee' until a mosquito chased me into bed.

I slaughtered the mosquito at midnight while it was examining my chart, swatting it with a tea-towel overprinted with a picture of a very big spider and Little Miss Muffet. When daylight came I saw that by killing it on the chart I had bloodied about four square miles of sea off the southern coast of Barbuda. The red mess was a horrendous omen, for until the mosquito had drunk it the blood had been mine. When it darkened on the chart, my blood speckle would look no different from all the other speckles around Barbuda, speckles which mark reefs on which more than 200 ships had perished by impaling themselves on

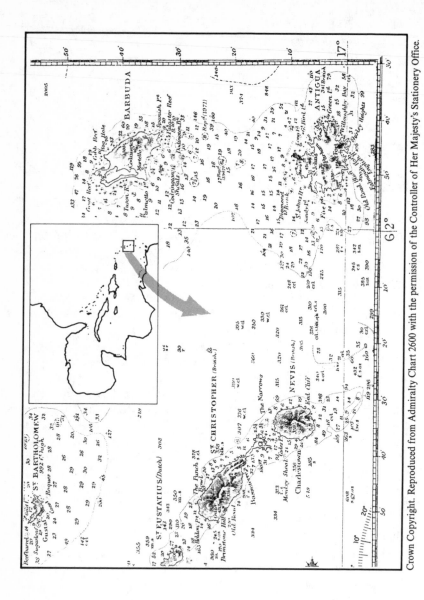

coral or, if the seas had been heavy and their scantlings had been light, by exploding into smithereens.

Made cautious by the omen, after scudding seaward through the Diamond Bank channel I brought the wind forward of the beam, heading ten degrees eastward to offset any leeway and current but still keeping slightly a-lee of the nearest reefs. Barbuda is mostly low-lying and sandy, and with a 25-knot easterly blowing dust and spray into the air, spotting the island would not be easy. Charting the waters in 1847 and making a cracking good job of it despite being made a bit gloomy by all the submerged dangers he was finding, Captain Barnett said that the first thing a mariner can see of Barbuda if he is coming to it from the south is a Martello tower, one of the hundreds of mini-forts which England had built on the coasts of not only England but also those parts of the Empire which Bonaparte had looked like invading. From what I could work out from the chart and the *Pilot*, however, an English mariner's first glimpse of the Martello tower might also be his last. The tower lies seven miles north of the outermost shoals but I reckon that even in clear weather the structure does not stand much chance of being spotted by the average Englishman – who attains a height of five feet eight when standing upright in his socks – until his boat is among the shoals or actually upon them, in which case he is more likely to be hollering for help from the masthead than pulling his socks on in the cockpit.

Kylie bounded through the seas toward Barbuda, spray flying over the weather rail. Three hours after leaving the Diamond Bank, having run a log distance which put me two miles from the shoals and nine miles from Barbuda, I backed the jib and heaved-to. Climbing the mast to a height of fifteen feet, I then stared northward. The sun was by now only twelve degrees from its zenith – a good angle for picking a way through any coral lying ahead. To the north the sea was wearing whitecaps, but among them were no signs of shoal water. What was not so good was that the visibility was reduced by a fuzzy veil which had draped itself across the horizon where Barbuda was supposed to be lying.

Opposite: Barbuda to St Eustasius. *Mt Misery is the 4313-ft mountain on St Christopher (St Kitts). St Bart is off the chart, 24 miles NxE of St Eustasius, and St Martin lies 31 miles north. The danger to navigation apparently lying 2 miles north of Codrington Shoals is really the blood of a dead mosquito.*

I let draw the jib, set the wind vane on course and went back to my perch. Though still seeing no signs of shoal water, I spotted a whitish patch among the folds of the veil. It was the Martello tower. Bearing twenty degrees farther eastward than it should have been and also looking lots nearer, its relative position told me I was clear of the outer shoals but was too far to leeward of Coco Point, where I wanted to anchor.

Half an hour of tacking brought Coco Point closer. My pencil was nearing the blood on the chart, so I eased sheets and stared downward into the water. Two fathoms below me the sea bed comprised weed, sand and coral. It looked awful. The weeds were the colour of roadside grass which has been raddled by winter salt and the coral heads had the appearance but not the texture of weathered molehills. The sea bed was uncannily like the verge of the A12 road on which I had thumbed lifts to the sanatorium where lay a wife whose beauty at 25 was already being airbrushed by nurselings of death.

The sun cast my shadow on the water and encircled it with a bright halo, so that besides seeing omens of death on the chart and on the sea bed, now I was seeing an angel of death on the surface of the water as well. Feeling I was in the first stages of calenture and would leap over the side babbling of green fields if I stared downward much longer, I dropped the anchor on a rare patch of sand and went below for a drink. A loud scrunch boomed through the hull as I poured it. 'Oh well', I thought, 'we've run aground.'

Impalement on coral is not the best way of dying and so I pulled on the anchor warp to drag *Kylie* free. Two more scrunches, three grinding noises and a shudder ran through the hull before she came clear. After checking that no water was running into the bilge I dived overboard to look for damage. From the noise of the impacts I thought that I would find lots of gouges but all the damage I could discover was a two-inch scratch on the rudder.

Swimming away from the boat, I came across the coral rock with which *Kylie* had collided. Coloured mostly green, with sporadic fawn patches and red buttons, it looked like a mock-up of a clown. But there was nothing comical about its hardness or its bulk. A yard in diameter, its mailed head lay only four feet below the surface. A shoal of tiny blue-and-silver fishes darted from its sides, slitting the thick water like scalpels cutting jelly. Though made up of a hundred individuals, each of which must have had its own fishy quirks and hang-ups, the shoal behaved as one body, streaking from the dark caverns of the coral into the sunlight, braking to a stop and hovering between the surface and the sea bed, trembling like tinsel in a draught. The shoal's delicate structure looked very frail, but the fishes' discipline was so good that I stopped my swimming and wondered at it. I did not wonder long. Suddenly the shoal lunged towards my stomach, and to me at that moment the tinsel became a cleaver. I turned away quickly and swam back to the boat.

The depthsounder claimed that *Kylie* had four feet of water below her keel, but above some of the coral heads all she had truly got was nil. I cranked the engine and motored another half-mile away from Coco Point until I was sure there were eight feet below her keel. Now anchored too far offshore to fancy rowing there, I wished I could be an eighteenth-century Governor on a visit, for then a boat's crew would be doing the rowing, a bigwig such as Sir Bethel Codrington would be presenting me with a fat sheep and I would be sitting down to a saddle of mutton for supper.

As it was, with the sun going down fast and the beach a mile away, I opened a tin of corned beef and washed it down with more of the fortified wine.

Rain drumming on the coachroof disturbed me in the early hours, and at daylight the sky was five-eighths cloud. Rococo cloud-castles trundled up from the west, moving against the prevailing wind. Thinking that bad weather was brewing and that Barbuda might soon become a lee shore, I weighed anchor and motored towards the castles, setting the mainsail as I went. By ten o'clock the wind had risen to more than twenty-five knots but had veered no further than south-east, and the barometer had steadied on 1020 millibars. Under an ashen sky and wearing a jib and single-reefed main, *Kylie* surged south-west at six and a half knots, cleaving through patches of saffron weed that tangled the log rotator. The swells were eight feet and getting higher by the hour. Then the peak of Nevis rose above the crests. Though supposedly corrected to the 1950s, my nineteenth-century chart said that the peak is taller than Snowdon, but the 1969 *Pilot* insisted that it is three hundred feet lower.

'. . . which means,' I remarked to a passing dolphin, 'that a century of hurricanes must have blown its top off.'

Some historical high spots also seemed a bit wobbly. According to one or two academics, Nevis had been called Nevis by Columbus because the cloud-capped summit had reminded the Genoese navigator of *nieves*, which is Spanish for 'snows'.

'. . . a line of thought,' I continued to the dolphin, who had come back to admire *Kylie*'s buttocks, 'which sounds only slightly less screwy than averring that Nevis was called Nevis because Mount Misery on St Kitts-Nevis is the same height as Ben Nevis, and Columbus was therefore a Scot.'

The dolphin jack-knifed out of a breaker and snorted.

Whatever its true height or its history, from the chart Nevis seemed a better place to be anchored at than was Barbuda. Taken together with its close neighbour St Kitts, the island has fewer dangers, and the two of them offer usable anchorages whatever the wind's direction as long as the wind is not a segment of a revolving storm. However, the place-names in the *Pilot* did not look inviting. The names Mount Misery and Fort Brimstone on St Kitts had a bitterness that was only slightly sweetened by a Sugar Loaf, a Nag's Head and a Horseshoe, but two local Saint Anthonys and one each of a Saint Christopher, a Saint Thomas and a Saint George seemed like weak attempts to sanctify the horror of Mount Misery, whose pagan slab-top was brooding darkly above everything.

At two o'clock the clouds broke. Instead of looking like the North Sea in December, the water to the south dappled itself gold but to the west and north it was still a muddle of whites, greens and blues. With some parts the blue of pre-War sugar bags, others the colour of bruised cabbage and all of it strewn with broken cauliflower heads, the sea looked like a market-place before the sweepers come along. Then the scud trailed away and the wind dropped, and slowly the sea tidied itself up, and before long it was a regulation navy-blue. The wind backed a point eastward and fell to 15 knots, so I shook out the reef, handed the jib, poled out a genoa and headed for the southern tip of Nevis.

Still doing six knots and chucking spray over her bows, *Kylie* rounded Dogwood Point three hours later to anchor off Charlestown, fifty yards from *Vår Flicka II*.

A masked form glided upward from the sea-bed, trailing bubbles.

'Hey, Sherm!' I called. 'How does the punchline of that story go?'

'Which story was that?'

'The one about Colonel Sanders and the Pope. Does the Pope say "We have lost the Wonderloaf account"?'

'No, he does not say "Wonder*loaf*". The product is called Wonder*bread*.'

'I get you. So the story ends: "Now for the bad news," says the Pope, "we have lost the Wonderbread account"?'

'That is correct,' said Sherm before replacing his snorkel and gliding off to look for sunken galleons.

Murmuring 'Wanderbread, Wenderbread, Winderbread, Wonderbread . . .', I rigged the awning and made a pot of tea. Soon after I had drunk it, four visitors came aboard.

Swimming in line ahead, each with a shiny black car inner-tube round his waist and grinning widely, from a distance the four of them resembled a cartoon of the Loch Ness monster flashing its dentures. As they climbed aboard over the stern, they said their names were Alfred, Henry, Patrick and Gene. The three who looked to me about 12 years of age but who claimed to be 15-plus accepted fruit juice. Alfred, behaving older and wearing an earring, permitted himself something stronger.

'Yeah, I'll have a beer with you, man,' he said.

But when he reached for the beer can I almost dropped it.

'Your fingernails,' I shouted, 'are painted *red*!'

His friends exploded with laughter but whether the laughter was triggered by my rudeness or by something else, I could not tell. Alfred just smiled.

'Yeah,' he said, 'my girlfriend did them.'

'And the earring too?'

'Yeah, the earring too,' he said, fingering the crucifix.

'And they're the *fashion*?'

The younger boys were creasing themselves, but again Alfred just smiled.

'Yeah . . . that's what *she* say: "Dey're de *fashun*!" she say!'

I looked away from their splitting faces, toward Mount Misery. With its volcanic top flattened by cloud, it looked more than ever like a sacrificial slab.

'Earrings didn't used to be just fashion,' I said sternly. 'In olden days sailors wore earrings so as to save their body and their spirit. They believed that one of two things might happen if they faced drowning: either St Peter would reach down and pluck them from the waves by their earring, or – if he chose not to and they drowned – when people found their body the earring would pay for its burial.'

The grins had gone from the younger faces but Alfred's smile had got wider. He drained his beer and squeezed the can until it crumpled.

'What about mah fingernails?' he said, pretending to be grumpy. 'Don't you know any stories 'bout zombies with red nails?'

Watching them swim back to the shore, flipping their inner tubes and hooting in the sunset, I thought it altogether likely that Mount Misery had been given its name by a black man in a fit of dark humour.

Then Mount Misery started to darken my white life as well. The name itself was spookish enough to haunt a morgue. After looking at the name Misery on St Kitts-Nevis for only a few hours, I marvelled that Barnett had not gone into a terminal depression and shuffled off this mortal coil before he had got as far as middle age instead of attaining the rank of Admiral and keeping himself hale and hearty well into his eighties like he did do. While drafting his charts he must have been writing 'Misery' every day for months.

The mountain lingered around for days and its presence made me uneasy. The feeling was like being aware that something was hanging around in your lung and thinking that perhaps it was cancer or TB. Whatever I did in the days which followed, a corner of my eye was always seeing Mount Misery. Because the other islands have sharper peaks I did not take any bearings of the mountain, and towards the end of my zig-zag passage to Anguilla I tried not to notice it, but this was difficult because it is higher than any others. As mountains go it is middling grand, and when sunshine is painting its slopes different shades of green it looks very beautiful. But many sea-miles from St Kitts, having written pages of figures which proved the patent log was slipping three per cent and having then made a sheepshank in its line which reduced the slippage to nothing and caused me to think I had got the Caribbean current nicely sewn up, Mount Misery was still glowering at me on the horizon when I streamed the log astern.

And later, touring St Eustasius in a taxi driven by a middle-aged elf called Josser, whose history of that island uttered in a cracked falsetto was a cataract of humour which left me gasping, we stopped at a toytown fort and looming above its embrasures was the bulk of Mount Misery. Turning my back on it to enter a bar, I thought the mountain was the shape of a wheel-clamp and was just as unshiftable.

I tried to lose sight of it by dodging into the island of St Bart and afterwards trailing Val and Andy across a 15-mile channel to St Martin. Crossing the channel, I again kept my eyes busy by taking a sun-sight and working a Marcq St Hiliare. When I plotted it on the chart, the position line was less than half a mile from cross-bearings of the Barrel of Beef and The Groupers. The closeness of this result gave me pleasure. The mechanics of taking the sun-sight would also have given me pleasure if Mount Misery had not contrived to slide itself into the eyepiece of my sextant and hang there like a morbid wen. To keep in touch with life and sanity, after anchoring at St Martin I dinghied to *Balize* and supped with Val and Andy. We sang till two in the morning, finishing off with 'The Leaving of Liverpool'. I rowed back to *Kylie* with a lump in my throat.

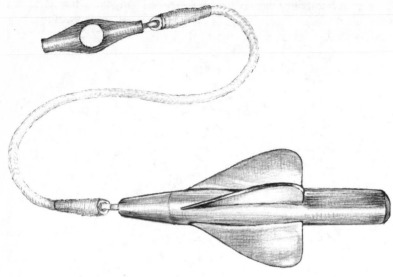

Log rotator

7

The Man in the Sulphurous Shorts

The leaving of Phillipsburg on St Martin brought more pain to my throat than thinking about the leaving of Liverpool did. Carrying a newly purchased cut-price holdall large enough to swallow a baker's dozen of heroes but also marvellously small enough after buckling a network of elasticated straps to serve as a rigger's toolbag, I went to the immigration office. Clearing customs before passing through Immigration in Phillipsburg was not needful because it is a duty-free port. Having to deal with only one lot of officials should have made the leaving of Phillipsburg easier but in reality it made it more difficult. Instead of having to jostle for power with customs like they did in other countries, here the immigration officers had all the power to themselves. Absolute power corrupts as absolutely in Phillipsburg as it does anywhere else. Here the immigration officers inflicted on the hapless traveller not only their own sectarian discourtesies, such as that of beckoning brusquely, plus those which the customs would have practised but also they practised tortures about which even the Caribs, not a race noted for the prevention of cruelty to hapless travellers, would have thought twice. If the Caribs of olden days had treated their captives in the way that modern immigration officers dealt with us visitors, the captives would have died long before they had been fat enough for the pot.

We visitors were mostly West Indians but we included a heavy sprinkling of Europeans, Americans and Asiatics. Standing alongside me was a muscular Norwegian in sulphurous yellow running-shorts. Slightly in front and to the right of me stood an Antiguan couple. The man was clutching an eight-foot oar and was chain-smoking cigarettes. Why he was carrying only one oar and not two I never found out. Because he was a chain-smoker and always needed one hand for his ciggy, it could have been that he preferred sculling his boat to rowing it.

Immigration started their tortures by tenderising us, broiling us in the hot sun for an hour past their scheduled time of opening. For some it was a time of grumbles, but I spent the time unbuckling and re-buckling the straps of my holdall. The holdall was terrifically interesting. The shorter straps were elasticated, but the longer ones were not. The shorter straps had enough power in their elastic to grip even something as small as the stem of my magnifying glass – a facility I discovered when my right index finger became entrapped between an over-stretched strap and under-buckled buckle. This was an exciting technological spin-off; now I possessed the means whereby I could bear the eyeglass to the masthead without having to tourniquet my wrist with old-fashioned string.

I sucked my sore finger. Other hi-tech scenarios dribbled into mind. If I buckled a shorter strap to a longer one and undid a draw string, the holdall became a sun canopy for the cockpit. By tightening the draw string and buckling one strap above the gooseneck on the mainboom, another through a luff cringle and a third through the upper part of the kicking-strap, perhaps I could create a rainwater-catcher underneath the boom . . .

Applications began to seem endless. Stealthily entwining a strap round the loom of the oar which the West Indian was now holding immobile to reserve his wife's place while she fetched an item of luggage from the periphery, I worked out that the energy stored by twisting all the elasticated ones very tightly about *Kylie*'s prop-shaft might even dispense with the need for an engine.

If the heights of happiness are reached by accumulating small pleasures, discovering the versatility of that holdall should have meant I was about to tread the foothills of ecstasy. However, it did not.

Balancing on her head a cardboard box big enough to hold an outsize teddy bear if she went in for that sort of pleasure but one which – taking into account her partner's addiction – probably contained thousands of cigarettes, the oarsman's wife, helpmeet, paramour or friend (which she was I didn't know, but happy is he who gets all four in one woman) was now forging through the crowd to reclaim her place. So as to make a space for the oncoming box, the oarsman raised the oar from the ground and after thrusting it forcefully sideways thumped it down on my foot.

Because the crowd's attention was elsewhere, my screech went unheeded. A window had opened, and a hand had thrust out a bundle of pink forms. Everybody except me and the burdened woman had jumped upward to grab at them and suddenly the air was filled with pink forms, most of which were wafting around above us like nervous flamingoes looking for landing spots.

According to what through gritted teeth the Norwegian said later, the person at the window then proclaimed that everyone had to present a pink form and a banknote at the office of the Federal Receiver three blocks westward and return it duly stamped to the speaker before an exit stamp could be stamped on their passports.

Roughly translated, this meant that two lots of crooked officials were going to rob us; the one at the window was arranging how they would split the loot.

What with deafness, tinnitus and attending to a busted foot, I heard nothing of this. Because everyone was still straining forward I thought that we were about to storm ahead into the office. Clutching my throbbing foot with one hand, I crouched down to slip the holdall straps onto my shoulders but by now the press of people was so great that my fingers could find only one of them. As there was little likelihood of my being able to find the other straps until the pressure eased, I slipped the one strap over my head and strove to stand upright. It was a brilliant move on my part but like almost all the other brilliant moves which I have so far made in life it was made a bit late. The person at the window had ended his proclamation before I had got myself anywhere near vertical. The crowd suddenly about-turned and galloped westward, yelling its head off.

Regrettably I was unable to go with it for the chain-smoking oarsman had knocked me flat. It was I am sure unintentional on his part but as I am not an irremovable object and the forces opposing me were irresistible the knockdown had to happen. Unintentional or not, though, I did not like it. What was surprising was that the muscular Norwegian had also been felled. One would have thought that his sulphurous shorts would have been at the forefront of the yelling horde.

It took me a while to work out why it was they were not. Dimly I perceived that he was trying to extract his left leg from one of my elasticated straps which somehow had twanged up his thigh.

Further reasons for his delay and also for the acuteness of my perceptions were that a buckle of the strap had entangled itself in his leg-hairs and, because the hairs were the same colour as the buckle, the disentangling operation was both delicate and time-consuming. I was incapable of helping the Norwegian with the unravelling because his labours were very private and he was doing them without first untwisting the other strap from around my neck.

In other words, the longer he took to avert castration, the nearer I got to being strangled. I drew his attention to this by kicking his backside.

Getting to our feet took ages. Feeling I had escaped death by what in happier moments I might have called a hair, I staggered with the Norwegian to the Federal Receiver's and back again to immigration only to find that it had closed its doors not just for lunch but for the day.

Stuffing the pink form into his bum bag and still slightly bow-legged from his ordeal, the Norwegian uttered a colloquial word for ordure and tottered off to get drunk.

All things considered, I cannot say I blamed him.

8

Boats and Coffins

Jennie's oil of geranium was soothing my neck when I at last made sail for Anguilla, two hours after Immigration had stamped my passport. In the light airs to leeward of St Martin I set both genoas, hanking them onto the twin forestays. This rig utterly spoilt the view ahead, but I was preferring it to other combinations. Crossing the Atlantic in strong east-north-east trade winds from the starboard quarter, I had set a small jib to starboard and a reefed mainsail to port. In moderate weather this rig was comfortable, rolling was minimal and the risk of dipping the poled-out jib clew in the wave-tops was low. When heavier winds came and seas built up astern, though, handing the mainsail became more difficult. If I held a downwind course while pulling down the sail, the chances of tearing it were high, and if I brought the boat's head up so as to spill wind from the sail before handing it I thereby risked a knockdown.

Except on short passages I did not use the spinnaker. The spinnaker is the bulimic in the sail family: it gulps and vomits wind compulsively. The spinnaker might boost the speed and give me a clear view ahead, but attending constantly to its needs was beyond me. However much attention I gave it, it always demanded more. It was a unstable teenager of a sail, bursting with high promise but gawkily inept; incapable, really, of looking after itself. When I went below to brew tea, the poor thing threw up. After an hour or so of tea-less labour my body was always suffering from tannin starvation and so eventually I stuffed the spinnaker into the sail bin and pretended that it had died. It hurt me to bury such a lovely sail, but if I had persisted in using it on

Opposite: St Martin to Sombrero. *The Sombrero Passage lies off the chart, to the west. Compared to heavily-hachured St Martin, Anguilla seems plain and dowdy. This is partly because a modern chart-reviser has rubbed out its elegant 19th-century linings, so now the island looks even poorer than Coleridge said it was.*

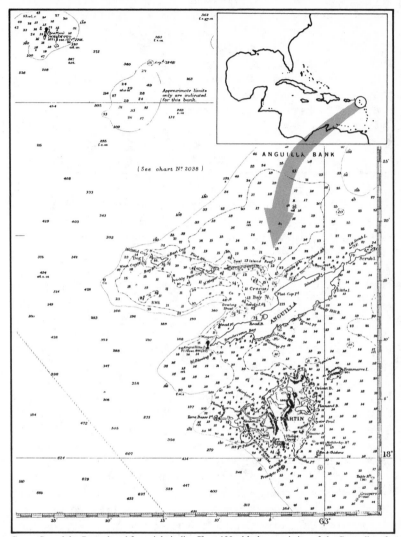

Crown Copyright. Reproduced from Admirality Chart 130 with the permission of the Controller of Her Majesty's Stationery Office.

long passages I would have gone barmy. The strange thing was, *Kylie* seemed to go almost as well without it, because, as Patricia and Jennie had seen, a couple of poled-out genoas gave her enough speed downwind to keep her level-pegging with boats wearing spinnakers, though on reaches we lost ground.

At sunset I anchored in Road Bay at Anguilla and breathed the odour of geraniums coming from my kerchief. It was a balm. Now that Mount Misery had at last buried itself below the horizon and St Martin was behind me, I was hoping no further neck-stretching incidents would happen in Anguilla for – except when I raised a gin-and-tonic to my lips without first leaning backward – the geranium oil seemed to be gluing my head onto my shoulders very well.

Unlike Antigua, the island of Anguilla really is British. Rowing ashore to wash my dirty linen, my back to the beach and my eyes on *Kylie*'s Red Ensign, I felt a glow of patriotic fervour coming on. I wondered if the islanders would share it. In the past they hadn't gone wild about British flags – or any others, for that matter.

In 1825 Coleridge had been astonished to see that Anguilla's flagstaff was not sporting a flag. Having almost completed his journey through the palm-waving islands of our West Indian empire, having seen the British flag flying over all of them, and having then landed on an isle on which no palm tree grew or English flag flew, Coleridge forsook his superlatives and felt slightly peeved. All the other British islands were flying their flags; why wasn't Anguilla?

The reason soon became plain: the islanders were stony broke. The thin soil and poor rainfall had meant that no crop of any value would grow there reliably, although the land was covered by a species of myrtle which the black slaves called maidenberry. The maidenberry looked pretty but it didn't bear pennies, and the islanders had no mineral wealth except the salt they scooped from a salt pond. By the early years of the nineteenth century most of the whites had given up the struggle to farm the land and had returned to the UK or moved on to pastures new, leaving their slaves – 2388 of them in 1825 – to scoop salt, pray to God and contemplate their maidenberries.

Life on other West Indian islands in the nineteenth century may have been hard and brutal but after trying to wrest a living from Anguilla the colonists would have thought the other islands were almost heaven. Moved to pity by the sight of a woman on Anguilla drawing water from a well using only a bucket and a frayed rope, a ship's carpenter had offered to construct a windlass. His offer came to nothing; an official certified that no timber could be found. This seems incredible. Not even a couple of lengths of four-by-four? Was the official hoarding the stuff to build himself a raft, perhaps? Given the choice of possessing ten yards of British bunting or the same length of hempen rope, the islanders would not have thought twice. Rope can draw bigger buckets than banners can. Why buy a flag for an island which has not even wood enough to build a windlass? The Honorable Benjamin Gumbs, returning officer for the island, told Coleridge that no enemy would ever bother invading Anguilla to see whether it had got a flag or not.

The grinding poverty had not made the people churlish. To Coleridge the islanders had seemed . . . *a good sort of folks, though they have been living for a long time in a curious state of suspended civilization* . . ., a comment which tells you as much about the speaker as it does about the subject.

The islanders were still suspended in limbo more than a century later. When the UK was hanging up its skylon to celebrate the Festival of Britain, Anguilla was still dangling on frayed colonial hopes, waiting for a twentieth-century equivalent of a windlass. In truth it was a forgotten island, where people raised a few livestock, collected lots of salt and built sailing ships from, presumably, imported timber.

Descendants of Benjamin Gumbs were not woken from their colonial slumber until 1969, when hundreds of British soldiers suddenly stormed up the island's twilit beaches to quell a black rebellion which a Mr Webster and another Mr Gumbs – this time named Jeremiah and lots less apathetic than Benjamin – were supposed to be fomenting. Finding the population asleep and the island's ancient Lee-Enfield rifles still locked up, the soldiers must have felt foolish, especially if they had blackened their faces. In 1982, when its own cheeks were also less dark with embarrassment, Downing Street tried to make amends by giving the Anguillans their very own Governor, complete with gold braid and a feathered helmet.

Having washed my clothes in fresh water cadged from a man rinsing glasses in Jonno's Bar, I walked into town in search of this new golden finery. I did not find any finery, nor did I see any gold. Judging from the dozens of new-looking banks in the high street, however, there must have been plenty of money around.

I returned to Jonno's thinking that although their township looked a bit dreary, after 300 years of poverty the islanders had at last struck it rich. I bought a beer and was asking Jonno why so many banks had suddenly set up shop on the island when a man wearing a shirt with only one sleeve began complaining about his lack of money. At first his voice sounded like gravel being swilled by a low-pressure hose, but when – because nobody was taking any notice – the voice raised its pressure, obscenities were soon spraying everywhere. Jonno went over to deal with him. I walked towards the beach to drink my beer and look at the sea.

The picture was one of leisured ease: gulls gliding, clouds drifting, a blue sea softly lapping the sand, and *Kylie* snoozing under her awning.

From Jonno's Bar behind me came the sound of angry voices. The contrast between the two scenes could not have been greater. Perhaps I would not have felt the contrast so strongly if I had not seen the notice. Standing half-way between Jonno's Bar and the edge of the peaceful sea, the notice could have been put there by Jeremiah Gumbs – or, indeed, by any other Anguillan who had been named after the prophet of doom.

Done in black paint, it said:

BOATS BUILT AND COFFINS MADE

A wavelet crept towards my feet. I floated the dinghy and stepped in.

With each stroke of the oars the noise from Jonno's bar faded. Twenty yards from the shore all I could hear were the squeaks of the oar-looms in their rubbers and the splashings of the blades. In a very few minutes I was making sail and looking at the next islands on the chart.

I hope the people will be happier, I thought.

9

A Sinking Off Sombrero

From Road Bay I sailed towards bird-haunted cliffs and discovered a turbulent cove which could have been a Gothic vision. A few miles farther north the scenery became less disturbing. From a sandy islet rose a stand of seven palms with trunks of different thicknesses. Viewing the trunks against a setting sun might be like looking at a bar-code on a plastic orange, I thought, but I did not linger to test the truth of this theory.

I sailed onward, anchoring at noon off Prickly Pear Cays, where I scrubbed the cockpit teak until it changed from being the colour of plain chocolate to chocolate of the dairy milk kind. Afterwards I spread a clean sheet over my berth and slept for two hours, for that night I would not risk sleeping or even dozing; instead, I would be keeping a lookout for ships in the Sombrero Passage.

The Passage is a section of the shipping lane often used by vessels to-ing and fro-ing between the oil islands of the southern Caribbean and Europe. It was many years since I had last been in the Sombrero Passage but when I sighted the lights of another vessel crossing *Kylie*'s course from starboard I remembered what an elderly Third Mate had said and done to me when I had failed to make a similar sighting forty years previously.

Getting on for what now seemed a lifetime ago, while standing my watch as lookout on the bridge of a tanker three hours before moonrise on just such a night, with the wind warm and my eyes heavy, someone had kicked me from behind.

'Dozing again?'

'No, sir!'

'Then how is it that you haven't reported yon ship? Its lights are brighter than Blackpool's are on Wakes Week.'

No reply; replying wouldn't help. Another blow comes from behind.

'And what about t'other?' A huge finger spears the darkness and points to starboard of the oncoming ship's lights.

'That's the loom of Sombrero light, laddie, flashing one every five.

A little glint of the Empire, is that! Three thousand three hundred miles from Bishop Rock by great circle, yet 'tis run from London by the Brethren of Trinity House*. And *you* didn't see it! The Elder Brethren will be turning in their graves, laddie! Now just you get me a bearing of Sombrero while it's rising, an' then you can go aft and fetch me a mug of well-mashed tea.'

I climb to the monkey island, adjust the prism above the compass and call out the compass bearing of Sombrero, whose finger of light is now stroking the belly of a cloud every five seconds.

Stumbling along the flying bridge to the galley, I try to remember whether the Third Mate takes two spoonfuls or six. In the galley I stir condensed milk into his tea until its colour changes from Walker's Warrington Ale to Honduras mahogany, and wonder what Elder Brethren look like when they are dead. Eye sockets crawling with maggots, leg veins like knotted electric cables, shrouds stinking like cheesecloth and all of them spinning indignantly in their coffins, they were unlikely to be likeable.

By the time I stir the sixth spoonful into the mug, I am finding it hard not to shudder.

Gimballing his tea by placing the mug in a bucket, I make my way back to the Third Mate, who tells me that because the engineer has now re-packed the leaking gland I must go below and pump up fresh water so that the Captain can take his shower. Below decks it is very warm, and the engine is pedalling its con-rods in a rhythm which sends me to the brink of sleep. This is not to be wondered at, because sleep is what I am very short of, having been made to work a 'four-hours-on, four-hours-off' system of watches on account of having sung a bawdy song at the shipboard Christmas party between the Azores and Falmouth three months ago.

'Since you are unwilling to behave as officers and gentlemen,' had said the Captain on Boxing Day, when the First Mate had stood three of us before him and itemised our crimes, 'you will stand watch-and-watch for the remainder of this voyage.'

'. . . which means,' had growled the Third Mate when I'd reported back to the bridge, 'for the rest of yer natural life.'

* Wrong. Sombrero was then being run by the Leeward Islands Government and/or the Imperial Lighthouse Service, but the error is entirely forgivable. Whatever organization they are in, officials like to wear uniforms to infuse awe. The dazzle of gold braid can be confusing, so it was no wonder the Third Mate got himself mixed up. In wartime Liverpool the doorman of the Palais de Luxe cinema was sometimes mistaken for the Admiral commanding the Western Approaches.

To add spice to my punishment, the Third Mate, who had lost a fortune at the dog tracks but was a wizard at mental arithmetic, devised exquisite tortures of his own, tortures derived from the thirty-one articles of the International Regulations for the Prevention of Collisions at Sea which had so perplexed Bill Fowler's acquaintance.

Lulled by the knowledge that if I was not pumping water to the Captain's bathroom the Third Mate would be setting me up for his nightly torture session on the bridge, I nodded off.

Readers who are rendered sleepless by accounts of mental brutality should now jump eight paragraphs while I reveal in harrowing detail what usually went on.

Licking tea from his moustache, the Third Mate would glare at me from the shelter of the wheelhouse and growl:

'You are steering north-by-east and the wind is south. You sight a green light bearing north-by-west. What is she, how is she heading and what action will you take?'

Eyes shut tighter than when being dosed with syrup of figs, after telling my brain that the green light is that of a sailing vessel under way, I gallop mentally hither and thither round the compass card thus:

The vessel can be heading in any direction within a 10-point arc to the left of the reciprocal of the given bearing; that is to say, between south-by-east and north-east-by-east. But because she can sail no closer than four points to the wind she must be heading somewhere between south-east and north-east-by-east, which makes her a crossing vessel, one which I shall have to keep clear of, if her bearing doesn't change, by altering course to pass under her stern, not forgetting as I do so to sound two short blasts on the whistle or siren, each blast being of one second's duration.

Having ensured by prodding me that my eyes had opened, the Third Mate would twist his mouth into what he supposed was a smile. To me it looked no different from the leer worn by Charles Laughton when the boatswain of the *Bounty* is about to lay 200 lashes of the cat-o'-nine-tails onto the back of a mutineer. The leer was the Third Mate's way of telling me to get a move on.

Even when they were correct, my answers bore little relation to 1940s shipboard practice. Telling anyone to steer north-by-east was as dead as dear old Barnett. True, we still had a dry-card magnetic compass in the wheelhouse and, true again, the card was resplendent with a fleur-de-lis, broad arrows, not-so-broad arrows, fine-cut diamonds, and what looked like – but couldn't possibly have been –

stone-age flint knappings, all of which marked off four cardinal points, four half-cardinal points, eight intermediate points and sixteen 'by' points. It was an impressive hierarchy but even in those far-off pious times it may have been redundant. Navigation was a black art masquerading as a formal science. I reckoned that although for the preceding 600 years gamblers like Columbus and the Third Mate had been pretending to navigate scientifically around the oceans with magnetic compasses, all the time they had been doing it by hunches.

After half-closing the wheelhouse door behind him so that I could not see what he was up to, the Third Mate would walk over to the dry-card magnetic compass and tell the helmsman to alter course. In the glow from the binnacle light the Third Mate resembled the late Adolf Hitler. Though he was standing next to – and skilfully pretending to look at – the dry-card compass with its cardinalled, its semi-cardinalled and its uncardinalled-but-ever-blessed host, he would not be looking at the magnetic compass but at a much less conspicuous gyro-compass repeater which was graduated not in points but in degrees. And although he would tell the helmsman to alter course, the course would be given in degrees, not compass points.

But the ultimate Barnett was to plague me with the supposition that we had encountered a sailing vessel. The idea was ludicrous. Having steamed 55,000 miles in ten months without seeing one, I assumed that they had ceased to exist. And until that evening off Sombrero, I believe that I was not the only one to think so.

The clanging of the engine-room telegraph woke me. By the time I had closed down the water pump and was climbing the ladder to the deck, the engineer had shut the steam-inlet valve to the main engine and the vessel was tilting slightly. Making a big circle to port but losing way, she was upright when I got to the bridge. The Captain was in the wheelhouse, tightening a bath towel round his midriff and staring ahead through an opened window. On the port wing of the bridge the Third Mate was staring astern but was also questioning Able Seaman Harris, who had been on lookout on the foc'sle head.

'You're sure? A schooner? And with no lights?'

'Aye, sir. Must've been on port tack and crossing. I rung the bell, but by then she were close aboard and her foremast were toppling.'

I was sent to rouse the Radio Officer, and soon messages were being morsed to other ships, telling them we had run down a sailing vessel and asking them to help search for it. We criss-crossed the Sombrero Passage all night. Our search was helped by a large moon, but nothing was seen or found; no bodies in the water, no wreckage . . . nothing; and by the time the First Mate came on watch at four in the morning, people were wondering whether we had really run down another vessel or whether Harris had dreamt it. Certainly, no one else had seen anything – the Third Mate had been in the chartroom, laying off a running fix of Sombrero when Harris had rung the foc'sle bell. And when at seven bells in the morning watch the bo'sun reminded the Mate that between staggering out of the Dewdrop Inn at Port Arthur and entering the bosom of the Seventh Day Adventist Church at Galveston Able Seaman Harris had claimed to have seen some very disabling visions, descriptions of which had entertained his messmates for weeks, it was not long before we had resumed our course for Bishop Rock and were telling each other that we hadn't run down no sailing boat and that Harris needed either his bald head or his eyes examined or better still all three.

Half a lifetime later, sighting not the single green light of a sailing vessel but the red and two whites of a steamship at – where else? – north-by-west, and this bearing not changing in ten minutes, I muttered 'Article 20* to you, Mister Mate!', put *Kylie*'s helm a-lee and altered course until she was close hauled on the starboard tack.

With miles of water to play with, the steamer should have given way, but I was not going to get close enough to argue the toss. When the steamer's lights were well abaft the port beam and I was about to turn back on course for the Virgin Islands, I saw the loom of Sombrero dead ahead.

Its ghostly finger was still stroking the belly of a cloud, and Harris's voice was saying '. . . she were close aboard and her foremast were toppling'.

So, instead of altering course I lit a pipe and steered for the loom of Sombrero light, anchoring off the western side of the island during the second hour of the graveyard watch. Although there was little wind and no swell I parcelled the anchor warp in way of the bow roller. The moon hanging in the southern sky was so very bright that even with the curtains drawn I could see well enough to pour methylated spirit into the bowl of the Primus stove. I lay on the starboard berth and drew a sheet over my body and up to my chin. Brighter than the moonlight, Sombrero was painting the deckhead every five seconds, flashing onto the loaf in

---

* International Regulations for Preventing Collisions at Sea (1929), Article 20: *When a steam vessel and a sailing vessel are proceeding in such directions as to involve risk of collision, the steam vessel shall keep out of the way of the sailing vessel.*

the hammock. It was my very last brown hero and in the flashes from Sombrero I saw that parts of it were black and mouldy.

I pulled the sheet over my face and slept.

For someone who was trying to evade the police, the man at the cliff top was wearing a shockingly loud shirt. It was a solid, pillar-box red. I decided that if he wasn't a drug-runner he had to be an itinerant fisherman.

He lowered an aluminium ladder from a ledge half-way down the cliff and lashed the top of it to a ring set in the rock. I hitched the painter of my dinghy to the lowest rung, threw an anchor astern and climbed the ladder. The man's handclasp was as rough as the rock we stood on, and his forearm looked pretty rugged as well. Burnt sienna in colour and deeply pitted, it reminded me of the ancient cannon outside the Harbour Inn at Southwold, one which the landlord had fished up out of Sole Bay.

I had not reckoned on getting a handshake. Indeed, I had not expected to meet anyone. Sombrero was supposed to be uninhabited. Whatever else the man was, he could not be a light keeper because Simon Winchester had reported that the light station had been de-manned.

The man in the red shirt did not speak, and he shook hands reluctantly. His shirt and trousers looked too clean to be fishing in, and so I re-classified him as a drug-runner again.

The drug-running notion was not far-fetched. After stating in his book *Outposts* that the light on Sombrero had been automated and its keeper brought home, Winchester goes on to tell of a big drug-busting operation which had happened nearby. On Scrub Island airstrip, only 32 miles from Sombrero and a stone's-throw from Anguilla, a billion dollars' worth of cocaine had been seized by Anguillan police in 1983 while being unloaded from a Colombian plane onto an American one. Four drug-runners had been arrested. Released on bail of half a million dollars, they had not returned to stand trial. Presumably, they were still on the loose.

Presumably, too, now I came to think of it, drug-running might be one reason why Anguilla had so many brand-new banks.

Ascending the cliffs of Sombrero six years after the drug-busting, I am thinking that if the island turns out to have an airstrip the man must be one of the cocaine Mafia and the pitting of his forearm is either where the needles have gone in or is what happened when he met a Royal Anguillan Constable who had been armed with a 12-bore shotgun.

73

At the cliff top on Sombrero

At the cliff top I see that the airstrip theory is unsustainable. The surface is so jagged and creviced that landing an aeroplane on Sombrero would be impossible. The surface is like a gigantic meringue which has been made by whisking molten limestone instead of egg-whites. Even parachuting onto the island would be barmy because the surface terrain would tear your body to shreds. The only place on which you could put your foot down in safety would be the narrow concrete path which runs from the cliff top to a flat-roofed building beneath the light-tower.

With its marzipan-coloured walls, as we walk the path I think the building looks like a Battenberg cake. What with the heat of the sun, the fearsome terrain, the spindly light-tower and the Battenberg cake, Sombrero was becoming like a film set for *The War of the Worlds*, or – to gladden those who have put money into nuclear electricity – Southwold after a meltdown at Sizewell power station.

The man leads me through a doorway into a high-ceilinged room. Its blank walls, painted concrete floor and large plain table make it an ideal room for the man in the red shirt to play ping-pong in if he feels like it and can get someone else to feel likewise, but it is also, I think with mounting anxiety, the ideal sort of room for the cocaine Mafia to interrogate visitors who are suspected of being FBI agents. Nothing in it suggests that it is a fisherman's home-from-home or that whoever lives there has any distinctive personality or interests. The walls carry no pictures. There isn't even a clock.

Three other men come in and sit facing me across the table. The red-shirted man pulls out a metal-framed chair and sits down so as to block the entrance door.

So now we have four men: the same number as are still on the run.

Each is of average height, each is of average build, and each seats himself in a similar posture: legs slightly apart, both feet flat on the floor, forearms resting on thighs, and hands hanging loosely between the knees. Their gazes are steady but their faces are blank. I get the impression they are waiting for me to speak.

'Forty or so years ago,' I begin, 'and about twelve miles south of here, some men may have drowned . . .'

It does not take more than a couple of minutes to tell the story but by the end of it I am sweating.

'Want a drink?' says the one in the red shirt.

But before I can answer, another says 'You can look at the graves if you want.'

There are supposed to be seven graves but I can find only five. One is a sarcophagus more than it is a grave. The sides are made of limestone slabs and its lid is nearly the height of my waist. The lid has been wrenched askew, and I can neither lever it back into place nor shift it further askew so as to look at the skeleton within. The words which had been inscribed on the lid have been weathered almost away. The graves that are really graves are just shallow pockets which someone has blasted or chiselled out of the rock. They have no lids and they are empty.

Though the island is under a mile long and is less than a quarter wide, it takes me three hours to explore it. Dynamite and the elements – including the occasional forty-foot swell – have hewn the limestone into such cruel shapes that I cannot walk its surface. Instead, I have to pick my way, one step at a time, from one razored ridge to another.

When they think I am not looking, black lizards scuttle among the graves.

I do discover a skeleton but it is a steel one. With its bony legs twisted and buckled, Sombrero's first light-tower, the one which a Third Mate had bidden me take bearings of forty years ago, lies on its side in a quarry.

One of several, the quarry had been blasted by miners who had been recruited on Anguilla in 1856 and shipped to Sombrero to dig out its phosphate rock. Bonnetted by thousands of seabirds and their guano, the island would have appeared no different to the first miners from what it had done to Columbus and his fifteenth-century *marineros* who had thought it resembled *un sombrero*, a hat.

Compared with poor Anguilla, though, Sombrero was encrusted with riches. During the years which followed the miners' landing, Sombrero became a busy place, with a railway, workshops, barracks, and – after 1867 – one of the finest, tallest and brightest lighthouses in the Caribbean. Since the barracks were large, the population must have been counted in scores, and so in addition to being a busy place Sombrero would have been a lively one too. But after thirty-four years of blasting and hewing, years in which hundreds of thousands of tons of Sombrero's head-gear was torn off and carried away to be spread over American cornfields, by 1891 the riches had been plundered, the last miner had departed (the birds had flown away long since) and the place had become the forlorn, hatless waif it is today. The only things still remaining from the miners' days are the boiler-house chimney and the ruined light-tower.

And, of course, some of the graves . . .

I do not discover all this history till I get back to the Battenberg building, by which time I have decided that either someone misinformed Winchester and the lighthouse had not been de-manned, or the island has been invaded by four hard cases who have gone a bit soft.

The man in the red shirt makes a fresh pot of tea and cuts a plateful of Spam sandwiches while I tell him what I have been doing and what I am searching for. Because of the unexpected sandwiches and some encouraging smiles, I also reveal that I had thought that he and his three companions were cocaine *mafiosi*. When he has reacted with hilarity to this information he straightens his face and tells me that three of his companions are light-keepers and he is the cook.

Carrying a fishing rod, one of them emerges from a back room and goes off to catch their supper. After setting the sandwiches before me, the cook returns to his seat in the doorway.

He isn't blocking my getaway, he says with another smile; he is sitting there because it is cooler.

'Look,' says a keeper who has not previously said anything, passing me a periodical called *Flash*, a title which might excite dribbles down some macintoshes until their wearers discover it is about light-stations and nothing else, 'Sombrero is listed as one of the manned stations.'

It is, too. Left-handed column. Sixth from the bottom. Between 'SARK' and 'ST ANN'S HEAD'.

'Got anything else? Anything about those graves?'

The one who has handed me *Flash* brings out the station logbook and a photocopied history of the island. The logbook goes back only as far as the 1960s. The photocopied history starts with Columbus and deals in some detail with the late 1800s:

Monthly rations 1895: 6 boxes smoked herring, 2 sheep, 7 lb butter, 100 lb family bees . . .

'2 sheep' makes sense, but 'family bees' doesn't. What are 'family bees?'

'You need longer arms,' says the cook, leaning over my shoulder. 'It doesn't say "bees", it says "beef".'

'Alright,' I say. 'So what is "family beef"? Chunks for stewing?'

Nobody knows. What is more discouraging is that nobody seems bothered that nobody knows.

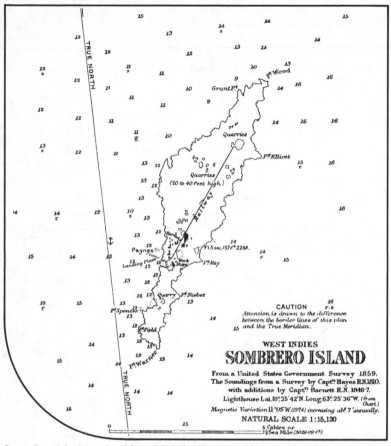

Crown Copyright. Reproduced from Admiralty Chart 130 with the permission of the Controller of Her Majesty's Stationery Office.

After an American company leased the island to quarry phosphate, the work of Captains Hayes and Barnett, RN, was superseded by the US survey. As printed, the chart contains a typographical gaffe: it is the island which is 20 to 40 feet high, not the quarries. This slip may have amused Queen Victoria, but Barnett would have felt like keel-hauling Her Majesty's Hydrographer.

And why 'smoked herring'? Herrings are eastern North Atlantic fish. To get them to Sombrero from, say, Lowestoft would have meant a voyage of 4000 miles. What a way to victual a lighthouse! Doesn't a freshly caught bonito taste better than a kippered herring? Did the Elder Brethren have shares in the Lowestoft herring-smoking houses or something?

I scratch my head and read on:

> *1960: Work commenced on new light-tower . . . Twice monthly schooner from Anguilla . . .*

A schooner . . . Harris had said it had been a schooner. If a schooner was still to-ing and fro-ing from Anguilla in the 1960s, it must have been doing the same when I took the bearing of Sombrero in the 1940s . . .

'This logbook is about the sixties,' I say. 'Can you find me the logbook for the forties?'

'Do you want another sandwich?'

'No, thanks. You do *have* other logbooks, don't you?'

'More tea?'

'No, thanks. I've had enough, thanks.' He is picking up the cup and saucer. He reaches for the plate but I hold on to it.

'Please, I'm asking about other logbooks, logbooks that can tell me about the nineteen-forties. I need to find out if a schooner was sunk . . .'

'Sir,' he says, taking the dirty crockery to the door, 'that's the only logbook we got. We don't know nothing about the nineteen-forties. The forties was a long time ago. We wasn't born then.'

Feeling rather elderly for the second time that day, I put on my hat and walk out into the bright sunlight.

'I s'pose the answer to what you're asking is somewhere else,' says the cook when we are standing at the top of the ladder and I am preparing to descend it.

'Where's that?' I say.

A black lizard scuttles towards the graves and he chuckles.

'With the Elder Brethren,' says he.

79

10

The Capetown Crew

Like other solitary, single-handed activities, solo cruising can raise distressful emotions but loneliness is not one of them; at least, it isn't for me. The farther off the land, the closer the company.

The earliest visitors to *Kylie* embarked years ago, during a gale in Biscay when I was feeling a bit whacked. Their colourful but unseamanlike attire, which had included the wearing of pink bedroom-slippers in the cockpit, may have been imaginative but their bodily presence was not. I suppose they might have been phantoms, but I swear that they had been in *Kylie*'s cabin because while I was pulling myself together in Portugal I discovered that each and every visitor had written his or her name in the logbook.

Since that time people have often come aboard in mid-ocean. They always come silently and singly – rather as if they are entering an intensive-care ward – and they come not only when they think I am on the danger list but also when I am off the drugs and doing quite nicely. Sometimes they bring me practical tidings, such as that another vessel is in sight, that the kettle is coming to the boil or that a chart pencil has fallen down a crack in the woodwork, but this is by no means always the case; sometimes they drop in because they want merely to pass the time of day. Settling into a cosy corner of the cockpit, they will then comment on topics of enduring interest, like the physiognomy of the late Margaret Rutherford, the vivacity of West Highland terriers or who in Southwold fries the best cod-and-chips, going on until I notice that a halyard needs setting up or a sail needs changing, at which point they steal quietly away.

Because most of them live in England their visits must involve long journeys, but none of them ever looks as though he or she has come very far. However many miles from England I happen to be, my visitors always give the impression that they have popped in for a chat from next door. Their homely table-talk and the casual nature of their comings and goings suggest that England lies just beyond the next wave-top, so to speak.

Another country, one which I used to think was utterly remote, seems to lie even nearer. She does not drop in often (and when she does, it is not to say much), but Pip seems to be dwelling so near to me that sometimes all I have to do to get in touch with her is whisper. I do not hear many of her replies but of course this does not mean she is not making them; it is more likely that my equipment is not up to receiving them.

Therefore I feel slightly embarrassed whenever I let on that I am cruising alone. Apart from the primary reason that my listener will think I am sailing solo because I am vainglorious or nutty, there is also the reason – from all I've said above – that I do not feel alone at all.

Though the rest of the world is content to believe that I sail around in permanent solitude, this belief does not always help me. Insurance agents and their actuaries think that sailing alone is so risky that anyone who does it must be a certain goner. On learning of my single-handed status, all but one of a clutch (an excess? a loading?) of insurers – including, ironically, a company which included Robin Knox-Johnston's surname within its title – rebuffed me. Eventually I did find an insurer who offered – after a bit of arm-twisting – to cover *Kylie* for the transatlantic passage, but only for the beginning and end of it: that is to say, for the times when I would be less than a day's sail from Europe, Africa or America and their adjacent islands. Since the most difficult moments of my voyages seem to occur when I am nearing the land, this insurer was offering me almost all the cover I needed for passaging the Atlantic and for cruising the Caribbean. I filled in his form and he took me on.

Now, crossing the Sombrero Passage and beholding Virgin Gorda ahead at sunrise, I spread a spoonful of marmalade onto a crust of bread and blessed my insurer for allowing me to sail alone. If I rationed myself to two sandwiches a day and kept it hidden from chance visitors, the marmalade – a 7-lb tin of my favourite thick-cut Dundee variety, not to be had for love or money in the West Indies – seemed likely to last me another month so long as nobody else came aboard to eat it.

A marina sidled round a headland at midday. I was nearing dangerous country. Marinas are jungles in which marmalade-hunters prowl around at all hours of day and night, and any blighters who get wind of it will spring into your cabin as soon as you have levered the

81

lid off. Therefore I sneaked past the marina and anchored off an island in Virgin Sound, stowed my marmalade out of sight and slept only lightly.

While I was sleeping, a letter telling me of a strong objection to my solitary condition was being unloaded from the Heathrow flight at Antigua.

I remained forty hours at this anchorage. Until a Welsh boat anchored close abeam, the nearest neighbour was sixty yards distant: far enough away for me to hide the marmalade if a dinghy headed towards me. Feeling that even the most pernickety insurer could not accuse me of the barratry of her provisions, I turned my attention to *Kylie*'s gear. Setting to work soon after the sun rose, I emptied and scrubbed the food lockers, painted the boathook, cleaned the carbon deposits from the burners of the Primus stove and polished its brass tank till its reflected sunbeams were sparkling on the deckhead.

By this time the insurer's letter was either aboard the inter-island flight which had landed at Beef Island or was already awaiting my collection at the post office on Tortola.

The Welsh boat weighed anchor and straight away ran hard aground – for the third time in twenty hours, so its crew said when I rowed across to offer my help. Their misfortune made me glad that *Kylie* was insured. Except for the time when I had run her onto the sand in Freeman's Bay so as to careen her, so far she had not grounded in the West Indies at all. However, much of the water on her route ahead – and especially the water around the Bahamas – would be shallower than the knoll on which the Welshmen had grounded. Laden with stores and extra gear, *Kylie* was drawing four feet four inches – four inches more than her designer had intended but still a good nine inches less than the other boat was drawing. Four feet four inches of draught would not give rise to pilotage problems in most of the small-boat channels and anchorages of the Virgins, but when she reached the Bahamas *Kylie* could be running aground as often as the Welsh boat was now doing. The huge increase in the numbers of shallows, pirates, learner-drivers, cocaine *mafiosi* and bad-tempered officials which was reported to occur as one sailed northwards made insurance as needful to small boats as featherdown is to small ducks.

The Welshmen kedged themselves free and motored away. I backed the headsail and broke out *Kylie*'s anchor. Her bow swung clear of the shallows and then she too was away, creaming through the western exit from Gorda Sound in no more than six feet of water. After beholding, open-mouthed, an amazing jumble of rocks called Fallen Jerusalem, I anchored off Virgin Gorda, made a mugful of tea and reminded myself that *Kylie*'s insurance cover would be due for renewal during the coming month.

Other boats were lying at anchor there also, but again I did not row over and visit their crews, for so much of interest was to be seen without stirring from the cockpit to seek human company. A hint of menace was in the air too, and so I needed to stay aboard and keep watchful. Armed with a bottle of rum, I studied the skyline. From time to time clouds poked their heads above the parapets of nearby hills like enemy infantry peering from their trenches. You could never know in advance when or where the next head would show itself. They were an enemy who could not be trusted. Just when you thought you had negotiated a two-minute cease-fire, half a dozen of them would crawl into the blue no-man's land while you were putting the kettle on, and by the time you returned to the cockpit, hordes of unprotected refugees on the hillsides would be threshing their green arms about and frigate birds would be dropping like arrows.

Compared with the free cadences of nature, commercial entertainment was expensive and flat. After sitting for an hour over a two-dollar beer in a bar called The Last Resort, listening to a singer whose English I could not understand though my eyes were fixed on his lips all the time, I rowed back aboard and played 'Rule Britannia' to a smiling moon.

On another day I had to work harder for my pleasures when, beset by a squall in the Narrows, I handed the genoa in a hurry, bent on the smaller jib-sail and beat into the lee of Norman Island. Anchored there in a wind which sang a Gregorian chant in the rigging, I watched sparks stream from barbecue parties on neighbouring boats while I consumed the third marmalade sandwich of the day. I had thereby exceeded my daily ration, but I do not remember feeling guilty, and certainly I did not feel envious.

I sat in the cockpit until late, watching silent legions rush across the moon to storm the dark caverns of the west.

Kylie was plunging from side to side like a dog worrying its lead, but the anchor did not budge. Ahead in the moonlight, other boats were plunging also.

'Easy, girls,' I said, watching them.

Downwind through the waves came a dinghy. From its steady rate of drift I judged it to be of solid construction – an inflatable would

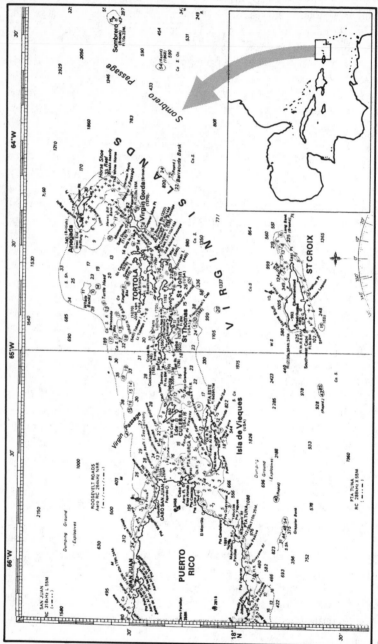

have been skittering over the waves – and as it came towards me I saw that it was empty. Plucking the boathook from its place in the backstays, I stood in *Kylie*'s stern, leant outboard and locked the boathook under the capping of the dinghy's sheerstrake. *Kylie* sheered in the opposite direction, canting me away from the dinghy, but after a struggle I made fast its painter to a stern cleat. I returned the boathook to its place and wondered rather smugly if the dinghy's owner had insured his property as certainly as I had insured mine.

The first hint that people such as insurance officials might regard me and my solitude with disdain came when a passport inspector on Tortola glanced towards *Kylie*, then looked at me and pulled a sceptical face.

'You an actor?'

'Sorry?'

'I asked you if you were an actor.'

'Aren't we all?' I countered.

Stomping across a dusty street to the post office, I tried not to feel angry. An actor? What on earth was he driving at? That I was camping things up in the Caribbees? Aye-aying with Cathusalem, the harlot of Fallen Jerusalem? Or did he think I was about to misplace my identity in Tortola in the way I had lost it in the Canary Islands, where I had been reduced to a gibbering wraith until someone had found my passport in a plastic bag, next to a tin of pilchards?

Fingering my body-belt through my shirt to make sure the passport was still in it, I clumped into the post office and asked for my mail. The clerk shook his head.

'There aren't no letters for anyone called Hancock.'

'Try looking under "K".'

' "K"? "Hancock" start with a "K", do it?'

'No, it doesn't, but my boat's name does.'

Opposite: Sombrero to Puerto Rico. A section of a chart reproduced here by permission of Imray, Laurie, Norie and Wilson Ltd., whose founders began publishing charts in 1670. On passage-charts such as this, many details are necessarily left out. Fallen Jerusalem lies off the southwest tip of Virgin Gorda, the Narrows is between Tortola and St John, and the Virgin Passage is between St Thomas and Culebra. The Boca de Infierno is on the south coast of Puerto Rico, while Isla Mona and the Dominican Republic lie a whole day's sail farther west of it.

He found five letters: four had been filed under 'K' and the fifth — from my insurer — under 'P'.

Not only because I was drinking beer while reading it, my insurer's letter made me sweat. He had had, he said, a change of mind. Things in the insurance market were not what they used to be, and so if I wanted *Kylie* to remain covered for the ensuing 12 months she must carry at least one, but preferably two, other crew members aboard.

This was a facer. I took a taxi to a supermarket to buy groceries and think the problem through. Feeding two extra males would be impossible: the porridge pan was not big enough. And if both were the size of the sulphurous Norwegian, where would we all put our feet? I stared at the taxi-driver's head, the back of which was peculiarly flat. Above it was stuck a notice which suggested my fears were well founded:

I Edwe Johnson do not want you to put your feet on the glass screen behind this driver's head. And not on the seats too. Your feet should be on the floor at all times. That's what floors are for.

I could have chosen to sail on uninsured, but 200 shipwrecks on the coralline shores of Barbuda argued that I should try to find just one person to sail with me until I'd at least reached the American mainland.

But dammit, how long can two human beings put up with each other when they are confined to a cabin which is the size of a wine tub? Diogenes had enjoyed living alone in his tub for months on end, but he had been a cynic — and what's more there had been nobody else in there to scoff his marmalade. Jennie and Patricia had lived aboard *Kylie* for two weeks and their company had been fun, but we had known each other's foibles in advance, their feet had been small and their stay had been short. Recruiting a stranger who would like to cruise to the USA might be easy, but finding a stranger who would endure *Kylie*'s cramped cabin and her crabbed skipper for a couple of months without contemplating mutiny, murder or suicide would not.

Drafting an advert of my crew requirement took ages. After tearing up three attempts I eventually stuck a thirty-word postcard in a shop window on the island of St John, not expecting much good would come of it. The only other shop window in which I had placed an advert had been a tobacconist's in Falmouth, England, when I had been seeking a crew to accompany me to Gibraltar. That advert had elicited five responses, but for several good reasons – one of which had been the impossibility of heaving on halyards when one has broken one's wrist and another of which had been the ditto of stowing a six-foot surfboard in a five-foot forepeak – the earliest attempt to recruit a crew had fallen flat and so I had set out from England alone. Two weeks went by without any replies to this latest advert, and so I was thinking of giving up. Then news came of yet another vessel wrecking itself on a reef, and so I redoubled my crew-finding efforts by replacing the thirty-word advert with another which ran to sixty.

Three days into the third week of the extended advertising campaign I received a 28-word reply. Soon afterwards *Kylie* was heading for Isla de Vieques under full main and small genoa, dodging heavy squalls in the Virgin Passage, being helmed by a new crew-member who at two o'clock in the afternoon had leaned protractedly over the side and afterwards written '*Adiós mío desayuno*' (Goodbye, mine breakfast), in the logbook before burying his nose in a tome which had been written by Jung. Though the new hand was unwell I ought to have been feeling comfortable. So far he had not consumed any marmalade, and as long as he stayed alive his bodily presence was meeting the insurer's requirement and was thereby keeping *Kylie* insured.

Long before Isla de Vieques came abeam, though, I was viewing the crew-member with an acidulous mixture of envy, sympathy and suspicion. I felt envious because he was the only person I knew of who could read Jung with manifest pleasure, and I felt sympathy because he was afflicted by seasickness, but I was wary of someone who appeared to be leading not just a double life but a triple or even quintuple one. Before embarking in *Kylie* he had said he was a South African, but he had produced a British passport when we were leaving St John, and now he had just penned a farewell to his breakfast in Spanish and was reading the work of a Swiss psychiatrist which had been written in German. What, in heaven's name, was he up to? I bade him put down his book and tell me. As the result of what I learned I must now conceal his true identity by calling him just Capetown.

The reasons why I do not refer to him by his real name are both general and personal. The general reason is that at that time in history white South Africans – for so he proved to be – were beyond the pale, and trafficking with them provoked punitive responses from other governments. Although I wrote his real name in the logbook every day for the ensuing six weeks and although a civil war and the horrors which attend such catastrophes seem now, seven years later, to have been avoided, things could change for the worse again – look what has happened in Bosnia and Chechnya – and then there would be a chance that some querulous official like the one who had doubted my *bona fides* would think Capetown had bamboozled him and would raise merry hell.

The personal reason – though neither of us knew it then – is that a South African friend of his in London whom Capetown was intending to visit had either just died, or was about to, in tragic circumstances.

Capetown's dubious citizenship, his absorption in Jung, and his seasickness were marginal concerns so long as they did not affect the well-being of *Kylie* and her skipper. But traces of other, more dangerous ailments were beginning to sprout. Like the old Third Mate, Capetown showed signs of being a wizard at mental arithmetic. The other disease which was worrying me was his ecology.

Commendable though this practice is, when I am at sea in *Kylie* the high sierras of ecology are unclimbable. If you are days or weeks in a small boat, what else can you do with rubbish except throw it overboard? Capetown was having none of that sort of selfish nonsense. Before we had left the Virgin Islands astern a waste bag had been strung up in the cockpit and I was depositing my empty beer cans into it. I felt a bit miffed.

Rolling to the south-easterly swell which was making him queasy, *Kylie* headed for a sheltered bay on the coast of Puerto Rico and roared into it with both my hands on her tiller and almost out of control, down the faces of six-foot breakers, through a passage called Boca de Infierno, the Mouth of Hell.

'That was almost as good as riding a surfboard,' said Capetown when we had anchored *Kylie* near a dreary vista of grass and mud and were getting our breaths back. 'I wouldn't have blamed you if you'd chickened out.'

As *Kylie* wended through the Greater Antilles, the Turks and Caicos Islands and the Bahamas, the pleasure of receiving this compliment was alternately soured and sweetened by a medley of other incidents.

After exploring the subterranean passages on Isla Mona with the aid of a reel of thread in the way Theseus is supposed to have done and encountering not, thank heavens, the Minotaur, but a three-foot black lizard which turned out to be harmless, Capetown celebrated our adventure by chopping the top off a coconut and pouring a libation. Drinking it beneath the shade of a palm tree, we both felt enormously happy. I went for a swim and he dipped into Jung.

On the northern coast of the Dominican Republic another adventure ended more sadly. With its trees and its flowers, the main square of Puerto Plata had seemed a pleasant place to loiter. For all of ten minutes it was. Then, while drinking beer and taking in the scene, we were befriended by – or were pretended to be befriended by – Francisco, an oval-faced *mestizo* who spoke fluent English (not something many do in an island which was once the Spanish Main), and who bedundered us with endless information about local persons, places or objects, over which gringos like us reputedly went moony.

We told him to buzz off.

The blighter was still with us two hours later. Having drunk umpteen beers and required us to pay for them, having trailed us into and out of three shops in which Capetown had sought but failed to find a new sombrero to replace the soiled canvas headgear he was wearing, all at once Francisco began demanding money.

'Do come off it!' said we.

Francisco was making these demands while we were passing through a seedy part of the town, a street behind a bottling plant whose crumbling walls were propped up by knots of *mestizos* clutching bottles and from whose portals wheezed gouts of vapour and trickles of what looked like yesterday's beer. It was not a tourist attraction.

Francisco appeared to be threatening us. The proximity of men who were not only compatriots but were also bonded to him by skin colour, poverty and blood (for all of them had the same oval faces) made it a classic apartheid confrontation, the sort of thing which, despite his iron-hard nature, had for years been making Capetown sick. In the course of hectoring us for a ten-dollar fee for guiding us round the sights of Puerto Plata, Francisco reached his hand behind his back as though to draw out a knife.

Capetown skipped sideways and put his fists up. Francisco looked shocked.

'No, man, no-o-o!' he cried. 'You have got things wrongly!'

The *mestizo* was holding aloft a plasticated card which bore his photo. We moved closer and inspected it. The picture showed a smiling Francisco, and printed words testified that he was a licensed guide.

With Francisco standing there bolt upright, holding the card before us in the manner of Columbus holding the cross in front of earlier men who had peopled the land on which we three interlopers were now standing, it felt as though we were reeling backwards into a filmed history of the Caribbean, most of it depressingly vicious and bloody.

'Ten dollars,' said Francisco, waving his talisman and descending to the nitty-gritty, 'is all that I'm asking you for.'

Though Capetown and I did not confer before doing it, we each gave him a dollar. We gave him the money not because he deserved it (he was an extortionist rather than an honest beggar); nor because some of the other oval faces had edged closer (they'd got rid of the bottles); nor yet because it was the easiest way to escape from his wheedlings (the dock gates lay only a hundred yards away and were guarded by a policeman, albeit a grossly fat one): we gave him two dollars because we wanted the historical film – with Charlton Heston and other Caucasians in the leading roles – to re-align itself on the sprockets and fast-forward to the present day.

Kylie sailed out of Puerto Plata as the sun was setting behind a gigantic cross which stands on a green hill high above the town.

Turning our back on the cross, we headed for the Mouchoir Bank and the Turks and Caicos Islands.

Sand Cay, the nearest of these low-lying islands, lies ninety miles from Puerto Plata, and Grand Turk is twenty miles farther north. The approaches to the islands are beset with currents which vary in direction and are therefore difficult to reckon with. Because the lights on the islands had been reported to be unreliable (nothing to do with the Brethren, one shouldn't criticise one's Elders), I did not want to approach them during the hours of darkness. If I needed any reminders, three wrecks in Puerto Plata would testify to the unforgiving nature of the local coral.

Weighing these facts, I had decided to make a landfall on the Turks Islands in mid-morning, when the sun was high enough for us to pick our way through the coral.

'We shall head for the Mouchoir Bank,' I told Capetown before leaving harbour. 'It's only sixty miles from Puerto Plata and its southern edge is a sheer cliff, rising from hundreds of fathoms to only fourteen in less than a mile. What is just as helpful is that the cliff runs roughly east and west. When we locate it, the cliff edge will give us a non-skid position line which will cross nicely with a morning sun-sight.'

'That sounds logical,' said Capetown. 'Is the depthsounder working okay?'

I switched it on to show him.

'Look,' I said, 'it's as clear as a bell: twenty-one feet on the shallow-water scale.' I glanced at the chart. 'How high is your Table Mountain?'

Capetown skipped sideways and put his fists up

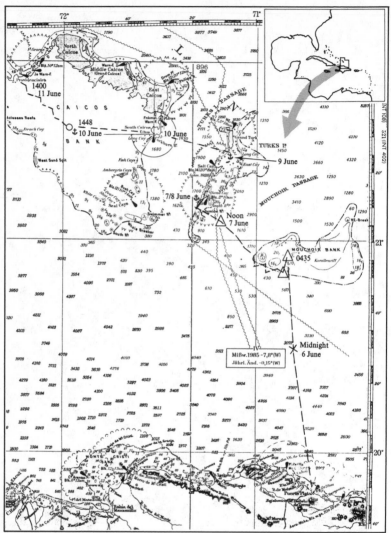

Reproduced by permission: Deutschen Hydrographischen Institut, Hamburg.

'Three thousand five hundred and eighty-two feet.'

'Once outside the harbour we'll soon be out of soundings. In a while we'll be in 2400 fathoms of water – that's . . . er . . . 14,400 feet. If you were to stand four Table Mountains on top of each other, how far . . .' – doing it in my head and forgetting which figure I was carrying forward –' . . . how far underwater would the mountain top be from the surface?'

'Eighty-four feet,' said Capetown without blinking. His hat was at its Jungian angle, deadly serious.

'Oh? . . . Er . . . Would it really?' I said. 'Eighty-four feet? Fourteen fathoms? With nothing left over . . .?'

'Yes.'

'I stand amazed,' I said, 'at my own brilliance. Fourteen fathoms happens to be exactly the depth we'll be looking for when we come onto the Mouchoir Bank.'

Table Mountains excepted, the foregoing was the theory of how we would find, fix and navigate the edge of the Mouchoir Bank. What happened in practice was that on a pitch-black night, half an hour after my dead reckoning had said we ought to be crossing the submarine cliff-face, the depthsounder was still telling us we were out of soundings, over an abyss.

'What does this knob do?' said Capetown, twiddling it.

'It switches over,' I said, 'from one scale to the other, and . . . and Good Lord!'

Capetown had stopped twiddling. The instrument was now reading fourteen fathoms, as clear as a bell.

I had forgotten to switch over from the shallow-water scale we had been using in Puerto Plata harbour.

Hurriedly gybing in the darkness which was temporarily even darker because I had been shining a flashlight onto the chart, I put *Kylie*'s head on a new course, the opposite of the one we had been sailing. For sixty minutes my glances went from the compass card to the depthsounder and back again. For one hour – five miles by the

---

Opposite: Dominican Republic to Turks and Caicos Islands. *On this German chart a depth of 14 fathoms is 26 metres. Luckily, one sea mile (one minute of latitude) is the same distance in English as it is in German, otherwise my navigation might have strayed even farther adrift.*

Walker log – the depthsounder recorded that we were in fourteen fathoms of water until all of a sudden the red flashes slid clockwise round the dial and vanished. *Kylie* was at the cliff edge, teetering on the brink of the abyss, the place where she should have been an hour previously.

'Take over for a moment, please,' I said to Capetown, handing him the tiller before going below and pouring myself three fingers of rum.

The unusual largeness – even for me – of the measure must have roused his suspicions.

He waited until late morning before analysing the data to find out what else had almost happened.

Meticulously drying his hands before picking up the dividers, Capetown bent over the chart. Though I was scanning the horizon ahead, I could picture his fingers measuring backwards with the dividers, backwards from the estimated position at 0900, the one where a sun-sight position line crossed the contour which marked the edge of the Mouchoir Bank.

'The bank is labelled *Korallenriff* and has crosses printed on it,' he said, putting his head out of the companionway. 'Because it's a German chart, I've only just realised that "*Korallenriff*" means "coral reef".'

'But I thought you could read German!' I said. 'Jung wrote his books in German, didn't he?'

'My copy's an English translation . . . And I suppose the crosses show where the coral is sticking up out of the water?'

'I think I can see Sand Cay!' I cried. 'Pass me the binoculars, quick!'

He withdrew his head but after a few seconds stuck it out again and handed me the binoculars.

'I reckon we were only three point five miles from a couple of those crosses when we did our about-turn this morning. Doing five knots, it works out that we were forty-minutes from a . . . er . . . *brush* with the coral?'

'It's Sand Cay alright!' I told him. 'And . . . and . . . yes, you're right. Doing five knots, we would've had a brush with the coral, and . . . er . . . the brush would've been quite a stiff one.'

'I hope *Kylie* is insured.'

Lowering the binoculars and looking him in the eye, I said: 'Yes, she most certainly is.'

11

To the Lighthouse

The cock-up on the Mouchoir Bank had rattled me. On arriving at Grand Turk I thrust full astern with the engine so as to bury the anchor flukes very deeply. I was not disposed to take any more chances with coral than I needed to, even if Columbus had.

Some scholars believe that Grand Turk was Columbus's first landfall in the Americas. According to the great navigator, *Kylie* was now anchored securely in . . . . *a port for as many ships as there are in all Christendom*; was lying, perhaps, above the very spot where the crew of his *Santa Maria* had uttered thanks for their salvation.

They must have been blind. From *Kylie*'s masthead the area seemed to be crawling with coral. On returning to the deck I also said a fervent verse or two on the same lines as the Spaniards. My feelings towards Capetown, though, were distinctly un-Christian.

For, as I have said already, the mess-up on the Mouchoir Bank had rattled me. When one's sanity is in question, the point is worth making twice. How much farther would *Kylie* have sailed toward the *Korallenriff* if Capetown had not twiddled the depthsounder? His intervention may have saved *Kylie* from impalement on coral, but it had punctured her skipper. I was hissing mad. Knowing he was reading *The Portable Jung* did not bolster my self-esteem either, especially as its author had written lots about senile dementia and the psychology of everyday life.

But only spiritual journeys are free of faults. Earthly voyagers make mistakes every day. Marmalade sandwiches which have been left unattended fall onto the cockpit sole, or someone puts salt instead of sugar into the tea. When you are the culprit, such failures are much easier to live with if you are voyaging by yourself. If you are alone, the cost of having put salt into your tea is merely the price of a teabag. All that has suffered are your taste buds. You pull a face, pour the spoilt tea over the side and brew another mugful. Making the same mistake when you have someone else aboard is more costly: your reputation

95

goes overboard with the teabag. Even if afterwards you thrill them by sailing into hundreds more Bocas de Infierno, your companion will still remember you as the idiot who made a balls-up on the Mouchoir Bank and afterwards handed him a mugful of salty tea.

It seemed apposite that the main export of Grand Turk was – or had been – salt. An elderly man who Capetown said looked like Nelson Mandela willingly lifted his walking-stick to point out the places where piles of this commodity used to be raked upward into the trade winds by gangs of black slaves. He declined to agree with me, however, when I suggested that tastable quantities of it could possibly have blown into the white man's tea.

Brooding on the difficulty of advancing (well, adjusting) Science to accommodate Art, I squatted outside the post office on Grand Turk while Capetown loped off to dump a bagful of *Kylie*'s garbage and buy himself a fishing lure. The bag was unusually bulky because I had emptied a bottle of rum in two days.

I did not drink more liquor until we had crossed the Turks Island Passage to Cockburn Harbour on South Caicos. Capetown tried out his new lure on the way there but, having caught nothing with it, rowed ashore in search of a better model. Alone for the first time in days, I broached a bottle of Glenfiddich, made myself a marmalade sandwich and sneaked a glance into *The Portable Jung*. What I read was not reassuring:

> *The nearer we approach to the middle of life, and the better we have succeeded in entrenching ourselves in our personal attitudes and social positions, the more it appears as if we had discovered the right course and the right ideals and the principles of behaviour. For this reason we suppose them to be eternally valid, and make a virtue of unchangeably clinging to them. We overlook the essential fact that the social goal is attained only at the cost of a diminution of personality. Many – far too many – aspects of life which should also have been experienced lie in the lumber-room among dusty memories; but sometimes, too, they are glowing coals under grey ashes.*

I pulled out a pencil and my mouth-organ, blew a doleful chord and copied down Jung's words.

Before we left South Caicos I also wrote some notes to myself. Mostly, they were ash-grey reminders in which were embedded more than a few glowing coals of paranoia, schizophrenia and spleen:

> *He is watching me again! This morning he re-scoured the porridge pan after I'd already washed it. Be careful! Think Glenfiddich bottle has been marked.*

96

Must stow marmalade in different locker. Also, must check depthsounder and Walker log before crossing Caicos Bank. Despite signs of impending mutiny, am determined to stay cheery!

Resembling on the chart the handkerchief after which it had been named, the Mouchoir Bank had solicited only my tears. The Caicos Bank might want heavier tributes. Shaped like the blade of an executioner's axe, the Caicos Bank looked as if it was after my head.

Streaming the log from one quarter and a lurid plastic lure from the other, we left Cockburn Harbour at 12 minutes past nine o'clock on the morning of Capetown's twenty-sixth birthday, heading westward across the Bank for the harbour of Sapodilla Bay on the island of Providenciales. Both of us wore grins, but mine may have looked fixed.

Sapodilla Bay lies some fifty miles from Cockburn Harbour. In moderate following winds, *Kylie* could just about cover this distance between sunrise and sunset but it would be foolish to try doing it because the Bank is peppered with coral heads. To avoid the thickest clusters we would need to steer dog-leg courses, which would stretch the mileage to more than sixty, and after three o'clock in the afternoon we would be steering into the sun. Shining onto the water ahead from a decreasingly low angle, the sun would then make pilotage impossible because even someone at the masthead would be unable to spot any coral heads which lay within 60 degrees of either bow. Rather than press ahead blindly, we would anchor in mid-afternoon and await the rising of the next day's sun.

Because it was his birthday, at noon I offered to make Capetown a marmalade sandwich. To my dismay he declined it. I became instantly suspicious. Had the blighter nosed out my marmalade and gorged himself already, then?

Standing on the stern, he tipped his ridiculous canvas hat backwards and remarked that though the log rotator was wriggling nicely in our wake, his lure was not attracting any fish. Just then a large one hurled itself into the air only yards away. Capetown whooped, and commanded the barracuda to take his lure as it sped across our wake. It didn't. Feigning commiseration, I plotted a bearing of the last of the Turks and Caicos islets we could expect to see on that day or much of the next one, and noted down the log-reading alongside it. Then I checked the depthsounder. It was working well, reading three fathoms. I was also relieved to discover the marmalade was still in its hiding place.

Outside the post office, Grand Turk

Shortly after two in the afternoon, when we were depending entirely on dead reckoning to reach an area where the coral heads were clustered less densely, Capetown suddenly yelled 'The log has gone!'

We hauled aboard the lines. Capetown's lure was still attached to his line, but a fish had taken the log rotator from the end of the other. Remembering my self-instructional notes, I produced a large smile and said brightly: 'I s'pose it was snapped up by your barracuda', Capetown coiled up his line and frowned.

'Climb the mast and hook yourself onto it,' I said with a hint of malice. 'We'll look for a place to anchor.'

The place we chose was not the best, but it was the only one which Capetown could spot as *Kylie* wound among the coral heads. In water which was clearer than any I had seen elsewhere, the black coral heads were impressive. They looked, also, a bit frightening. Made columnar by refraction, they stood around on the sea bed at irregular intervals, like well-helmeted policemen who have been drafted onto a city square in case any hanky-panky goes on. Whenever we sailed near one – something we could not help doing because there were so many of them – our bow wave set a policeman fidgeting beneath his flak-jacket, and sometimes he swung his truncheon.

Capetown remarked that a poet might look upon the coral heads as objects to inspire his muse to take wing. I said I didn't know about that, but they certainly put the breeze up me.

Some of their forbidding appearance and attitude may have been due to their savage remoteness. We were now far out of sight of land – the nearest inhabited island was 16 miles away and its direction lay athwart the wind. If one of the coral heads were to pierce the hull and sink us, it would be a long row to reach safety, even if we could do it. Rowing the dinghy sideways-on in a wind which was now blowing at more than 20 knots and raising steep seas would more than likely be beyond us. The only possible course to safety would lie downwind toward Providenciales, still 25 miles distant.

Apart from coral heads, other impediments to safe pilotage were the remarkable clarity of the water, the whiteness of the sandy bottom and its featureless surface. Around Antigua and all the other intervening islands of the Caribbees the water had been of a gradual opacity which allowed the eye to grade depths at a glance, and knolls, furrows, stones and weeds provided a range of natural punctuation marks which helped the reader to comprehend the text spread out below. The Caicos Bank offers no similar help to the mariner's eye. It comprises dazzlingly white sand and it is as flat as a ballroom, with hardly a hummock for fifty miles. Its only distinctive features are the black pillars of coral, so that trying to read the depth of water on the Caicos Bank is as easy as trying to make sense of a page of exclamation marks. For the previous two hours the depthsounder had indicated that we were sailing in nine feet of water. To anyone looking down at it from the cockpit of a small boat, however, the sea-bed seemed only inches away.

Kylie brought up – for those who have a soft spot for Barnett – on 11 fathoms of five-sixteenths calibrated chain in one and a half fathoms of water over blinding white sand at 35 minutes after two of the clock. I veered out such a long scope of cable (more than seven times the depth in which we had anchored) because the wind was gusting at 25 knots and my boat was pitching heavily to short, four-foot seas. Two sun-sights – the first taken at three o'clock that afternoon but the second not taken until eight the following morning – put us at 21° 32′N, 71° 58′W. If I had not been cooking a four-course dinner during the previous evening I could have taken star-sights to cross with the afternoon sun-sight.

But dammit, I told myself when Venus appeared soon after sunset in the western sky while I was trying to chop garlic with a Taiwanese knife, the star-sight can wait. The boat is firmly anchored, Capetown is 5000 miles from his home near Table Mountain, and today is his birthday; moreover, I am almost persuaded that he has not filched any of my marmalade.

I opened two tins of Tomsp and, finding that they did indeed contain tomato soup, was highly delighted.

It may have been because of the extra wine which I was obliged to drink – for Capetown is abstemious and the bottle was large – that I thought it to be one of the jolliest dinners I had ever attended. Wearing paper hats made from the business pages of *The Times* (the editorials were discarded on the grounds of their levity), we dined off *Crème de Tomate, Broccoli Grande Turque con Beurre Liquide, Poulet de la Montagne de la Table con les Pommes de Terre Frites et Poids Mushy.* We finished off, to Capetown's amusement, with Spotted Dick. Then, lounging on *Kylie*'s comfy red settee berths and having eaten from nine-inch plates which had stayed on her eighteen-inch-square table without any help from us when she was pitching her bows under, we clinked glasses and toasted our hostess.

During the night the wind speed dropped by ten knots and the wave heights lessened, but by the time I had taken the morning sun-sight the sky was three-eighths cloud and I was uncertain whether conditions were safe to continue. When clouds are darkening the water, collisions with coral heads are as likely to happen as when the sun is in your eyes. On much of the Caicos Bank which lay between our present anchorage and Sapodilla Bay, we would find that the coral heads were scattered more thickly, I remarked to Capetown, than currants in our Spotted Dick.

From the masthead I scanned the sea in the direction of Providenciales. Each cloud shadow looked to be the size of three or four soccer pitches end-to-end, and the shadows were moving westward at a moderate clip – about 15 miles an hour. If we carried only enough sail to make, say, 3 knots, the apparent speed of the cloud shadows would be reduced to 12 knots. Did this mean that *Kylie* would be in a shadowed area of sea for about only one minute at a time or didn't it?

I put the question to Capetown. Pulling his hat forward until the tails of its headband were streaming forward horizontally along its brim, he agreed that it did.

'We'll make sail, then,' I said. 'If the sky becomes too cloudy we can always anchor again.'

On and off, between the time we weighed anchor at nine in the morning until we arrived at Sapodilla Bay at two in the afternoon, one or other of us was in the rigging for four hours.

As though calculating all the lovely overtime they were clocking up, the policemen stopped swinging their clubs and nodded us cheerfully through into the anchorage, but I was pleased to be able to write 'End of Passage' in the logbook when the anchor cable was cleated down. It was a passage I could not have made readily without the assistance of a crew. Had Capetown not been with me I should have remained at anchor and awaited a lessening of the cloud cover.

'Let us up-anchor and sail tomorrow to another lighthouse,' I said to him at Sapodilla, at the end of a day on which I had told him about my landing on Sombrero and had opened another tin of Tomsp which had turned out to be rice pudding, 'so that we can eat better grub.'

In the event, it took us three days to cover the 150-odd miles between Sapodilla Bay and the lighthouse on Castle Island, which lies at the southern end of the Bahamas chain.

We sailed toward its gleaming white tower and red-capped lantern on a glorious morning, with the sea smooth, the sun high, and hardly a cloud in the sky. There was no need, now, to tear our jeans or graze our feet and legs on the rigging by piloting *Kylie* from aloft. Because we were nearing civilization, Capetown pulled on a pair of cleanish white shorts and stood in the bows, whooping at dolphins and pointing the way through the reefs to an anchorage near a spectacular beach.

The camera and a notebook, I told him when I had twanged its straps, were in the ultra-marvellous holdall. He had launched the dinghy and was ready to ferry us ashore.

'What about food and water?'

'There is a pint of tepid liquid and a couple of soggy choc-bars in the holdall as well, but we'll not need them. After Sombrero, this place looks plushy. They'll probably offer us iced tea and Black Forest gateaux.'

From whichever angle one viewed it, Castle Island was both tremendous and twee. Tremendous, because the lighthouse itself erupted from an ocean of greenery in the way that the waterspout from an eight-inch shell fired by HMS *Effingham* had risen in HB pencil and wax crayon from the inside back covers of my school atlas; and twee because cottage-style buildings – too small to be barracks and not large enough to be houses – with cosy verandahs and dappled gardens could be glimpsed among the trees. Surrounded by palms, banana plantains and a profusion of what Capetown said was hibiscus and oleander, and having a foreground of what both of us admitted later was well, er, just sand, but with everywhere else – and there were endless miles of sky and water – done out in regal shades of blue, the scene produced feelings of lushness. It was an island on which the sort of millionaire about whom Eartha Kitt used to sing would be happy to put his feet up.

Most certainly, I confided to Capetown, eyeing the cottages over his shoulder as he rowed towards them, the residents would not be eating Tomsp or Spotted Dick. It seemed more than likely that several cubic feet of Black Forest gateaux, double-decked with ice cream, might be on offer.

And even when we were standing on the nearest verandah, the ice-cream idea seemed sustainable. From the expanse of solar panels on the roofs, we knew the keepers had electricity. The white clapboard of the bungalow looked recently painted; the porch and verandah were uncluttered; no jalousies hung askew.

Capetown removed his ridiculous hat and combed his hair with his fingers. I emptied sand out of my shoes and rapped on a door.

'Not so hard,' he said. 'They'll be having their siesta.'

The door swung inwards and I stepped forward.

If Capetown had not been close enough behind me to grab my belt I should have fallen into a void because all the floorboards had been taken up and removed. Except for insects and reptiles, no creatures inhabited the place. For all its loveliness to the human eye, Castle Island was deserted.

We forced a way through shoulder-high weeds to reach the oleander and hibiscus, where we sat down and ate the choc bars, compensating for their sogginess by chewing nuts of philosophy.

'Automation has to happen,' said I.

'Yes?'

'Progress is unstoppable,' I insisted.

'Who says it's progress? You can only call it progress if you benefit. What are those keepers doing now? Yesterday they were eating home-grown bananas and their children were fishing the reefs; today they are eating their hearts out and their children are fishing for reefers.'

'Don't be so emotive. You don't know what they're doing. Perhaps they are putting their feet up and enjoying Jung. Perhaps their children are reading Jung, too.'

'Pass the water bottle, please, if there is still any left.'

We drank the last of the water while standing at the end of the railway line on which the last keepers of Castle Island light had hauled up their boats. Sand had drifted over most of the railway but the spindle of the windlass still bore traces of grease. The barrel was wooden and it looked very old.

Before Capetown weighed anchor I looked back at the windlass and wondered if it had been constructed by the same carpenter who had tried to build a windlass for Anguilla. If he had succeeded, wouldn't the black woman have thought it was progress?

At least, I sniffed, turning my eyes to the compass, the windlass would have meant she'd have had more time and energy for saying prayers and contemplating maidenberries.

We were making about one mile an hour, heading for Governor's Harbour from Little San Salvador, the wind had dropped, and I had been reading *Six Characters in Search of an Author*.

I was not complaining, I said, but for the past four weeks he had been writing so many E3s in the logbook that anyone who looked into it later might think that we had been residing in the Mile End Road.

He eased the sheet of the ghoster, but he did not laugh. I wrote 'E 1' in the 'Wind' column and returned to the cockpit holding my nose.

'What's up *now*?' said Capetown.

His 'now' was a bit much.

'Don't you know *anything* about London? We are surrounded by rotting fruit. The 'E 1' postcode includes Spitalfields market.'

He did not laugh at that one, either. He just said: 'I left England when I was 12', and went back to playing the sheet.

The Force 1 was unusual. Easterly winds of Force 3 had been just what Capetown and I had needed so as to maintain our agreeable lifestyle and amity. For four weeks there had been enough wind power to keep *Kylie* moving steadily through the Greater Antilles and the Bahamas, but not so much as to raise waves to make him queasy or to spill the gin-and-tonics, highballs, Bloody Marys, beers and tequilas which, between one sunrise and the next, had stood on whatever flat surface was handy till I had drunk them. Although the Force 1 was pandering to our sybaritic dispositions, as far as getting to Governor's Harbour was concerned the Force 1 was a let-down.

From the look of the sky it seemed other components of the weather might also be collapsing. I considered whether I should check the barometer, but, since this would have meant putting down the tequila I had just mixed and then raising myself from the cushions, I asked Capetown to do it.

The pointer was still on 1021 millibars, he said, the same figure on which it had been reclining for five days. I lifted my hand from the tequila and pointed at a cumulus which was rising from the western horizon.

'I saw another cloud which looked like that one when I was going from Barbuda toward Mount Misery,' I said. 'The wind blew at twenty-five knots but it didn't veer much. It stayed between east and south-east.'

'What little wind we have here and now,' Capetown said as the ghoster drooped onto a spreader and a cap shroud, 'seems about to take leave of us.'

We anchored in two fathoms of water at a quarter to seven, still thirty miles short of our destination. No wind stirred the water. The sea was a mirror in which lay a pink-and-yellow sunset.

After swallowing a corned-beef hash while gazing at Venus, we filleted the subject of the Bahamian clergyman who had been an architectural phenomenon. According to what I had been told while goggling at one of his buildings, this man had designed and built a church with two very grand towers. People had walked miles to marvel at their grandeur, and his congregation had multiplied so exceedingly that other shepherds must have suspected that he'd been rustling their flocks. Then, after years of being Anglican, he'd changed his mind – like my insurance broker had done – about the relative importance of the Unity and the Trinity, and had defected (if that is the correct term in these equable times) to the Roman Catholics, in whose pastures he had built another church, identical to his Anglican creation except that all its dimensions were increased to the nth power. Out-topping its rival by miles, the new church had drawn even larger crowds of admirers. Hundreds of sheep had deserted the Anglican folds and become Catholics.

'It made no difference to them in the end,' I said, one eye on the sky. '*My Father's house has many mansions*, and all that.'

'How can you *say* it? Building the second church made a *heck* of a difference,' said Capetown. 'Did he build it on the *same* island?'

'Yes, I think he did.'

'He did wrong, then. It was done out of spite. He should have built it on another island or better still in another country. How could he preach morality from a pulpit built on spite and sour grapes?'

As if shocked at the severity of this judgement (knowing he was a rampant ecologist, though, I myself had seen it coming), the mirrored sunset cracked and shattered. A wind had come from the north-west.

Casting the dinner plates into a bucket, I squared up the cockpit while Capetown set the mainsail. Under the small jib, the reefed mainsail and a thickening sky, we weighed anchor and beat towards Governor's Harbour. Handicapped by the lack of our Walker log (for a young barracuda had sneaked off with yet another rotator, in the manner of one who knows he is taking your last éclair from the cake-stand), I was obliged to guess our speed and distance run. To add to our problems, forty minutes after we had got under way we were set upon by a thunderstorm.

'Get the jib down!' I gasped above the roar of the wind and the drumming of the rain. 'We'll anchor till this lot has blown over.'

Before he could scramble to the foredeck, however, *Kylie* had run aground.

Of course, I told him when the squall had passed and we were lowering the anchor into the dinghy, the bottom was unblemished sand. There was no coral for miles. We had sounded around with the boathook, and if he would kindly row out forty yards of our eight-plait nylon on a bearing of 080° and allow me to tip the anchor over the stern of the dinghy into the six feet of water which undoubtedly lay there, we would have *Kylie* kedged-off this here sand bar in no time.

In what seemed like hours later, having laid out the anchor, heaved taut the eight-plait nylon, jumped up and down in unison on the foredeck, canted the boat from side to side by careering back and forth across the coachroof, and larked about, in other words, like a couple of school-leavers on the last day of term, we retired to the cockpit for a breather.

Or even, as far as I was concerned, for a laugh. Capetown poured himself a drink of water and eyed my Glenfiddich with the mien of a seriously permanent (as opposed to a frivolously part-time) member of the teaching staff who had come upon a first-former puffing a ciggy.

'We'll have to wait for the tide to lift us off,' I said, regarding him darkly through the plastic beaker which occasionally, in fits of euphoria, I called a glass.

'I thought you said that one of the delights of cruising the West Indies was the absence of tides?'

'At the time, I was referring to the matter of entering harbours. A tidal range of seven feet can often stop me from getting into Southwold, but a two-foot-seven-inch tidal range won't stop us from entering Governor's Harbour.'

'It seems to be having a good go. We haven't shifted an inch.'

'Ah, but this isn't the harbour entrance, is it? We shall just have to be patient.'

I sipped my Glenfiddich in the cockpit and went on looking at Venus. Capetown went below and began another chapter of Jung.

Venus sank below the western horizon, the moon moved, and several zillion tons of water sluiced through the Tongue of the Ocean, the Mira Por Vos ('Watch Out For Yourself') channel, and other delightfully-named gullies, and, as the result of this stupendous activity, two hours before midnight, when Capetown was well into Part II, Section 12 ('The Spiritual Problem of Modern Man') and I was into another Glenfiddich, *Kylie* rose half an inch and floated off the sandbank.

Each uttering his own private sigh, we put aside our impedimenta of happiness, unbent our calloused fingers and made sail.

12

The Charleston Landing

A day's sail north of the Bahamas we whizzed out of the Gulf Stream and headed for Charleston. I pricked off the noon position on the chart and shortly after I had done that our amity got damaged.

'Look,' I said, 'it's *Kylie's* best-ever day's run: one hundred and ninety-two miles, noon to noon. This calls for a celebration.'

Though I knew he was watching me I dug out another beer from the bilge. The trouble was, the beer was lukewarm and my hand was shaking with glee. I yanked the ring-pull and beer geysered onto his shorts. Capetown was less than pleased. He changed into another pair of shorts and then he ran a steely eye over my figures.

'Wasn't the horizon fuzzy when you took the morning sight? Don't you think the fuzziness might breed a few errors?'

'Here he goes again,' I thought, wiping foam from my chin. 'Twenty-six years old, hardly knows a bowline from a backsplice, and he's getting up my nose again worse than gassy beer.'

I stowed the sextant away and despite my self-discipline tapped hard the barometer.

'What did I say about the three "L"s? About Lead, Log and Lookout? If you were keeping a lookout instead of reading Jung, you would've noticed that buoy ahead. It's the Charleston landfall buoy.'

'It's not a buoy,' Capetown said, proffering the binoculars; 'it's a fishing boat.'

The Charleston buoy did not make an appearance until two hours after I had claimed it had already done so, by which time I was in a black mood. Plainly, all my faculties were silting up. My ears had been choked up for centuries and now my eyes were going, too. If things went on at this rate, soon I would be marooned like a Cinque Port, haunted by mud-hoppers and people who once ate whelks. If my eyes were mistaking fishing boats for landfall buoys and false horizons for true ones, I might as well pack up and go home. That noonday position must have been all of *twelve miles* in error . . .

I pulled the harmonica from its locker, intending to blow myself a cheery tune, but it was choked with marmalade and fluff. Also, I noticed, the rust on its casing had spread. *Kylie* must be leaking as freely as Liverpool Lou.

'And like that lady,' I murmured at her hull while mopping out the locker, 'you are poxily osmotic down below.'

I had thought I had cured her of the boat pox back in Norwich six years previously, but before setting off northward on the axis of the Gulf Stream I had dived overboard to scrub the slime from her hull and had come across a large pimple on the turn of her bilge. I had hardly dared to touch it because it looked so venereal.

'You should have been more careful,' I said. 'It was probably that smooth Italian job which was rubbing against you in St Martin.'

Kylie cackled down the front of a swell. Out of Capetown's sight-line, I poured a whisky and thought: 'Have a good laugh while you can; it may well be your last. You are less commodious than an alligator's armpit and you are damper than it, too. You know what . . .? I am going to sell thee into bondage when we get to Carolina! My fund manager says my nest egg is incubating nicely, and so I'll change up to a forty-footer when we get to Charleston. I'll arrive in style at the wedding in Baton Rouge . . .'

'Sorry to interrupt your conversation,' said Capetown, putting his head into the cabin and eyeing the whisky with a hint of disdain, 'but would you please pass me my hat?'

I passed it up politely enough but really I could have thrown it at him. Cobbled out of canvas, stiff with salt, sweat and speckles of blood, yet sporting a multi-coloured headband whose tails jigged flippantly behind, it symbolised the paradoxes of its owner's character and situation. The headband declared that Capetown had a frivolous attitude towards life, but the stiff canvas and the utilitarian shape argued the opposite. At first he had worn the hat with frivolity on the back of his head, and had canted it forward only when he was being stern or having a session with Jung. It had been on the back of his head when we had surfed into the Boca de Infierno and had explored the caves on Isla Mona, but these days he was wearing it canted forward more often than not.

Capetown, I decided, was becoming a prig.

I swallowed a mouthful of whisky and scratched my head.

On the other hand, I thought when the whisky had warmed my stomach, he'd worked with a will, he had stood his watches, and (though it was irksome to think so) he had saved my boat from disaster on the Mouchoir Bank.

'It's me who's the meanie,' I murmured, stowing the bottle away. 'I'm a hollow, slothful meanie.'

Capetown put his head into the cabin to look at the chart.

'What does Jung say about it?' I asked him.

'About what?'

'About what is running or – as your mentor Jung might have noticed – ruining my life. Jennie says my Karma is running it. What does Jung say?'

'In principle, Jung says we are either introvert or extrovert, with one or more significant functional modes predominating . . .'

'Oh dear me,' I said, pulling on a jacket, 'that sounds a bit ominous. Let's get into Charleston.'

Kylie arrived off Charleston at three in the morning, just as a fleet of shrimp boats were leaving. The shrimpers were holding their nets aloft with their derricks and jostling each other merrily, rather like Victorian farm-girls might have done when they went on seaside outings to Southwold. Holding their skirts up and titupping at the prospect of a paddle, they barged past with throaty gurgles, knocking all the wind from our sails.

When *Kylie* had got her breath back and was on course again, I said that though I'd never been into Charleston before and it was a dark and moonless night, we had a large-scale chart of the harbour and so we wouldn't wait until daylight but would enter straight away.

I told Capetown to stand at the chart table, tick off the buoys as we passed them and call out the courses to steer. The sails were now drawing nicely but in the entrance channel we made slow progress against a two-knot ebb tide.

'A buoy flashing red every four seconds is abeam,' I told him after a while. 'What's the next course?'

'That will be number eight buoy. Hold the same course.'

'It can't be number eight, you clot! We passed it way back, for Christ's sake!'

We were off Fort Sumter, the place where the American Civil War had started. A whiff of insurrection must have still been hanging around, for straight away Capetown shot out of the cabin and thrust his face close to mine.

'I don't need glasses and ear trumpets, even if you do! When you last spoke you said we were *approaching* a flashing red light. You never did say we had *passed* it! Since your eyesight and hearing seem to be giving us dangerous problems, I suggest we double check all communications until such time as this boat is docked someplace where I can leave it.'

'That time,' I shouted back at him, 'will not be a second too early!'

It took an hour to slog a further two miles up-river, by which time *his* temper, at least, had cooled.

In the early light he came out into the cockpit and looked at the mansions on the riverside, all with their Stars and Stripes glowing in the sunrise.

'Peter,' he said, 'do we really have to bust our braces to get to the City Marina? Can't we moor up over there and wait for the flood to carry us up?'

'It's too shallow,' I snarled, not even bothering to look at the chart.

He rubbed the stubble on his chin and took up the binoculars.

'H'm,' he grunted. 'Over there, a bigger boat than *Kylie* is lying alongside a pontoon . . .'

'That doesn't mean there's enough water there for *Kylie*, does it? It could be a centreboarder; there's a lot of them around these parts. Why don't you stop telling me what's what? If I say we're going to berth at the City Marina, we're going to berth at the City Marina, even if it takes us all day to get there, and that's that!'

So, a few minutes later we are moored at the nearby pontoon and Capetown is watching pelicans diving for their breakfasts while I am making ours.

I stirred the porridge and said: 'I'm sorry about my bad temper . . . The thought of wearing glasses and ear trumpets is a bit off-putting.'

'That's foolish, isn't it? Sooner or later, facts have to be faced. If your sight and hearing are below par, you'll just have to wear specs and hearing aids.'

I gave a few more stirs before answering him.

'Do you want me to ladle a ton of salt onto your porridge,' I said; 'or would you prefer sugar?'

'I'll tell you what,' said Capetown: 'because your hearing is down, why not let *me* go ashore and phone the US Customs?'

It was strictly against the rules, of course: only skippers are permitted to go ashore and check in. But before I could stop myself I had agreed to it and he was off. I watched him lope along the dock, the ridiculous hat on the back of his head, carrying three bagfuls of trash which consisted mostly of beer cans and liquor bottles. Perhaps it had not been a bad trip, I thought, leafing through the dog-eared pages of the logbook before writing 'End of Passage' and lighting a pipe. Capetown wasn't bad, really . . .

The smoke of two further pipefuls had drifted above the Stars and Stripes in our rigging before his shadow fell across the companionway and *Kylie* listed as he stepped on her side-deck.

'What terrific self-discipline!' he grinned, holding up a bundle. 'Our first mail in months, and yet I keep mine unopened until I get back aboard so you can open yours at the same time.'

We read our letters and fell silent. After a while I put mine aside and decanted methylated spirit into the bowl of the Primus.

'Tea?'

'Yes, please; I think I need it.'

'Oh?'

'That friend of mine in London . . . he's dead.'

'I'm sorry.'

'They say it was suicide . . . He'd received his draft papers for the South African army.'

The flame of the Primus guttered and died. I fumbled for a match.

The match flared. Capetown blinked twice, and then he burst out: 'He'd no *right* to do that! Trying to dodge away from facts . . . making other people clear up *his* mess! You can't *navigate* by feelings, can you? Feelings can power you, but only logic can navigate. You can know your *true* position only if the horizon's clear and the figures are in their right columns . . .'

I dumped a spent teabag and said: 'You don't have to leave *Kylie* straight away, you know. You could stay longer if you wanted to.'

'I thought I heard you going on about . . . saying something about selling her and buying a bigger boat?'

'I can't do that, I'm afraid. One of my letters said my fund manager has blown my nest egg. So it looks as if *Kylie* will be mine for a while longer . . . and so . . . er . . . you could stay . . .'

'Thanks, but no. I have to look for a flight.'

'Oh, yes . . . of course. You'll need to get to London.'

He looked out at the British ensign and shook his head.

'No, not London: not any more. I may have been born in England, and I may have been using a UK passport to get around the world, but where I *really* belong is South Africa . . . and it's time *I* faced up to *that* fact.'

He stacked his letters neatly in his berth, alongside *The Portable Jung*. Then he took off his hat, flicked the headband, and tossed it into my lap.

111

Startled, I flinched away. The hat fell to the cabin side.
'Go on,' said Capetown; 'take it! I know you think it's a great hat.'
I looked at the hat but did not move to pick it up.
'Who's flung Jung?' I said. 'Who's navigating by logic now?'
'D'you *hear* what I am saying? The hat is now yours.'
'That's just sentiment,' I said; 'just fuzzy sentiment.'
But sometimes, even on grey days in England, I still wear it.

13

Dogdays

Anyone who has cruised the Norfolk Broads will recognize the Intracostal. Enchantingly misty at sunrise, scratched by catspaws an hour later, merely ruffled when the wind is with the current but rucked into steep waves which dollop onto your foredeck when blowing contrary, the wider sections of the US Intracostal Waterway can be both as lovely and as lousy as Breydon Water. Narrower segments, where the Corps of Engineers has dug channels but where birds with long legs still teeter on their own reflections, are not unlike the higher reaches of the River Yare, – or, now I think of them, the Thames, the Severn, or the Warwickshire Avon.

In its length, though, the Intracostal has all England's – and most of Europe's – waterways beaten. From Florida to Virginia, its east-coast section stretches twelve hundred miles. To cover the same distance in what Nelsonic die-hards and the few remaining Hull trawlermen still call British waters, you would need to sail from Lands End, up the Channel and North Sea to where the Arctic Circle skewers Iceland. Add on the mileage of the Gulf Coast wiggly bits, and the journey would land you on the bleak island of Jan Mayen, when you would be in the same latitude as the North Cape of Norway and wondering, if the whisky can de-frost your skull, why on earth you had jolly well come.

Unless they are the ghost of Peter Tangvald, who sailed his 50-foot gaff yawl 190 miles from Beaufort, North Carolina, to Great Bridge, Virginia, and found the passage easy, the same spine-chilling question might penetrate mariners who try sailing the length of the Intracostal. Even a nippy, fin-keeled boat with a full crew and a self-tacking jib would find that sailing it is not a doddle. The waterway's fixtures and fittings have been aligned to accommodate powerboats rather than sailing boats, and though many American 'sailboats' migrate the twelve hundred miles with the coming and going of the seasons, they do not cover the distance without cranking their motors. And why

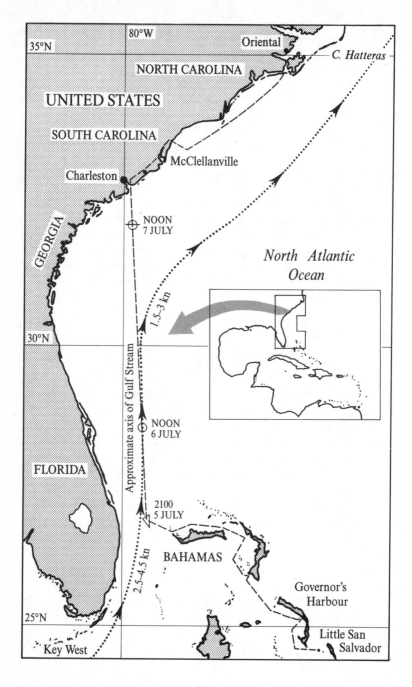

114

should they? Successful Americans – whether named Juan Poncé de León or Richard M. Nixon – have advanced gloriously to Florida, Washington or wherever without quibbling about how they were getting there. Americans are not cranky purists. Any method of progress has always been okay in America so long as the boat gets to the fountains of youth or the motorcade gets to the White House.

Mariners who hail from less desperate cultures may find passaging the Intracostal is quite difficult. When Bill Cooper had suggested in Menorca that Philippe Fau could travel its whole length in his 25-foot sloop, Philippe had doubted it, for his boat has no engine and he would have to pass through or under 200 bridges, whose keepers would lambast him with their tannoys – something they are quite good at – when they saw him sailing past their windows instead of motoring past them like the regulations said he should.

'Have a go! I'm sure you could sail it!' had urged Bill, pouring more red wine into Philippe's glass; but the Frenchman had shaken his head and merrily demurred.

Now, having twice in four hours run *Kylie* onto mudbanks, I thought that even without the bridge problem Philippe would be wise not to try it. I had been using a six-horsepower engine to motor along a stretch which had no bridges but I had still got myself into a mess. My six horses had panted towards the western shore so keenly that I had been unable to keep them heading up-channel for the Pamlico Sound and the Outer Banks of North Carolina, an area in which my six-dollar tour-guide atlas insisted they could get . . . *interactive hands-on multimedia experiences* . . . (such as, presumably, eating grass) . . . *for free*. Unfortunately, though, the horses had begged to differ; in their opinion, grass on the Outer Banks was bound to taste too salty. This line of sweet but selfish reasoning may have satisfied the horses, but by the time I had kedged myself off the second mudbank it was driving me crackers. If they bolted towards the Appalachian foothills again, I reckoned *Kylie* could be high and dry until the Second Flood.

I bucketed mud off the foredeck and puttered onwards.

Water in less cataclysmic amounts was gushing out of the Carolinas, ebbing from not only the Intracostal Waterway but also a sprawling hinterland of lakes, creeks and rivers. Some of their oceanic outlets are

---

Opposite: Cape Hatteras to Key West, showing *Kylie's* track through the Bahamas to the Outer Banks of North Carolina.

ten or more miles apart, and so a boat which is being carried forward parallel with the coast by the outflow at one moment will find itself stemming an adverse current when it gets past the gap. As well as that, when crossing an outlet or a river, the boat will be carried sideways by cross-currents too. In winds which were as light as I was finding them, even Philippe Fau would be lucky to make a dozen of his measly Napoleonic kilometres – let alone miles – between sunrise and sunset. If he wasn't abeam of an outlet at or near slack water he might have to stay anchored in the same spot for hours, or – if the wind died and he felt disinclined to row out anchors and kedge his boat onward like I was doing – perhaps days.

North of Charleston I hauled *Kylie* off yet another mudbank and nosed her into McClellanville, a harbour insulated from the Atlantic by a scarf of sedge, at a time of day when the shrimp-boat skippers were grooming their nets and their boats were purring like coddled cats. Everything looked clean and neat. The dockmaster hitched *Kylie*'s bowline to a cleat, popped a cola and said 'How're yuh doin'?'

Deducing from the cast of my facial mudpack that I hadn't been doing too well, a disabled war veteran pulled me a beer and said 'McClellanville's a nice city . . .' adding, like many other Americans do, '. . . to be at.'

McClellanville was nice place for a muddy Englishman to be at alright but it did not look big enough to be a city. It seemed to have fewer houses and people than did a Suffolk town. The evening I strolled its streets I found lots of antebellum gentility around, but some of it was oddly named or positioned. A clapboard building which the dockmaster called the city hall but which was not much bigger than a Southwold beach hut though it was painted less jazzily, squatted beneath huge oak trees on a roadway which was grand enough to be an avenue in England but in McClellanville was still labelled only a street. The height and breadth of the live oaks was magnificent, too, but with Spanish moss dripping from their branches, the trees seemed rather off put and miffed, like elderly aunts who had wandered into a teenage rave-up and become embrangled in the party fuzz. Shaking glitter from their shawls in the moonlight, they exchanged pleasantries about the olden days and complained about the doings of the young.

Middle-aged people dwelling in the houses under those trees were less stuffy. Someone in a rocking-chair folded his newspaper, tilted his specs and murmured 'How're yuh *doin'*?'

116

As *Kylie* stumbled through the Carolinas and south again to Baton Rouge, 'How're yuh *doing?*' was on the lips of many other Americans who made her welcome. The 'doing' separates the Americans from the English more deeply than their accents do. Accents are the skin colours of a language but words are its flesh and gristle. Between the American 'How're you *doing?*' and the English 'How *are* you?' lies a difference in attitudes which is wider than the Atlantic, and deeper too.

In the English greeting it's your health which is being asked about. With his 'How *are* you?' the Englishman wants to know how soon you'll be entering your grave. In America, though, your health is taken for granted; the questioner is not asking about your state of being but your busyness.

For, whichever way we spell it, business is everything to American people; and so it is natural that American flies should think likewise. American flies are not content just to *be* flies; they have to *do* the fly thing all the time. Your English fly is content to hang upside down and philosophise for minutes on end, but the US fly has hardly got himself upside down before he must be airborne again and busily buzzing. He is not – as you might think – showing off; he is merely telling you he means business. Since he is the size of a toy helicopter and is armed to the teeth, the business is aggressive.

Another distinction is that, apart from the Suffolk bluebottle who tries to batter through my windows in Southwold, the flies of South Carolina are the only flies I have ever heard. At least, they are the only flies I *think* I have heard. Their attacks always coincided with the advent of extra-loud buzzings in my ears, and so I thought the buzzings were coming from the flies. Looking back into the logbook, I think I may have been deceived, for I now see that the fly attacks and the buzzings started on the day I consumed the last of my thick Dundee marmalade and started drinking (*sic*) a jar of American jam. The jam was labelled 'Orange' and had been concocted in California. It was thin enough, said a Scot who tried in vain to stop it dribbling off his bread, to ascend your wee capillaries and ooze out of your sconce. The jam made the Scot dizzy; for me it just gave rise to more buzzes.

Attacking singly and in waves, biting through jeans and thick socks, the Carolina flies did their best to buzz me insane just when I was needing to focus on the currents of the waterway.

It happened on a Sunday, when I had given the six horses the day off work so as to kid myself that I was sailing the Intracostal without using the engine. Becalmed, and having made only seven miles since eating my porridge, I dropped a mud-hook in mid-channel and waited for a helpful current to come along. The atmosphere was very like a Sunday afternoon at the end of the White Hart race, when you are sitting outside the pub at Blythburgh, waiting for the ebb to carry you back to Southwold and the Harbour Inn. A bird resembling an English heron was contemplating its reflection in the shallows. Mugfuls of Broadside Ale drifted to mind. I tipped Capetown's hat over my eyes and determined to be restful and content. After all, Sunday was Sunday . . . People in God's Own Country didn't need to be busy seven days a week . . .

There came the sound of a two-stroke lawnmower with its throttle jammed open, and a squadron of anti-sabbatical horse-flies zoomed out from the banks. Pulling the hat over my ears, I stood to arms and brandished something hissy called Off.

'Eff off!' I cried, pressing the button till the Off was on.

I enveloped myself in a cloud which hung about so densely that I had difficulty in seeing the flies. This did not at first seem to matter. The idea wasn't to target individual marauders but to encompass them *en masse*. I had faith in the vapour's deterrent properties, for it had fazed several mosquitoes in Charleston and had routed a posse of gnats in McClellanville. This latest cloud, I thought, should be large enough to deter all the flies in South Carolina. Enveloped in mist, I waited for them to buzz off.

Instead, their buzzings got louder. The horse-flies charged straight through the vapour, attached themselves to my body and started to consume it. I squirted more vapour and made a bigger cloud, but the only creatures affected by it were myself and the heron. My left eye started watering. The heron raised its head above the droplets and took off.

By this time the can had run out of Off. However much I shook it, only unmiasmic hisses came out, so now I started slapping at the flies. Watched by eyes which in Florida would certainly have been an alligator's but in the Carolinas might have been only those of a frog on a log, I thrashed around mightily, well on the road to madness.

My frenzy was arrested by a sudden bellow. Laden barges and a tumbling cliff of water were bearing down from the north. I started the engine, heaved up the mud-hook and motored to the side of the channel. Steering with my backside and beating the air, I sped towards the only remaining haven of refuge: the sea.

Ten miles offshore, at midnight the rising moon looked like a scoop of ice-cream dripping onto a mirror. The thermometer stuck in the high seventies till sunrise but rose to 89° for the fourth day running as I headed for the land.

'It's the dogdays,' explained two gentlemen of Oriental, the only town I know that has been named after a ship and not vice versa; 'it's our dogdays.'

Their liking for the unusual was evident not only in the naming of their town or appropriating the hottest days of the calendar unto themselves: it included matters maritime as well. Local sailors thought the dogdays were sensible days on which to be on the open water, where the air was cooler and less fly-blown, and they also thought the dogdays were good days for holding regattas. Unluckily for the competitors, the dogdays were notoriously windless.

'Hell! Wind or no wind,' said the gentlemen, 'the Dogdays Regatta is our big *fun* thing, y'know! It's the time we go partying and such. You never been to a Carolina Dogdays party? Grab yourself a six-pack and come along.'

In company with three other boats I motor-sailed 38 miles in nine hours to the regatta on the Pamlico River, which lies inside the banks of Cape Hatteras. Finding more wind on the way than I'd ever expected, for two hours *Kylie* glided sedately, her engine silent, through water which varied in colour from heron-grey to smoky blue; but in the afternoon the wind came and went three times in as many hours. I set the ghoster whenever the wind came, but *Kylie* did not overtake the others.

It must have been the frequency of my sail-changing rather than its effectiveness which inspired Sal and Lena to pop the question.

'Hey! How 'bout you 'n us doin' it together?' said they, thrusting their cigarettes into my Zippo. 'Looks like you got loads of experience.'

'When would you like it to happen?' I said.

'Tomorrow's the only time we got.'

'Okay, we'll do it tomorrow on yours,' I said. I tried to blow a smoke ring. It buckled, sagged and failed to rise. 'What'll I bring?'

'Don't bring nothing. We got the gizmos; you got the know-how.'

'What about some cushions?' I said. 'My bones are awfully close to my skin.'

'Heck, we got *loads* of cushions,' they said.

The ancient cannon which made the bang to start the race looked authentic, and the bang itself was utterly convincing. Wearing what could have been a Confederate uniform which, from the shine on its cuffs, had been worn not just on dogdays but on cooler days too, a man named Frank James boiled his coffee in an enamelled coffee-pot, gazed into the smoky distance and cranked the barrel higher. Since the cannon was not intended on that day to be firing live shells, until I noticed the sticker on his truck his reason for adjusting the barrel was obscure. THE SOUTH WILL RISE AGAIN, however, said it all. Could this here Frank James, I wondered, be a grandson of the famous outlaw? From the net of creases around his eyes and the whiteness of his beard it looked entirely possible. And he wasn't the only one to perhaps be stepping out of the pages of history. Also present was a man in a coonskin hat who was oiling a Winchester rifle. People with other anti-Union stickers gathered round, drank colas and eyed the duo with respect. Him and Frank weren't partying at no goddam fun thing: they were readying to have a shoot-out and re-start the Civil War.

'Hell!' said Frank, eyes misty as he loaded a blank. 'I need to be firing real ammunition.'

He let off his cannon at mid-morning. The smoke rose above the trees and hung there. On the start line a faint wind puckered the water like a thread being pulled through a swatch of sateen.

With Sal at the helm and Lena on the jib sheet, we travelled a hundred yards before the wind died. In an hour and a half we had made two miles but our concentration was flagging. Under the hot and greasy sky the river looked like used cooking foil. Boats were annealed to its surface, pointing all ways. Somebody fell overboard and was whooped and cat-called. Sails flapped like the wings of dying butterflies; Sal opened a bottle of gin.

'My boyfriend had a wheeze,' said Lena. 'He sold condom-vending machines which carried the motto *Let Us Come Before You Do*.'

Somehow, on her third gin Sal passed me a thicker cushion and murmured: 'The darnedest thing 'bout life is, women's sex drive increases as they get older.'

Also floundering on the water were insects, rafting up with the cigarette ash alongside the boats until they eventually died. More people fell off decks or were pushed. Frank's cannon emitted another puff of smoke and somebody's radio said the race had been abandoned. We motored back to the shore, singing *The Elephant's Bottom*. After taking a shower we smoked and ate popcorn while Frank loaded the cannon onto his truck.

The dogdays proceedings were not totally unrewarding: in a raffle that evening I won a twelve-speed bike.

Frank James prepares for the Dogdays Regatta

14

Gabrielle and Other Wild Ones

By September I was sailing offshore again, heading south for Cape Canaveral, snatching sun-sights as *Kylie* balanced on the swells from hurricane Gabrielle. Though the name may sound charming to those with normal hearing and unflattened insteps, to me Gabrielle was an apt name for a powerful disturbance.

Gabrielle had been the name of a World War II Belgian Land Army girl who had driven her tractor over my left foot and made it flatter. She had been hastening to a wedding, and the wedding had been her own. The tractor had skidded on a muddy Warwickshire bridleway and its offside rear wheel had gone over my foot. Luckily, the tractor had been wearing soft tyres, I had been wearing stout boots and the ground had been quaggy, else I might have passed out. Gabrielle had hitched up her white bridal gown, jumped down from the tractor and wiped my nose with a lace hanky. Bystanders said afterwards that white was the wrong colour and that the wedding was a shotgun affair. At 14, I had thought they'd meant she should have been wearing khaki and going to the war.

Pregnant with a cargo more explosive than children, hurricane Gabrielle became larger as she closed with America. Her oceanic bulges were huge, being all of thirty feet from trough to crest. Climbing the mast to look for a sea buoy near Cape Canaveral, I misjudged a mast step and mangled thereby my other foot.

Hurricane Gabrielle swept across the coastline hundreds of miles distant, flattening many buildings. SHIT HAPPENS cried the car-stickers, and next day people started rebuilding their shattered homes. I breathed easier and looked around Florida. In creeks off the waterway I saw alligators with custard-cream bellies, and orange-coloured snakes which looked as if their backs had been stencilled with black diamonds. They gazed at but did not hinder *Kylie* as she, too, wriggled westward across the Okeechobee shallows of the Intracostal. The only organisms that hindered her progress were water hyacinths,

Gabrielle hastens to her wedding

which clogged the propeller and fouled the paddle of the windvane steering gear until I removed it.

But by the time I reached the Caloosahatchee most of the glamour had departed from Florida and the remainder had tarnished. Perhaps this was because by then I was seeing carrion birds feeding off the corpses of headless alligators and also by then the flies were thicker than anywhere else since Carolina and I was worrying about when and where the next hurricane would hit the mainland.

The lock-keeper at Ortona thought sportsmen had sawn off the alligators' heads to mount them on the walls of their gun rooms, but he said nothing about flies or hurricanes. Mounting an alligator's head would pose a leverage problem, I thought: they would have to through-bolt the head to the wall. Mounting flies' heads would be even more difficult but, pending the arrival of a hurricane to blow them away, I thought mounting flies' heads would be more helpful to unseasoned travellers like me.

A terrapin waggled its green head at me and submerged. Terrapins had been around for millions of years. Was submerging themselves all that terrapins did when hurricanes came through? I coiled *Kylie*'s bowlines, beat at the flies and headed for Tampa.

September is the worst month for hurricanes, and before I reached Tampa another was trundling towards the Atlantic coast. Like all the rest, this hurricane had been given its name by NOAA even before it came into the world, which it did on the 10th of the month. NOAA* (said as 'Noah') is supposed to be an aerial and oceanic soothsayer, but some of its doings are not unlike those which might go on in a TV sitcom set in an up-market fertility clinic; it assigns names to its hurricanes long before anyone is aware that they have been engendered, and it prophesies which gender they are going to be as well. The names are not run-of-the-mill, though the genders are conventional. NOAA's hurricanes are alternately of the male or female gender, but their names are a bit odd. The choice of names makes me think that either NOAA is a reincarnation of T.S. Eliot or it is run by people who keep his cat poems under their pillows. Giving a hurricane the name Gabrielle is one example of NOAA's nancifications. Unless you have previously encountered the tractor-driving

---

* National Oceanic and Atmospheric Administration. *On discovering what the initials stand for, I was astonished. Admittedly it was Man, not God, who created Holland, and aeroplanes can sometimes make rain fall, but these achievements are not global. To administer [i.e. manage] the smallest ocean would take more power than even America has.*

members of the Women's Land Army, it is highly likely that the name would mislead you. When they hear that something named Gabrielle is approaching, many people will think they are about to meet up with one of Eliot's nicer cats or, if they have been reading regularly their Bibles like many Americans do, the female offspring of a high-flying angel. Even in America, hyping up a meteorological phenomenon to this altitude is absurd. Hurricanes should have much baser names. NOAA should be staffed by readers of brutal James Bond novels, not cat books. If NOAA had told the American public that, for example, selecting a nasty one, Oddjob and not Gabrielle was about to come through their back yards, it would have encouraged them to prepare themselves for the event more thoroughly by, for example again, tying down the lids of their trash cans.

Turning over another page of cat poems, NOAA announced that the newly born hurricane had been named Hugo. *Hugo*? Hugo still sounded feeble, but it was better than Bombalurina, Jellylorum or Gabrielle. Hugo's *Les Misérables* was currently a smash hit. I made for Tampa and wondered when he would turn right.

Give or take those which go bananas and loop the loop in mid-Atlantic, hurricanes usually make a right turn when they are nearing the US coast or soon after they have passed over it. Generating wind-speeds of more than a hundred miles an hour and storm surges which rise higher than houses, hurricanes are nasty to meet with anywhere, but they are absolute horrors if they catch a seaman with all his sails up or with his anchor or his trousers down.

My Liverpool uncles used to ask for three times the usual nineteenth-century wage rates when they signed on for voyages to the West Indies during the hurricane months. They got their danger money and by golly they earned it. If Uncle Tom's captain found himself in the path of a hurricane while his vessel was at sea he escaped it by steering into what Barnett, after a spasm of cynical chuckles, would have called the 'navigable' semi-circle of the storm. The difference between the 'navigable' semi-circle and the 'dangerous' semi-circle was – and still is – that in the dangerous semi-circle the winds might be as much as 175 miles an hour but in the navigable semi-circle they might be only 60. In my uncle's sailing ship days it was the difference between having all of your masts, boats, hatches and deckhouses swept over the side and only one or two of them.

A hurricane which came upon my uncles when their ship was in port could be just as nasty. If the storm surge did not lift their ship onto the

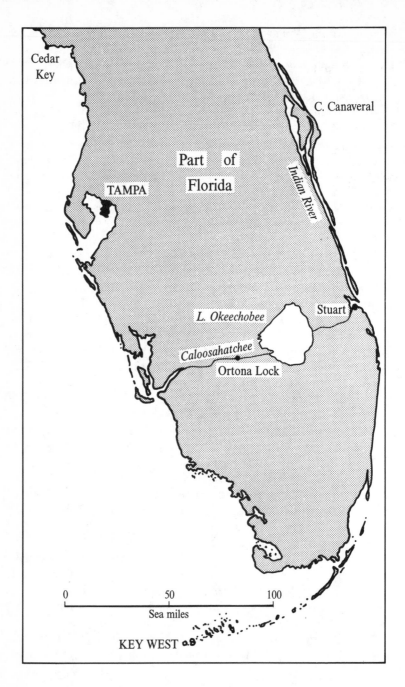

quay and impale it on the harbour ironwork, if the force of the waves and wind did not uproot the anchors and hurl the vessel onto a neo-Palladian city hall, then it would still be sunk by other ships which would be torn from their moorings and would batter holes in its hull.

Kylie was hardly bigger than my uncles' longboat and was one five-hundredth the size of any of the three- or four-masted barques in which they had come through their hurricanes. I had no intention of trying her against Hugo. Hugo's *Les Misérables* had slain thousands on Broadway; now it looked as though he was going to be a smash hit in the deep south as well. If he made a bee-line for Tampa I would moor *Kylie* in a creek and thumb myself a lift to the Appalachians.

I inspected as much sky as I could see between the skyscrapers. It looked a bit thundery. The radio said the centre of Hugo was 305 miles south-east of Savannah, moving north-west at seventeen knots. I locked up the boat and went ashore to replenish my food stores.

Downtown Tampa may have lots of foodstores but I could not find them. A claustrophobic rain shower which howled itself into a frantic gale when it became entrapped among the skyscrapers, set the traffic lights swaying on their wires, tailgated a taxi and held open immovably its door when I hunched inside and attempted to close it. The driver tried to converse but because his back was towards me I could not hear him. Tossing umphs, huhs and yerps from behind my holdall, I rhubarbed to a shopping mall.

Conversation became possible only when I was standing outside the taxi and could see his face. Giving him what I hoped, at 12½ per cent of the fare, was a tip and not an insult, I made a bet with myself on how he would word his farewell. 'Have a nice day' would win me a self-awarded strawberry sundae; 'Thanks' or 'Thank you' rated a chocolate milk-shake. Anything else would allow me to present myself with merely a mint-flavoured skyrocket.

His 'Have yourself a good day, now!' landed me with an unscripted variant. Did it rate a strawberry sundae or a skyrocket? Did the extra words disqualify me for the sundae or did they garnish it with, say, pecans and chipped chocolate? Attending to the niceties of this verbal

---

Opposite: Florida: Cape Canaveral to Tampa. *The Intracostal Waterway follows the line of the Indian River.* Kylie *left it at Stuart to head west on the Okeechobee Waterway.* (*From a map copyrighted by the H.M. Gousha Company*).

127

problem quashed any impulse-buying. In under ten minutes I was able to get myself to a less-than-ten-items checkout, where the cashier told me 'to have an iced day now' and the *National Enquirer* informed me that an American lady had birthed a Martian.

Leafed through during the strawberry sundae, even *Time* seemed to be obtaining its home news from a different planet. Reading those magazines, you would think America was populated by maniacs and the country had gone to pot. From what I had so far seen of America, the same high proportion of kindly-disposed people were still living there as when I had first visited it, but the national magazines seemed not to know it. The high-school students with short haircuts who had Sir'd me under the live-oaks in McClellanville appeared no different from the ones who had Sir'd the middle-aged Third Mate on his way to a betting shop at Bayonne, New Jersey, in the 1940s; and – take or stretch a vowel or two – Frank James of North Carolina was the same bearded veteran whom Able Seaman Harris or myself had encountered at a soda fountain in Port Arthur, Texas, forty years previously. The grass in America was just as green and springy as it always had been, and nowadays there seemed to be more of it. But between then and now it was as if some intergalactic Oddjob had doped the home news editors and had made off with all the old American signposts. I had had to carry my holdall of groceries into and out of two tucked-away places which had been tarted up with plastic oak beams and ye olde Englishe tea-shoppe tablecloths before I had found myself a genuine American strawberry sundae. Where had the soda fountains, Norman Rockwell and the *Saturday Evening Post* gone?

'Sir, would you fart cake in my Hoover?'

White female. Thirty-ish. Short haircut. Blue-grey eyes. Upper lip a shallow 'M'.

'Sorry, I didn't catch that. Please say it again.'

'Would you partake in my movie?' she said, and then: 'You're English?'

The least one could do in such dreadful emergencies was stand up.

Her smile was different, of course, but even identical twins don't have quite the same smiles . . .

'I'm afraid I'm only here a day or two. Just passing through . . . on the way to Baton Rouge . . .'

What on earth was the other thing she had asked me?

'Oh, yes; I'm English,' I said, and studied the table.

She'd put her handbag on the table. Now, she placed her left hand on the bag, lifted the strap and returned it to her shoulder. My eyes followed her hand. Except for the rings, it was the same.

'Baton Rouge needn't be a problem,' she said.

'I'm sorry, but I have to go . . . I mean, you see, I have a boat, and so I must find out what Hugo's doing . . . what the weather will be getting up to . . .'

I picked up the holdall and fiddled with an elasticated strap. She scribbled some figures on a card and slipped the card into my shirt pocket.

'Phone me,' she said, 'when you have time.'

The man in Antigua had said I'd got all the time in the world; but I'd be unwise to spend it making a movie with a ghost. I buckled my holdall and went looking for a taxi. The thunderclouds had gone and Tampa was having itself a nice evening. Arms on each other's shoulder and heads touching, a man and woman were checking out of the marina when I got back. They took over my taxi and headed downtown. I fingered the film-maker's card. Making a film with her would have been a thrilling expedition, I thought, but I'd do better travelling alone.

Travelling is cheaper per capita for couples but it is not easier. Besides enduring the embarrassment of sometimes spooning salt instead of sugar into each other's tea, couples are always having to unbuckle and re-buckle their straps while their conveyance is in motion. On the way downtown, perhaps she suddenly thinks that she'd prefer to eat Indian instead of Italian, and so before the cab gets to the next stop-light someone will have had to unbuckle and give way. Tomorrow she wants to do Disneyworld but he wants to watch a ball game. Next week he'd like to buy a Folkboat which is equipped with a Porta Potti but she isn't going anywhere in a boat which hasn't a flushing loo. In order to stay coupled, couples have to flex themselves, breathe deeply, adjust their straps and pump lots of psychological weights. These activities may make them strong and supple and can be a source of pride and pleasure, but they can also rupture arteries and thicken skin.

Shared pleasures are sweeter, not deeper. Two-way communication with a companion has to go mostly sideways and so its depth range is shallow. Telling her your thoughts about the sunset means that besides concentrating on the sunset you are also having to keep half your mind on what you are speaking and hearing. If you don't match each other's range and pitch you fumble the catches, and that can sour the sweetness.

129

When you are alone you have to pitch questions in all directions, and catch bounce-backs from unlikely quarters; from clouds and cabbages, from custards and kings. You are the pitcher of the questions, the striker of responses, and catcher and umpire too. You miss the sweetness of sharing the experience, but the questions come quicker and the responses go deeper and farther.

Watching the cab glide away downtown, I knew that I would rather keep on travelling alone. Parting from Pip had been a sorrow, but in part the sorrow had become sweet. Sometimes the single-person surcharge exacted on all lone travellers had seemed a lot to pay, but I would go on paying it. Privacy (as distinct from loneliness) was getting to be as rare as turtles: NOAA was naming next year's hurricanes even before they had been fathered, up-and-coming businessmen were coming before their customers did, and women were birthing Martians . . .

Taking a part in a film with someone who looked like Pip would be like heading into the dangerous semi-circle. If I picked up the phone *Kylie*'s mast would crash over the side and I'd drown.

I stowed away my groceries and turned in.

Hugo stormed into South Carolina at midnight and blew McClellanville from the face of the earth.

Prairie chicken

15

Twelve Nights Out From Tampa

I kid myself that I act unselfishly but I do not. All I am concerned about is me and my boat. When Jennie had disappeared from *Kylie*'s cockpit in the Bay of Biscay I had not turned back to look for her. Now, McClellanville had been wiped out but I did not think of sparing a dime to help rebuild it. To me, the disaster at McClellanville meant only that when *Kylie* headed out across the north-eastern corner of the Gulf of Mexico I had to be extra wary. More hurricanes could happen. NOAA was still compiling this year's genealogies: *Abendego begat Quaxo who begat Macavity who begat alternate males and females even unto Gabrielle and Hugo* . . . September had not ended yet, and NOAA would not stop unscrolling the dynasty until November, so Inez, Iphigenia or Iriadne still had plenty of time to be birthed.

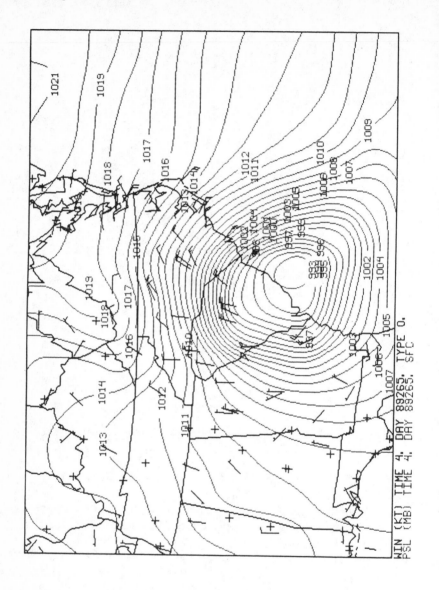

Hurricane Hugo approaches the US Atlantic seaboard.

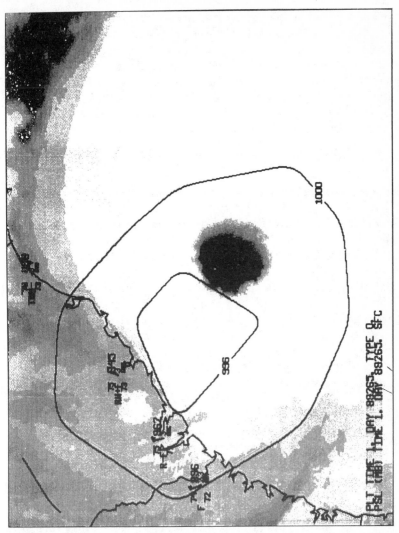

Hurricane Hugo about to devastate McClellanville. *The hurricane's 'eye', shown here densely black, is, in fact, clear and starry sky, and the white area is dense cloud. Hugo stormed onto the coast at 138mph and the Atlantic Ocean rose 20 feet. The hurricane killed 35 people in South Carolina, injured hundreds more and caused $7 billion of damage. (Credit: Steve Sokol of the Spaceflight Meteorology Group, Johnson Space Center, NASA).*

The buoy off St John's Pass fell astern. I knotted a new rotator onto the logline and streamed it. It was good to be at sea again, working the boat and making a passage. I lashed down the dinghy, tied the anchor onto its chocks and started a new page of the logbook. On the left-hand side it was just a matter of writing figures in columns: Time, Compass Course, Compass Error, Log Distance, and so on. Filling in the right-hand side of the page was more interesting, because what I wrote there was mostly words:

'KYLIE' from CHARLESTON towards BATON ROUGE at SEA.
CREW : NIL.

Not '*to* Baton Rouge' but '*towards* Baton Rouge'. Barnett would have approved of my using 'towards'; it conceded that winds might baffle *Kylie* and prevent a perjured commoner from getting there. And the writing of 'CREW : NIL' was as powerful a tonic as making a good landfall or reciting Sonnet CXVI. One of the benefits of 'CREW : NIL' was that when apportioning victuals I never lost out. Bligh's bo'sun, making the incredible journey to Timor in the *Bounty*'s crowded longboat, would have pointed to a portion of a dead seabird and said 'Who is to have this?' In *Kylie*, where the captain, bo'sun, cook and cabin boy are commonly inseparable, putting the same question would be silly.

Two miles offshore I sawed a cake into three unequal portions, held up the middle-sized piece, shut my eyes, and diplomatically altered the wording:

'Which watch is to have this?'

I opened my eyes, looked into the area of sky and water framed by the companionway and began counting off the seconds:

'Half one, half two, half three, half four . . .'

By the time I had counted to ten, two birds (one a gull and the other a sooty tern) had come and gone in the frame of the companionway. Two birds meant that the answer to the question was that the second, or middle, watch should have it. I wrapped the portion in paper, labelled it '0200' and held up the largest piece.

'And which shall have this?'

This time no birds flew into the picture but a powerboat creamed out of St John's. Seeing just one moving thing or creature meant that the first watch should consume it. I labelled the largest piece '2200 hrs', and pulled a face. Today Dame Fortune was flighty. Given a free choice, I would have prefeered that the largest portion should be eaten at 0500, when the body temperature was at its lowest. *Ché sera, sera*, of course, but a sailor boy must enjoy his ups and downs, as Lady Hamilton huskily observed on meeting Nelson.

The snacking programme never got started. An earlier forecast of five- to ten-knot southerly winds was followed by the prediction of a north-easterly wind-shift and a small increase in its strength, but twenty hours later *Kylie* was still struggling to make westing in light airs which boxed the compass and raddled my patience. Where were the moderate north-easterlies? All I was getting were zephyrs.

The wind-shifts kept me hard at it on deck. Instead of eating slices of pre-packed fruit cake at regular intervals I was having to gulp down whatever I could lay my hands on in between sail-changes. Between one noon and the next I set and re-set the sails more times than my pen could find an available space on which to record these matters in the logbook. Thunderclouds piled up in the east and the sun drowned itself in an ocean of what looked like leek soup. Till well after midnight NOAA was promising moderate north-easterlies but by six in the morning the wind had faded completely. I trussed the sails, spread out my jacket to dry on the coachroof and went below to make tea.

While I was stirring it the weathermen looked at the thumbprints on their charts and changed tacks. NOAA divined that something unusual was happening among those thumbprints: it seemed that a small pimple was beginning to fester among the whorls and loops in the eastern Gulf of Mexico. They would examine the disturbance and let us know.

'And meanwhile, boaters . . .,' I imagined them adding as they scrambled a Lockheed P-3 turboprop reconnaissance aircraft and asked it to find out what the hell was going on, '. . . have yourselves a nice day!'

I fished out my Zippo and puffed my pipe: the first point to consider was that *Kylie* was in the eastern part of the Gulf of Mexico . . . The second point was that calling something a disturbance is another way of saying it is a depression . . .

Admittedly, a tropical depression is the lowest form of cyclonic life. In it the wind is what my Uncle Tom called 'a soft gale'. If they were content to snooze their way softly through the West Indies and the Gulf of Mexico, tropical depressions would not be a worry. Boats the size of *Kylie* would put to sea in a 'soft' gale if the skipper was reasonably sure it would not worsen. His passage would be wet and uncomfortable, but a well-found boat would be in no great danger from the wind and waves.

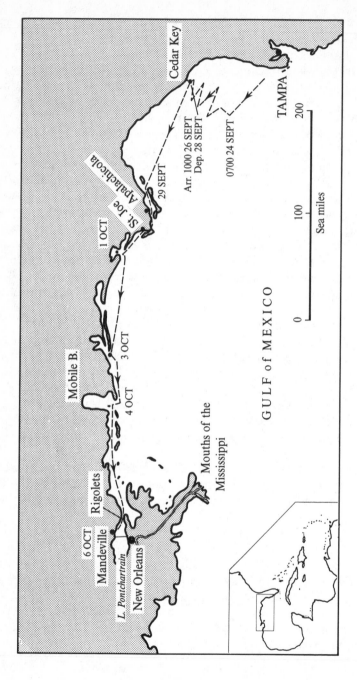

The trouble was, tropical depressions often wound themselves up into more vigorous cyclones such as tropical storms of 34–47 mph, severe tropical storms of 48–63 mph, or hurricanes with winds which – according to my *Ocean Passages for the World* – gusted at speeds of more than 175 mph.

I sipped my tea and pulled my Mrs Thatcher-reprimands-blocked-lavatory face. Whatever the airborne lookouts might be telling NOAA about the goings-on in the cistern up above, *Kylie* ought to get out from under it.

I drew on my pipe and peered at the chart. Which way should I go? Ahead lay ninety miles of open water, a town called Apalachicola and an unknown coast. Astern lay only forty miles of water, familiar sea-marks, and towns with Anglo-Saxon names.

Just as I finished my tea, a 12-knot breeze came in from the east. I bent on the genoa, pointed *Kylie* as high as she would go, and headed back the way I had come.

By noon, 26 hours out from St John's Pass, I calculated that I had sailed 92 miles by log and was making 4.8 knots. If the wind held at east-south-east and 15 knots, *Kylie* might reach Cedar Key by nightfall.

At this point in the narrative you may be expecting a bit of seascape or graphic action. I am afraid that you are not going to get it. This is not to say there was no seascape or action: there was a lot. Indeed, during the ensuing 46 hours there was far too much of both of them to suit my frugal taste. Even a Texan might have found the busy-ness a bit much. Do not expect me to give details of the barometric pressure, the wave heights or the set and drift because I did not write them down and I do not remember them. My time was so taken up with keeping *Kylie* afloat that I could not find time even to make tea. All I can tell you is that at about two in the afternoon the wind backed seven compass points to blow straight from the direction of Cedar Key, and that a few hours later it had turned into one of Uncle Tom's 'soft' gales.

Ordinarily, the wind-shift and the 25–30 knot wind-speed would not have been anything more than a wearying annoyance. Under deeply-reefed mainsail and storm jib *Kylie* should have been able to beat into the lee of the coast and get to Cedar Key by the next morning. For a

---

Opposite: Tampa to New Orleans.

couple of hours she was indeed able to punch into the seas and make headway, but then the soft gale became a hard one and her distance made good fell to under two miles in each hour.

Putting it another way: the whorls and loops had become a watch spring and the watch spring was winding itself up into a tropical storm.

Whether the bilge pump clogged before the sail-car shattered; whether the parting of the tiller yoke-line caused her head to fall away from the wave or the wave knocked her head off the wind before filling the cockpit are questions which insurance assessors might put. Good luck to them; I do not know the answers. I can, however, confirm that in a storm, whether tropical or otherwise, repairing sail damage, bailing water out of the cabin, re-setting the mainsail and getting small sailing boats back on course are tasks which take more minutes to complete than to write about.

I can also tell them – though it will have nothing whatever to do with their questions – that laying himself down to sleep after being three days awake is the most profoundly pleasurable experience which any man can enjoy.

Discovering anew when he goes ashore in the cool of a bright morning in Cedar Key that eggs can be cooked and served in five different ways is also quite pleasant.

She placed the cutlery in a napkin alongside my plate and chanted: 'Boiled, poached, scrambled, fried over easy or sunny side up?'

Sunbeams slanted through a blind and patterned her face. Between the slats I could glimpse *Kylie*'s cabin-top and golden mast against a blue sky. Also at the dock lay a ketch more than twice her length and ten times her tonnage. Both of us had come through the storm. The morning was young, no insects were abroad, and my scalp was tingling from the shower.

'Sunny side up,' I said; 'no grits but loads of waffles.'

The girl wrote the order onto her pad and slid the pencil behind her left ear.

'Goddam,' said the ketch's owner, a Texan whose bright black eyes, small hooked nose and brown-and-white barred tee shirt gave the impression that one was breakfasting with a prairie chicken, 'the Gulf can be one helluva place. You ain't seen nuthin' yit. December we were comin' from Galveston to Isla Mujeres and were hit by a sonofabitch storm. The seas were so goddam high and we were rolling so much that it shitted up the Weatherfax.'

He buttered a stack of pancakes and poured maple syrup.

'Goddam! When the Weatherfax was shitted up we didn't know what sonofabitch weather we were in. "Is it blowin' a gale, Captain?" they kept askin'.

' "How the hell should Ah know what the fuckin' weather is doin'?" I told them, "The Weatherfax is shitted up." '

I slid an egg onto a waffle and slit the yolk. The Texan folded a pancake.

'Ah knew it was bad, though. The seas were half as big as the mast.'

'What did you do?'

He pulled the peak of his baseball cap over his right ear and rolled his eyes.

' "The Weatherfax is shitted up," Ah told them, "but Ah knows this is a bad storm 'cos the seas are half as big as the mast. As captain of this here vessel Ah'm going to make a decision 'bout what to do next."

' "Go right ahead and make it, Captain," they said. "You make your decision just as soon as you want, and that'll be just fine".'

The yolk had run into – and filled the indentations of – the waffle. I shook pepper over the waffle, cut a segment and impaled it on my fork.

' "Mah friends," Ah told them, "what we are in is a sonofabitch storm and the seas are half as big as the mast, so I guess that we'll quit headin' for Mexico an' we'll head for someplace where the sonofabitch seas'll be smaller."

' "That's fine by us," they said; "the liferaft has been washed off of the deck and a shroud wire has busted. You tell us the name of the place you wanna go for, Cap'n, and we'll head for it whenever you say".'

'So what on earth did you do?'

He swivelled the peak till it was above his left ear, then rolled the eyeballs again.

'Ah shut down the fuckin' Weatherfax an' Ah headed for Tampico.'

With time uncoiling fast and the Texan's Weatherfax displaying looser whorls, I set out again for Apalachicola. Line squalls blustered in from the east, but at teatime the wind steadied at Force 5. *Kylie* surged westward at six-plus knots, bow wave arching high, seeding the blue valleys with pearls.

I perched on the pulpit and glanced astern. Unless they are oarsmen training for a coxed boat race, now and then everyone should glance backwards. If they did so, fewer of us might be sleeping in cardboard boxes and more of us might reach the land of our dreams. Glancing at the angle between the lie of our boat and its track through the water, we can see how much the wind and waves are skewing us from the course we want to make through life.

For me and *Kylie* at that moment the angle looked like five degrees. I hardened the mainsheet and clicked the latch of the steering gear a notch upwind.

The foam trailed astern and was lost among crests and valleys. The vane canted and swivelled as the waves shouldered against the stern and the wind pressed against the vane. In the cockpit the tiller edged to windward, shock-cord looped and contracted or tautened and stretched. Pressures and counter-pressures . . . checks and balances . . . gently giving and gently taking . . . no forces applied to excess.

The windvane is a wonderful help. Using it, I can make the longest voyage and not be wearied by the labour of steering. I shall be weary alright, but not because I have had to spend long hours at the tiller. If I responded to pressures ashore as sensitively as the windvane does at sea, I would suffer fewer bruises and I would make better courses . . .

The bow wave was arching high, cascading into furrows and valleys.
. . . and possibly, I thought, I might even harvest a few pearls.

The vane was working smoothly, but other mechanisms were not. According to the patent log, *Kylie* had travelled only 1.7 miles in the past hour. A skein of weed had fouled the rotator. I straddled the cockpit, leaned over the mainsheet horse and unhooked the line from the log clock. Passing the hook and line across the cockpit, I fed it into the sea over the opposite quarter. It was a task which I should have done earlier, because now the line had snarled into hard bunches. Reversing the logline and streaming it astern should have been done as soon as the rotator had fouled up. The longer you left it, the harder you had to work to bring it back to a healthy state.

Inch by inch, foot by foot, I kneaded the bundles. Segments emerged, crumpled and dishevelled. Some bundles looked like worm casts; others like models of the DNA chain . . . in which latter case, I supposed, my labours must be akin to those of a psychiatrist who is unkinking a patient. For both of us, the longer the interval between the snarl-up and the laying-on of hands, the tighter the knots and the harder it becomes to unravel them.

I plucked the saffron weed from the blades of the rotator, faked down the line in the cockpit and hooked the inboard end onto the eye on the back of the log clock. Because the rotator would start revolving and snarl the logline again if I did it any other way, I did not toss the rotator back into the sea until I had paid out half the line over the stern.

The rotator plunked into the water and sank slowly, quiet as a tickled trout. *Kylie* surged ahead for three boat-lengths and then the rotator suddenly twitched its nose and sped after her.

As with other jobs which sound tricky, straightening log lines is really quite straightforward. The thing to remember is that, as when dealing with immigration officers and people who affix alligators' heads to their walls, log lines need lots of patience.

The same can be said of statistics. Generally speaking, Floridans can be proud of their statistics. The *Almanac of the USA* informed me when I opened it in Apalachicola that Florida has 1350 miles of coastline and 8426 miles of shoreline. Though to my taste they are a little on the large side, the figures neither appal nor delight me. They are well-behaved statistics which present themselves unassumingly and do not clamour for attention; they are a credit to the state.

But not all Floridan statistics present themselves as modestly. Under the heading THAT'S INTERESTING I learned that in Florida . . . *alligators increased to become something of a nuisance, sometimes swallowing poodles and other pets.*

As you would expect of a state which builds sharp boats, Floridans are very good at making points. Sometimes, though, their points are so delicate that the needle bends, and once in a while it misses the target. Whatever the 'other pets' were, wasn't their death something more than just a *nuisance* to, say, neighbours who had baby children that were no bigger than poodles?

And *poodles*, for heaven's sake! Saying that the alligators were swallowing poodles is like saying that the state executioner fries his blacks sunny side up. That statistic may have been said interestingly alright, but was it rightly said?

On the same page the *Almanac* informed me that the state bird of Florida is the mockingbird, but I found the chapter otherwise unblemished by irony.

Another alligator was at Port St Joe. Statistically it was dead. It lay on a sunlit bank and it had a gaping hole in its stomach. *Pow! Goddam sonofabitch swallowed mah poodle!* The putrefying carcase was straddling the time zone line but at least it still had its head on. On the plus side, Port St Joe was one 'How're yuh doin'?', one extra hour of time-zone time and three US gallons of diesel fuel. On the minus side it was one dead alligator.

I motored past the alligator and put out to sea again.

At one in the morning a large seagull perched on the stern and fell asleep. *Kylie* pitched gently onwards through the night, heading for Mobile Bay. It had taken me 28 days to do it, but after 1108 so-called sea miles of journeying half-way down and entirely across a state which had seemed more riverine than nautical, I was at last leaving Florida.

'Which watch shall have this?' I asked the seagull loudly, but the creature didn't wake up.

It could have been the same gull to whom I directed the same question two hours after sunset on the third night at sea, for this next seagull was just as unresponsive. For 48 hours the wind had not varied from the northerly point. Mobile lay astern and I was heading for the Mississippi Sound. With the ghoster bulging as roundly as the moon, *Kylie* glided through glittering water, making three and a half knots. I shone the flashlight in the seagull's face. Its eyelids did not move. I put my head inches from its beak and emitted alligatorial vibrations. Still the bird would not awaken.

'GRR!' I said.

Nothing happened.

Hang on a mo'. 'Grr'? An alligator saying 'Grr'? The sound didn't fit. As far as I and T. H. Huxley knew, alligators ingested poodles' bodies without acquiring their personas. 'Grr' wouldn't do. One needed something amphibian. A bronchial croak, perhaps? No . . . the seagull might think I was about to change into a prince . . .

I retired to the cabin and savaged a pecan pie.

'Rwarll'? . . . 'Pshaaah'? . . . 'Howzt'? . . . 'Zok'?

Oh, well, I thought, picking up the flashlight, one ought to stay loyal to sterling: in for a penny, in for a pound . . .

I hoisted myself into the cockpit, switched on the flashlight and blasted out a wholly English oath:

'Featherstonehaugh-Cholmondeley!' I roared up its beak.

The seagull opened an eye and yawned.

Kylie snoozed too at one in the morning, but more briefly. In no wind I handed sail, lowered a mud-anchor and lit the Primus. Reflected in her deckhead, the pricks of blue flame were a circlet of opals and her cabin lamp was a large pearl. The moon was down, and the Mississippi Sound lay muslinned with a thin, tight mist. I sipped tea and tasted the silence. Astern, tugboat searchlights practised their fencing skills but even without them I could see that *Kylie* was penning her log. Water scrolled past the anchor warp, bearing curves, whirls and loops downstream in a fine Arabic script. From time to time *Kylie's* pen trembled and altered its angle of incidence, but it never once left the page. Lit by the sky-glow from distant New Orleans, her testimony went on, and all of it was being carried down to the sea.

Fluent and copious it may be, but was it structured? *There's no point in putting down thoughts which can't be understood, girl! What about crossing your t's, putting in full stops, indenting your paragraphs?*

I rattled the tea mug on the deck.

'Twaddle!' said I. 'You can't stay here scribbling all night. You should have finished your homework earlier. We must get moving, lass. There's miles to go before we sleep.'

There weren't that many more miles to go, actually, but *Kylie* might find that covering them was difficult. The idea of punching up-river through the Mississippi delta to Baton Rouge had been abandoned; the current was too strong and lay-bys for small boats were few and far between. Instead, I was making for one of the small towns on the north shore of Lake Pontchartrain, a shallow dish of brackish water to the north of New Orleans. Fifty miles long and twenty-five wide, about the size of Holland's Waddenzee or – for those who like darker English beers – the county of Suffolk, Lake Pontchartrain was discharging thousands of gallons of itself into the Mississippi Sound through a narrow gulley called the Rigolets. The water was flowing against me at around two knots. At just over half revs, *Kylie* was doing about four.

'In Louisiana we say "Wriggle-Ease" not "Rig-o'-lays",' Joe had told me when I had quizzed him by phone about the Rigolets. 'An' sailing the lake is as easy as pie once you're past the railroad bridge and the shallows.'

The railway bridge loomed up at three in the morning, when the darkness was at its thickest. I could see no sign of life up in its cabin but I had been told that the keeper would open the bridge on request if no train was coming through.

I backed the throttle, filled my lungs, blew on a platelayer's horn and waited.

Here the water was Indian ink surging past the piers, folding under itself, glinting in the fitful glimmers from ashore. In the beam of the flashlight the bridge's girders were as wide as horse troughs and the bolts were as thick as my wrist.

I filled my lungs again and blew the horn, but the bridge cabin did not light up. I stood in the bows, away from the mutters of the engine, blew the horn once more and cupped my better ear, listening for answering wails from the railroad.

The bridge piers were shearing through black shantung. *Kylie* machined a ruffle and gathered pleats. I lowered my cupped hand and returned to the tiller. I could hear no sounds except the whirr of the engine and the babble between my ears. *Sir, would you fart cake in my Hoover?* Like hell, Gabrielle. *Death to the French!* Mantovani playing *Rule Britannia* on his violin . . .

Open the bridge, *goddam sonofabitch* old chap, and let a tired man get his head down.

Motoring until *Kylie*'s forestay was no more than three boat-lengths from the nearest girder, I jiggled the beam of the flashlight onto the cabin windows and blew the horn again.

'I SAY!' I said. 'ARE YOU THERE?'

After half an hour of vain endeavours I was hoarse and *Kylie*'s engine was also beginning to croak. I revved up to clear her throat, stitching figures-of-eight in the water as the dawn came. Eventually the bridge swung open. By then the water had changed from black shantung to polished pewter. *Kylie* chugged between the piers and entered Lake Pontchartrain.

'Good sleep, was it?' I called to the windows, but the watchman didn't tannoy an answer.

At first Lake Pontchartrain was also unyielding. The mist thickened, cutting visibility to under thirty yards. A channel buoy loomed up dead ahead. I lowered a mud-weight, made tea and re-plotted courses, listing them in bold two-inch figures that I could see from the cockpit. Then I drained my tea-mug and set off again.

Until the sun dispersed the mist pilotage was difficult. Perched in the bows, with the engine running dead slow or stopped, I inched my way from buoy to buoy. They emerged from the mist gravely, deep in thought. Some inclined their heads as I passed; others revolved slowly where they stood, like old men looking for their slippers.

Sunshine filtered through the veil as I left the last of the channels and soon a breeze was raking the mist aside and wooded shores were drawing me north. The woodland looked dense, with here and there a water tower or a steeple poking above the greenery. Just from looking at them, it was hard to know where I was.

I heaved-to near an anchored powerboat. A young girl wearing a blue peaked cap with gold braid opened a window and offered me a smile. I pointed to a cleft in the tree-line and remembered that I was coming up to my twelfth night since leaving Tampa.

'What place, lady, is this?'

'This is Mandeville, sir.'

The phrasing was acceptable and so was the substance. Sir John Mandeville had tenuous Shakespearean links, had journeyed beyond Turkey, written a travel book, and finished up, one presumed, in Elysium or Westminster Abbey.

I let draw the jib and headed for the cleft in the trees, but before reaching it I had begun worrying again; not about my pilotage, but about the place-name. In sombre contrast with his lustrous achievements, John Mandeville had been a self-confessed murderer . . .

I peered above the sprayhood at the place which she had called Mandeville. Among the trees lay neat houses, bright flowers and – most unexpectedly – a children's adventure playground.

Though tired, hungry and twelve nights out from Tampa, I was still miraculously undrowned. Even more curiously, I was sailing my boat towards an adventure playground . . .

I stopped worrying about Mandeville. The girl in the powerboat leaned out of her window, gestured towards the trees and shouted the place-name a second time.

I pointed *Kylie*'s bows at the adventure playground and smiled: sometimes even the locals don't know where they're at. Whatever the lady says, this is *Twelfth Night* and this is Illyria, lady.

16

Louisiana Lay-days

It is a truth universally acknowledged . . ., began a widely-beloved writer of fiction.

. . . *that a single man in possession of a good story must be in want of a listener,* concluded my notebook, which concerns itself with facts.

Finding a willing ear among Sarah and Joe's wedding guests in Baton Rouge would be easy, but the tale would be truly enjoyed only if we shared the same values. When told to a vegetarian, for example, the story about fried chicken would fall flat.

But by the time the champagne was uncorked I knew the chicken story would go down nicely. Like me, the wedding guests were tucking into poultry breasts with gusto, and Sherm's belief that a Catholic audience would admire the wheelings and dealings of the Vatican had been confirmed by the *Almanac of the USA.* Before picking at the chicken, I glanced into the almanac and saw that Louisiana's four-year increase in retail sales figures was way ahead of what was happening in the rest of America. Another statistic – on page 126 if you find yourself as astonished by it as I was – told me that a whopping 94.7 per cent of its free-spenders were old-fashioned Christians. These facts were good news indeed. Whatever the song had said about the poverty of Bobby McGhee and her lover, not a lot of burghers in Baton Rouge were busted flat. So abundantly was wine flowing in the antebellum mansion that late arrivals from England were saying that Baton Rouge was feeling more like Bognor Regis by the minute.

On the other hand, not having been admitted into the USA until years after Nelson had bumped into Emma, Louisiana seemed a bit thin on history. This shortfall needed making good. Even the most affluent of nations, I suggested to the Americans, should put money into history: it is the only product with guaranteed growth. However, like other re-cycled commodities which are thought to be a bit stodgy, from time to time history has to be re-painted. To English eyes the most appealing colours have always been the darker shades of regal purple. As a local employee sighed to a tabloid: 'Without a king to bugger us, where would Bognor be?'

Clasping a third glass of champagne, I filled Louisiana's historical void by revealing that the state possessed lots of ancient links with the English monarchy. Because waves had demolished his sand castle on Bognor's beach in AD 1020, King Canute had made his notorious anti-tidal speech and the royal family had become fitfully hydrophobic. The fearful madness peaked during the reign of George the Third, who thought the waves currently demolishing His Majesty's sand castles in the Americas had been generated by Papal bulls. This notion became so obsessive that he expelled the Catholics from Nova Scotia and caused them to settle in New Orleans, where they consoled themselves by making – and in times of need eating – Mississippi mud pies.

In the light of all this ancient history, Sherm's up-to-date episode of the on-going saga of God's Own Country – in which Colonel Sanders gives dollars to the Vatican in the hope that the Pontiff will tell his flock to pray for daily chicken instead of Wonderbread – went down quite well.

'You tell stories better than you take pictures,' remarked Daniel the photographer. The wedding guests had seen Sarah and Joe off on their honeymoon, and now we were drinking the last of the wine and inspecting my snapshots of *Kylie*. Daylight had returned; though both of us were squiffy I could see that his lips were moving.

'Oh, I don't know,' I said, pulling out my snapshots. 'What about this one?'

'What the hell is it?'

'Heavy seas cascading into the cockpit during a monumental gale in the Bay of Biscay.'

'I'd never have known it. Next time, try holding the camera *above* the waves, not under them,' said Daniel.

'You ever been out in a gale?'

'No, I hain't never been in a sailboat.'

'Alright, clever clogs, come out in mine and show me how to take better photos.'

'It'll have to be soon,' Daniel said; 'in January I'll be flying to Australia to shoot kangaroo.'

It was then the middle of October. During the two hours it took me to find a missing cufflink and return it with the hired tuxedo, I worked out that re-commissioning *Kylie* by the end of November was well within my reach. Though scrawled on a crumpled napkin, the timetable figures were clear and the addition was correct: *Kylie* would be ready to set sail, declared my figures, in ten days' time. I de-crumpled the napkin by rolling it with a can of warm beer and checked the figures again to make sure I had got my facts right: two days to find and plug the deck leaks which were rusting my harmonica; two days to replace the teak capping which had been gouged by the anchor chain while a nameless idiot was guzzling wine on the Caicos Bank; two days to build a chart-rack to fit beneath the cabin deckhead; and a final two days to eradicate the botanical garden and slap on the anti-fouling paint.

I picked up the handset, prodded Daniel's numerals and readied an I'm-not-really-deaf gambit. It began with the customary lie: 'Listen, I've only got two coins, so this has to be quick. Can you be ready to sail as soon as Thanksgiving is over?' A 32-wheel lorry came roaring past. 'What . . .? Just say yes, no or maybe . . .! What's that you say . . .? WHAT . . .?'

He hung up in despair, but later sent me a letter which said: Yes, sailing after Thanksgiving would be hyper-fine, so I made my way back to *Kylie* to get ready.

Just walking towards where my boat is lying makes me feel healthier. Often in Southwold have I come out of my house with a dulling headache to walk to *Kylie*'s berth on the River Blyth. My eyes cannot yet see the boat, and so my mind has to stumble ahead. By the time I have trudged past the cast-iron head of the journalist H. M. Stanley, whose eyes are perpetually searching for Dr Livingstone (I presume) among the cygnets in Buss Creek, a wind will be stirring the gorse, I will be wondering if the mainsail will need reefing and my headache will have gone. Rabbits bobtail along the old railway cutting; my steps are still flat-footed but are quicker. Canada geese beat across Reydon Marsh. Beyond them, clouds as dark as blackberries hang over Blythburgh, and *Kylie*'s mast rises above the dyked skyline. Soon I am clunking across the Bailey bridge, slithering down the Walberswick earthwork as the first raindrops popple the river, planning which tack I will set off on, and feeling years younger than when I had shut my front door.

The same uplifting sensation occurred when Joe's father drove me back to Mandeville and *Kylie*; however, its life-span was short. At traffic lights outside Baton Rouge I spotted a neatly dressed, clean-shaven man carrying a placard which read:

I WILL WORK FOR BED AND FOOD

From that moment onward, work got in the way of pleasure. Instead of setting headsails I found myself lugging them ashore to a sailmaker for repair. Writing a work schedule had been easy, but sticking to it was going to be difficult.

Halloween loomed up, bringing rain. The adventure playground lay deserted, and water puddled the side decks of a double-ended ketch which lay nearby. Her name, *Nada*, Spanish for 'Nothing', suggested that her owner had a sardonic cast of mind. Children with painted faces flitted around the houses, hooting ghoulishly, their candles spluttering in hollow pumpkins. At the adjacent dock a geriatric sloop peed copiously into the bayou on the hour, every hour, day and night. Black mould was speckling the white paintwork in *Kylie*'s forepeak and, though I prodded its innards with a pipe cleaner, my harmonica gave out only squeaks. I swallowed Temazepam and drifted ashore, muzzily wondering how on earth I was going to affix a chart rack to the deckhead.

'How're yuh doin'?' enquired the yard boss.

'Pretty well,' I lied. Rain was thundering onto Capetown's hat and my left welly had sprung a leak. The work schedule was a week behindhand but I had no intention of speeding things up.

To procrastinate further I biked to a bar which dispensed English beer to an inmate who looked like Sir Toby Belch. He had worked as a deckhand on Mississippi steamboats, flown Flying Fortresses from Suffolk airfields and had once come close to greatness by inhaling the fumes of Churchill's cigar.

'How're yuh doin'?' I said, getting out the greeting before he did.

'Pretty well,' he lied back, picking up a glass of Watney's Red Barrel and sinking deeper into the upholstery. 'Ah hope this rain don't never stop. If it does, I got to paint mah chicken house.' He fluffed his beard and beamed. 'They say it'll be raining all goddam day.'

We played cribbage and tried inventing quotations to justify our idleness.

'How about: "Work fascinates me: I can sit and watch it for hours"?' he said.

'You pinched that from someone else,' I told him. 'Jerome K. Jerome said it fifty years ago.'

'How was I s'posed to know that? I was raised in Lebanon, Pennsylvania. They don't talk English in Lebanon, Pennsylvania. Anyways, anything I don't know about doesn't exist.'

'Alright, let's try this one,' said I: ' "If work is such a good thing, why haven't the rich grabbed it all for themselves?" '

'I heard that already.'

'Oh? Where?' I said.

'Outside a bar in Tegucigalpa.'

'You couldn't have done: if nobody talks English in Lebanon, nobody talks English in Tegucigalpa,' I said.

Five glasses of Red Barrel enabled us to agree only that justifying idleness is impossible because you have to work at it.

I pedalled back to *Kylie* on the wrong side of the road to confuse the Halloween witches. The rain had almost stopped, and puddles in the boatyard were blinking at a patchy blue sky. I wobbled through the gateway and fell off the bike near a small boy with carroty hair who was chasing an over-dressed witch around a parked car. His legs were a lot smaller than his intentions but he was not going to admit it. Chin down, elbows well against ribs and fists going like pistons, he was stomping through the gravel like a bull with a scorched tail. Though greatly hampered by a nappy, the infant was gaining ground. I propped the bike against a rubbish skip and laid bets. Being twelve or fifteen months older and almost as many inches taller, the witch should have been escaping her pursuer quite easily, but her chances of doing so were getting smaller by the second. Her ball gown had tangled with her broomstick and her feathered throat-wrap had caught on the car's mirror. I rated her chances of escape at five to three.

Aboard *Nada* a dark-haired woman was picking over a pile of mouldy root vegetables, watched by a one-eyed teddy bear seated on an adjustable wrench at the mast foot. Ten to one she's their mother; even stevens that when she turns around and sees what's happening she'll roar ashore and smack them.

The carrot-headed boy butted the witch in the stomach and both collapsed into a puddle. Correction: even stevens that only he will be smacked, and six to four that he'll be sent to bed without supper.

'Children, I'm so glad you're playing nicely!' cried the woman, who all the time had had her back to the fracas and was now examining a turnip.

A lanky man emerged from the companionway, strode briskly to the foredeck and set down a bulging plastic bag at the woman's feet. By this time the witch had dragged the younger child into the lee of the skip and was trying to throttle him. The odds tipped back in her favour.

'Terrie,' said the man to the woman, 'your garage-sale expeditions have to stop. All the lockers are full. No way can we carry this junk.'

'Nigel, that is *not* junk: those are Pippin's school clothes.'

'Hum! Schoolgirls do not wear high-heeled shoes and feathered hats.'

'Pippin and I have made a contract, Nigel: she has agreed to do one hour's writing every day, and I have agreed she can wear what she wants while she does it. If there's no room in the lockers for essentials, why not dump some of the luxuries?'

'Marmite and Earl Grey tea are not luxuries.'

'How was it we lived through eight winters in Oxford without them?'

The small boy sank his teeth into the witch's forearm. Her shriek brought the parents running. I bent over the bike and pretended to adjust a gear sprocket. To my surprise – for a passion for Marmite is an indicator of chronic Britishness even more ominously than Earl Grey is of degenerate Liberalism – the man did not administer a thrashing. Separating the combatants gave the adults a chance to widen the conflict and so they did, but where before they had been adversaries, now the man and woman joined forces and became by turns prosecuting counsel, defending lawyer, jury, judge and social worker.

Getting the evidence took all of three minutes, for the case was complex and the witnesses were sulky. Questioning established that Pippin had insulted the teddy by chanting 'Liar! Liar! Pants on fire!' when the teddy had claimed to be *not* wearing a diaper, and that Pippin's insult had rendered the teddy speechless. Seeking to defend his weaker brother and motivated – as all the world except his sister knew – by kindness, Paul had responded by calling Pippin a punk. This was hotly disputed by Pippin. Vital evidence was being suppressed: Paul had called her not only a punk but – if the court would forgive the vile epithet – a *raving* punk. Also, allegations that she had tried to strangle her brother were false: the ol' gen'leman with the bike would testify that she had been massaging Paul's neck.

To their everlasting credit the judges did not call upon me to bear witness; in fact, they ignored me. The man rasped his beard on the carroty head; the woman's eyes smouldered. The court, they said, had been held in contempt. Instead of bringing the dispute to arbitration the accused had uttered threats and practised violence. Their behaviour had been disgraceful; the court required that they apologise forthwith.

Pippin ruffled her feathered throat-wrap and pouted; Paul folded his arms and struck a Napoleonic pose; both gazed adamantly at puddles.

The sands of time, the court reminded them, were running out; if they didn't produce apologies pretty soon, they'd be late for the Halloween party.

It was not said as a threat but as a statement of fact, and it worked. In *Twelfth Night*, thoughts of a life without cakes and ale make Sir Toby Belch turn wrathful, but the idea that even a crumb of cake might disappear into someone else's stomach settled the children's distemper straight away. Apologies were cobbled, and soon the witch and her tormentor were scampering aboard *Nada* to prepare teddy for the party. The woman tumbled the turnips into a sack, the man retrieved the wrench from the bear and soon afterwards the family drove off.

I lit a pipe to get my breath back. In more than four years of bluewater cruising, these children were the first infant sailors I'd met. The dearth of the species had not surprised me. Mariners who have never yet set foot in Bognor Regis let alone lain – or been laid – there agree that taking small kids to sea in small boats is tragic folly. Much anguish might result: if small bodies plummetted down hatches they might spatter blood on the charts; their dismembered fingers could clog the winch pawls, and whenever infants fell overboard they always fouled the log. Even more to the point, where could their parents hide to get some rest?

But 'rest' did not seem to be a word which figured much in the minds of these parents. Nigel and Terrie Calder, said the yard manager, were always on the go. They'd fitted out *Nada*'s hull themselves, and when Paul was still in the womb had sailed to the West Indies and Venezuela. The Calders had waited for gale-force Northers to come along, had hared out into the Gulf Stream and had skittered south-eastward faster than a coon with a candy. Likely, they'd be off on another nautical hayride before Christmas . . . Jeeze, once Nigel and Terrie started work on *Nada* there'd be no seeing them for dust.

This prediction came near the truth. Before I had lighted my after-breakfast pipe next morning, the husband was destroying *Nada*'s cockpit with a chain saw and dust was rising in clouds. His wife's doings seemed just as unseamanlike: she had up-ended the sack and was scrubbing the mildewed turnips.

Aboard ninety-nine vessels in every hundred which are about to set off on a long voyage, the preparatory routine is much of a muchness. A dockside reporter will note down, for example, that at some stage in the goings-on every skipper will ascend the mast to check the soundness of its fittings while his crew squats in the cockpit greasing eggs. The tasks may look tedious, but though the observer may know little about ships and the sea, the activities will seem relevant to the intention; masts need to stay upright; eggs must be kept from going bad.

But watching the present goings-on aboard *Nada* would have driven a reporter dotty. Calder, the best-selling author of DIY books on pleasure boating, was the nautical equivalent to the bee's knees. So what on earth was he up to? Adjusting bottle-screws and applying egg-preservative would have been logical, but how could he and his crew be preparing for a voyage if they were sawing up the cockpit and scrubbing turnips? The yard manager had said the Calders were hell-bent on nautical adventures, but it looked to me as if they were about to destroy their ship and take up market gardening.

'Tea?' called the man a couple of hours later when the remains of the cockpit had been cleared away. He was polishing his spectacles and blinking. By now the two of them looked altogether agricultural: his trousers were rustic corduroy, and sawdust was lying on his weathered nose like hoar frost on a carrot. The woman had discarded the scrubbing brush and was coating the turnips with varnish. Both of them were chuckling; both looked slightly mad.

I laid down a bundle of teak laths. Until the Calders appeared I had been staring at the laths for ages, but they had shown no signs of assembling themselves into a nautical chart-rack. I wondered if I too should take up farming.

I abandoned my labours and went aboard *Nada* for refreshment.

Looking back, I think it was one of the most fateful cups of tea I have ever drunk.

Clearly, the ten days I had allowed for readying *Kylie* for the next legs of her travels were going to be nothing like enough. Extra repair jobs were going to keep me – and, if I played my cards right, Nigel – going for days. Before the tea kettle was drained I had allowed Nigel to persuade me that, so as to be nearer to his woodworking tools, *Kylie* ought to be lifted ashore. Soon her decks and cabin, like *Nada*'s, were thick with dust. After a morning of dry-throated misery which not even mugfuls of Earl Grey could swill away, I lengthened the straps of the holdall, filled it with whatever clean clothing I could lay my hands on and moved into rented rooms ashore.

I reviewed progress, quickly ticking the jobs already done and sighing lengthily over those which had still to be tackled. The list was becoming longer. Only today, Nigel had inspected *Kylie*'s cockpit and tutted.

'Hum! This is too flexible underfoot.'

'Nonsense! It's just . . . er . . . nicely *springy* to stand on. A sensible design feature, if you ask me.'

'How's that?'

'Really, Nigel, you are the blessed limit! Always asking the most ridiculous questions! Even to someone with a degree in philosophy the answer must be obvious: the springiness keeps the helmsman alert.'

'M'm?'

'Yes . . . When one stamps one's feet in the cockpit, a sympathetic tingle reverberates through one's wellies and goes up one's legs. To persons of my years and condition, the sensation is delightful.'

'Hum! All the flexing is making the cockpit leak at the joints. The sole has got to be *firm*. Tomorrow we must make it strong and solid.'

'But you can't afford the *time!*' I remonstrated with delight.

'And so . . . ah . . . if you would purchase sixteen feet of two-by-one teak before the yard shuts, I'll be along in the morning and see what can be done.'

'You're off your flipping rocker,' I said happily. 'No wonder your children are juvenile delinquents.'

Tut-tutting through his beard, he went off to put the kettle on.

But plainly, even with Nigel's help *Kylie* would not be leaving the boatyard till at least mid-December. Daniel obligingly altered his work schedule and said that so long as he could get to Australia in January, any departure date before Christmas would be fine.

Making *Kylie*'s cockpit watertight and putting right another fault in her engine took Nigel longer than he had led me to expect. Halfway through doing the jobs on *Kylie* he sneaked off to re-fashion *Nada*'s bowsprit, dismember her cabin woodwork and drag two immensely thick cables through her hull to power a new anchor windlass. I found his selfishness a bit trying, but not until he had finished the tasks aboard *Nada* did I lay aside a magazine and complain that his neglecting my repair jobs had left me feeling a bit narked.

'Hum! That's a pity. We were thinking of inviting you to our Thanksgiving dinner.'

I already knew something was in the air. For days Pippin had been measuring her parents' heads and designing party hats, and Paul had been asking questions about the size of the turkey. The things which looked like headless turnips but which turned out to be nodules of cypress trees had been transformed by Terrie into sumptuously gilded figurines.

I hesitated over Nigel's invitation a fraction too long.

Pippin threw her arms about my neck and studied my face.

'Peeder, you *godda* come to our pardy!'

'Why's that?'

She patted a stray wisp of my remaining hair back into place.

'Peeder, I guess it's 'cos you're so *old* . . .,' said Pippin sagely; 'maybe by Christmas you'll be *dead*.'

17

To Mexico in Midwinter

It sticks in my mind does that party, and the reason is this: at nine o'clock, when Pippin and Paul were still not asleep, one of them asked for a story. I spun them a tale which I had once made up for my Karen and Sarah, a tale entitled *How Giraffes Got Long Necks*. Many years previously a much better storyteller than I had woven a fable with much the same title. I had never read it, nor knew even the gist of it, but it sounded just the sort of story that was wanted, so, with a nod to Rudyard Kipling, I had made my story up.

Seconds after I had finished telling it, Paul and Pippin were fast asleep, but next morning it seemed that a few strands of the fable were still drifting around in their heads. Pippin raised her eyes from her muesli and said 'Tell me another one, Peeder'.

'Hey!' said Terrie, bent over a cypress stump she was metamorphosing into a Santa Claus. 'Seems like you're getting popular! Maybe you'd better sail with us in *Nada* so Nige and I can get some sleep.'

'Where are you planning to go?'

'Nige wants to write a cruising guide to the north-west Caribbean, so I guess we'll be going to Mexico and Guatemala.'

'Okay,' I said, 'how about *Kylie* and *Nada* sailing in company? We could do a deal. You could top me up with occasional teabags and I could top the children up with occasional stories.'

'Bedder start telling the stories right now,' said Pippin, snuggling onto my lap as we drove back to Mandeville, ' 'cos by den you'll be *dead*.'

With a concrete Madonna in the forecourt, opulent trees in the background and crazy paving all the way up to the door, from the road my Mandeville accommodation looked like the 1950s *Woman's Own* bungalow which my mother always dreamt of retiring to but never did. Nearer to, the enticement faded. The solid-looking walls were plastic sheets on steel brackets, and the kitchen was a windowless dungeon. Being only a three-minute bike ride from the boatyard and less than a hundred dollars a month, though, it was all the accommodation I needed.

Through Thanksgiving and into December the looks on the face of Lewis the landlord flitted between amazement and amusement when I told him of *Kylie*'s doings, but not once did he look wistful. Boats and the sea did not interest him. He had bought an acre of the American dream and built his house; and that, goddam it, was that. To underline that his dream had achieved reality he had laid a ten-foot-wide driveway up to a three-foot-wide front door and, in case his achievement had not got through to passers-by with spiritual leanings, he had plumped a statue of a pensive Madonna in the middle of the front lawn. He came outdoors every day to sweep the leaves off his driveway and to wipe the bird droppings off his Madonna, and then he went inside again. Cockroaches as big and shiny as pickled walnuts were scuttling through his rooms but outdoors the humidity was so high that he preferred to stay indoors with the air-conditioning, the cockroaches and the television. Never once did he yearn to spend a morning on Lake Pontchartrain, enjoying a breeze on his cheeks.

The nearest old Lewis got to open water all the time I was there was when he drove his Chevrolet to the boatyard to bring me a letter from England.

'Well!' he said, winding down the window and looking at *Kylie*. 'Where d'you s'pose you're heading for?'

The question caught me on the hop. I had gouged out and filled two dozen blisters, sanded the hull and was coating it with anti-fouling paint. The day after tomorrow *Kylie* would be afloat again, and yet I still had not decided exactly where I would be heading. The Calders would not be leaving Louisiana till after Christmas. If Daniel was to get his sailing, *Kylie* would have to set off a week earlier, but what port would we be heading for?

'Er . . . Isla Mujeres,' said I.

'Mexico? You going 'cross the Gulf in *that* . . .? Heh! Heh! Well, I'll be . . .' he said, winding up his window.

And he said the same again later, chuckling from behind the mosquito screen as I biked past the Madonna.

When next day I bade him goodbye and biked down the driveway, the gate behind me clunked shut. The gate was iron-barred and the fence was chain-linked. It was to keep stray dogs from peeing on his Madonna, he said.

158

The Mandeville Madonne

For two months his land-lauding had affected me no more than a gnat bite, but now the pricklings were like pins and needles in the brain. Trolleying *Kylie*'s Christmas groceries to the checkout, I could not remain tranquil. Taped carollers were insisting that the land is the *only* place to spend Christmas. Except for *I Saw Three Ships*, the carols were saying that all the gladdest things happened to people who stayed on terra firma. Kings, wise men, farmers and shepherds were being hosanna-ed often, but where oh where, I increasingly thought, were the sailors? There were carols about the ox-stall in Bethlehem, red-nosed reindeers, Good King Wenceslas trudging up snowy hills, and the night-time activities of shepherds. Of mariners, however, there was hardly a mention. Even in *I Saw Three Ships*, the nautical story-line was a logistical balls-up: *I saw three ships come sailing in on Christmas Day . . . in the morning . . .* Really . . .? Bethlehem is all of five hours by donkey from the Dead Sea. How could Joseph and Mary have journeyed from Bethlehem to a seaport so as to start and finish a sailing voyage before noon on the same day as Christ drew his first breath?

Inserting tins of turkey into *Kylie*'s lockers, I thought about the carol yet again and felt even more annoyed with the lyrics. It wasn't Jesus's fault, though. Jesus knew what he was doing when he chose fishermen as disciples: it was positive discrimination to offset the land-hype from his later scriptwriters. But dammit, even *I Saw Three Ships* reeks of land-lauding; the lead singer is going on about ships and the sea but he has his own two feet firmly planted ashore. He isn't *at* sea at all; he's only looking at it. He says that he is glad to see the three ships are coming into harbour alright, but why?

I stowed away the last tin of turkey and I decided that the lyrics had been written by either a very relieved Orthodox Greek shipowner who had forgotten to renew his insurance, or a Lebanese immigration officer who was keen to get on.

Ten days before Christmas I, too, was rather keen to get a move on. I spread out the US *Pilot Chart of the Gulf of Mexico* and saw that after jetting through the 100-mile-wide channel between the Yucatán and Cuba, the currents in the Gulf swirled and eddied in all directions. Looked at upside down, the Gulf of Mexico was like a boiling cauldron blowing its Cuban lid off. To get to the Yucatán peninsula from the Mississippi delta, *Kylie* would need to plunge into the cauldron and cross it, but I was not sure of the best route to take. In the second week of Advent I had been lobbied by two schools of thought. Led by Sir Toby Belch, the Cuban school said that I should hitch a ride on east-going swirls of the currents and make for the Dry Tortugas, islets a hundred miles off the south-west tip of Florida. From there, they said, I should steer towards Havana until I found an inshore counter-current which would carry me south-west to Isla Mujeres, the Island of Women, off the Yucatán peninsula of Mexico.

The opposing school, comprising a flag officer of the Pontchartrain Yacht Club, the owner of a Chinese junk, and Nigel Calder, argued for making a bee-line for the Yucatán, a course 200 miles shorter. Despite some grossly adverse currents, the direct route was the faster in midwinter, they claimed, because from November to March the winds often hauled round to the north.

I opted to sail the shorter course, with some slight bends in it so that *Kylie* would be pranged by the currents at less hurtful angles. From a position on the 100-fathom contour off the Mississippi delta I pencilled shallow dog-leg courses, hoping that some of these courses would allow *Kylie* to benefit from south-going eddies.

'. . . if you can find them,' said Mr Bedford Brown.

The very models of modern meteorologists, he and his buddies were doing their jobs in a nearby town whose Weather Center was another NOAA. With an address on a road which was called the Old Spanish Trail, it sounded as though NOAA had abandoned his sissy cat poems, oiled his Smith and Wesson and was now heading West. The address had evoked promising images: outdoorsmen Wyatt Earp and Wild Bill Hickock had to be better at reading the weather than was T. S. Eliot. Instead of Jeeps and Buicks, car parks on the Old Spanish Trail would surely be chock-full of chuck-wagons and six-foot cowboys chewing straws.

Disappointingly, the Weather Center turned out to be a bunker-like building which bristled with antennae and similar gizmos. Its car park contained nothing but cars, Mr Brown's head was only slightly higher above his shoes than mine was and he did not perceptibly chew anything.

We entered a darkened room which contained monstrous electronic machines. He ripped a print-out from the jaws of a stuttering, green-eyed leviathan and spread it out on a table. The print-out looked like a medieval star-chart. A button was pushed, the leviathan grunted and its eyes went bright red: we were going to play Dungeons and Dragons.

'Here's your termal analysis,' murmured Mr Brown.

The leviathan shut its eyes and gulped.

What had he said? A *terminal* analysis? There was silence while I worked out how to react. What on earth did one *do* on the Old Spanish Trail when one was faced with the prospect of death? Cock a Smith and Wesson at prairie chickens? Send for Wyatt Earp?

Mr Brown flicked on extra lights and tapped the table. I took my hand from the chart.

'As of now, we are doing our termal analyses of the Gulf waters every five-six days.'

'Oh . . . *thermal* analyses?'

'Uh-*huh*! That's what I said already.'

We bent over the chart. Where my hand had been, the chart was a bit damp.

'And the currents in those tongues will push me towards the Yucatán?' I said brightly.

'Uh-*huh*! And the winds, too, I guess. You'll have fifteen-knot northerlies Friday thru Monday – just what you need for a good passage. If you can get into those tongues and loops you'll be going real fast, with the wind blowing you from behind and the seas no bigger 'n five feet.'

'That's all very well,' I told Nigel, 'but how do I find his blessed tongues and loops? By the time I get out into the Gulf, that thermal chart will be five days old; the tongues may have lolled sideways by then . . . Is the tea alright? It looks a bit weak.'

We were back in *Kylie*'s cabin, drinking Earl Grey.

'Hum! The tea's fine, thank you . . . You'll need to navigate by a marine thermometer,' said Nigel, between sipping his tea. 'Water in the loops will be at a 25- or 26-degree temperature, but water outside of the current will be much cooler.'

I had a thermometer aboard. In my previous life it had hung above tomatoes in a Suffolk greenhouse. Its stem contained something alcoholic which looked like absinthe. Dunked now and then into a bucketful of Gulf currents, though, I thought the thermometer would convert to marine usage very well.

With Daniel aboard and the Calders waving from the boatyard, *Kylie* set off from Mandeville an hour before sunset on December 19th. The barometer was then at 995mb and was confidently rising. To reach the Gulf we had to sail more than 80 miles; across Lake Pontchartrain, then through New Orleans and an outlet canal which runs down the finger of the delta poking south-eastward from the mainland.

We ghosted down the canal under all plain sail in fading northerly winds. The last of America slid past. With its fringe of shrubs and dark grasses, it looked no different from a Suffolk backwater. The weather was also looking a bit English. At 0200 on the 20th the absinthe was at freezing point; and *Day opens,* I wrote in the log at six o'clock, *with 8/8 cloud.* By noon we were out at sea, but the daylight was sombre and shimmery. Oil rigs were stalking us, slinking up from leeward when we weren't looking. Two managed to creep to within a mile of us before we had wit enough to alter course and scuttle off into the thickening gloom.

Below decks Daniel wrapped himself in a sleeping bag while I unscrewed the thermometer from its bulkhead. By threading a yard of marline through its topmost screw-hole, I equipped it for its dunking.

Though delayed by bridges in New Orleans, 24 hours out from Mandeville *Kylie* had averaged 3.6 knots, which pleased us a lot. On the down side, Daniel was now battling against sea sickness, the air temperature was still only just above freezing and the sun was sulking behind dense cloud. I struggled into a second jersey and glanced at the green figures flickering above the chart table. After 14 years of navigating by the sun and stars, I had bought myself a cut-price satnav, thinking it might come in handy.

For a while after midnight the cloud thinned and broke. Under main and genoa *Kylie* was rolling to a light north-easterly wind and confused sea. We spotted what Daniel called the Big Dipper and I the Great Bear, but with no horizon to be seen the constellation was unusable. On earlier voyages the situation would have triggered a scowl or two; here it produced only a wistful shrug. Now that I'd got the satnav to help me, the sextant could stay in its box.

The wind remained light for another nine hours. In the early hours of 21st December I poled out the genoa and began to think we might be in for a slow but pleasant trip.

The idea came too early. At noon Daniel took his pocket radio into the cockpit. Faintly through the hiss and crackle, his ears picked out news that a strong cold front would sweep down the lower Mississippi during the night, bringing with it winds of 40 knots.

'*Wow!*' said Daniel, highly impressed.

'What are you *Wow*-ing for? We were supposed to be getting fifteen knots of wind, not forty.'

I hoped the forecast winds would not be long-lasting. Should a 40-knot wind persist for 24 hours, the waves might be fifteen to twenty feet high and our lifestyle might suffer: one's porridge pan, for example, might jump off one's stove.

I thought about the Texan whose Weatherfax had packed up; if *Kylie* was pitchpoled, would her crew be served over easy or sunny side up?

Assuming the weather front was moving southwards at 20 knots, I estimated that the strong winds would hit us soon after dawn on 22nd December. To be on the safe side we began to prepare the boat for heavy weather during the afternoon watch by putting extra lashings on the dinghy and anchors, and by reefing the mainsail. By then it was also time to think of heavy-weather preparations for our stomachs too, and so before the cabin grew dark I cooked a half-gallon potful of spaghetti bolognaise.

To my dismay, Daniel declined it.

Undeterred, at dawn I cooked a similar quantity of oatmeal porridge.

Daniel pushed it away.

'But in Scotland it is the food of kings!' I protested, raising the ladle so he could see how enticingly the globs plopped into the morass. 'Macbeth and Bonnie Prince Charlie were reared on porridge!'

'They must have died young,' said Daniel, turning his face to the wall.

The first of the 30-knot gusts came along soon afterwards, and with it came heavy, freezing rain. Daniel again scanned the local radio-waves for Christmas cheer but heard only that three inches of snow had fallen in New Orleans and that the Mississippi had iced-up. It was, said the announcer, the lowest low since records began. Feeling in need of more uplifting news, he switched to the short-wave band.

Across five thousand miles of land and ocean, the choristers of King's College Chapel in Cambridge were asking rhetorical questions:

> *And who were in those ships so fair,*
> *On Christmas Day, on Christmas Day?*
> *And who were in those ships so fair,*
> *On Christmas Day in the morning?*

Two days before our Christmas Day morning, the gale eased a little, allowing us bring *Kylie*'s head towards the wind and repair the steering-gear. One of the wooden cheeks which clamped the gear to the rudder head had split.

Replacing it was not a high-tech problem. Clipping my safety harness onto the mainsheet horse, I sat on the stern and requested tools.

'Pass me a five-sixteenth spanner,' I said to Daniel.

'A what? D'you mean a wrench?'

' "Wrench" is a better go-for-it, American word, I must admit. "Spanner" describes only the form, not the action. "Spanner" is a very *British* word, though: it keeps the sweated labour at arm's length.'

The windward bow rose to a breaker and a hillock of water filled my leeward boot.

'So what the hell is it you're asking me for?'

'Let's call it, say, a five-sixteenth thingy for now. It's the one with marline tied to its shank.'

He leaned aft and placed it in my palm. I put my hand through a loop of marline and fixed the jaws of the spanner onto the first of the nuts which had to be undone. In all, there were fourteen.

Hove-to, *Kylie* nestled in the seas like a sleeping child among bolsters and bedclothes, but I myself was not so comfortable. From time to time water swilled across the stern deck and whenever the bow rose to a breaker more hillocks of water climbed up a sleeve or re-filled my leeward boot. The water felt warm, but the wind was icy.

It took twenty minutes to unfasten the bolts and replace the damaged cheek, and another twenty to de-frost my numb hands above the blue flame of the Primus stove. Before letting draw the jib, we made a flask of coffee and chatted. Even in midwinter, I remarked to Daniel, it was not often that one had to thaw out one's hands when one was less than 150 miles from the Tropic of Cancer.

By five in the afternoon the wind had backed west of north and increased again, and the cockpit had been filled four times. We doused all sail and ran before the gale amid rolling wave-crests. Behind the breakers the foam lay as thick as Irish coffee. At six, we were towing 30 fathoms of eight-plait nylon to slow down our breakneck speed. This cut down the chances of pitchpoling but upped the number of cockpit-fillings.

Another inundation happened an hour before nightfall. A mile away, we saw the wave coming. It was a big one. Rearing high above the smeary horizon, its tumbling head was cascading white water down a dark and beetling cliff. Before *Kylie* sank into a trough, we saw the head had broken and was trailing a foamy mantle fifty yards wide. The boat rose to the next swell and we again looked astern. Now the wave had gathered itself for another go and was trying to frighten us.

I told Daniel not to bother with his camera just yet awhile.

The wave's shoulders had broadened, and it was stacking extra breakers on its head. We clipped more safety-lines onto our belts.

'Looks as if it's making us a club sandwich,' I said.

A hundred yards away it started burping, Daniel said afterwards, like it was Macbeth and had consumed a panful of porridge.

It fell upon us moments later. For three seconds or so the cockpit was full to the brim and the duckboard was doing its best to pop up and float away; then *Kylie* did a little roll and shrug and the cockpit was straight away half empty. A minute later most of the remaining water had gone down the self-drainers, Daniel was pumping like mad and I was forking soggy tobacco out of my pipe.

Peering into the cabin through the hinged half-moon of washboard, Daniel shouted that the bilge was full. Twenty or thirty gallons had spurted through gaps between the washboards and between the cockpit hatch-lids and their bearing surfaces. Apart from wetting sixty fathoms of coiled lines, dousing the plastic chart-cover and converting two pecan sandies into a pulp, the wave had done us no harm.

On its three-hundred-and-fifty-something stroke the pump sucked air, so we unshipped the pump handle and practised some warming but un-American – and therefore possibly illegal – activities, including the singing of *Rule Britannia* and the drinking of liquor while in charge of a seagoing vessel. Before the rum had quite gone down, a cunning little wave had coiled the trailing rope around the steering gear. We untangled the rope, hauled it aboard and stowed it below. These valorous exertions, we agreed, merited another reward, and so we uncorked the bottle again. After two more tots Daniel's hands were warm enough to allow him to beat time to another carol. According to his diary it was entitled *While Shepherds Washed Their Socks By Night*.

The vane gear gave no more problems after we had unbandaged it. Whatever tricks the waves got up to, the gear quickly corrected any yaws so that *Kylie* could present her backside squarely to the tumbling breakers still roaring down the olive-dark cliffs above Daniel's head. From time to time a rogue wave would attempt to scramble aboard, but *Kylie* always side-stepped at the last moment to leave the hooligan seething angrily astern.

Behind the shuttered companionway, I munched pecan sandies and inspected the satnav.

'How're we doing?' called Daniel.

'Can't really say. The satnav appears to be cussing.'

'How's that?'

'Four asterisks have come up. It's writing swear words for a Victorian novel.'

We heard later that the gale peaked at 45 knots during the afternoon, but the strong wind did not stay with us too long. By the early hours of Christmas Eve it had fallen to a steady 25 knots, the duckboard was damp-dry, and we were able to change out of our soggy clothing.

As if adorning the fir tree back home, we dressed our mast for Christmas. In front of it we set the little storm-jib and behind we hoisted the deeply reefed main. When the wind eased to below 25 knots these offerings were thought paltry and so they were improved on. Up went a small genoa and out came a reef. The sails bulged and the speed increased but the height and steepness of the seas went down as we surged into the shallower waters which lie above the Campeche Bank.

At the point at which *Kylie* reached it, the Campeche Bank rises from the 12,000-feet-deep basin of the Gulf of Mexico to a plateau 600 feet deep in the space of twenty-five sea miles; the bank measures 120 miles by 360.

'It's quite a whopper,' I remarked; and, when he didn't look suitably awe-stricken, added for good measure: 'The Campeche Bank is *as big as England!*'

'England? Where the hell's that?'

Daniel was not speaking wholly in jest. The question, unthinkable in my boyhood, unaskable even as late as the 1950s, was not now unknown. *England?* In Asiatic Turkey, a camel driver had looked blank; in Louisiana, a waitress also. Sometimes, though, ignorance of England would have been blissful. Months after the bloodbath at the Heysel Stadium, yachts flying the Red Duster were being given a hard time in foreign ports, and in Portugal, Britain's oldest ally, when the name of my homeland was mentioned the speaker was pelted with asterisks.

But now the satnav was stencilling not asterisks but figures. I plotted the position and went out into the cockpit. No doubt about it, we were twenty miles onto the Campeche Bank, supposedly in a

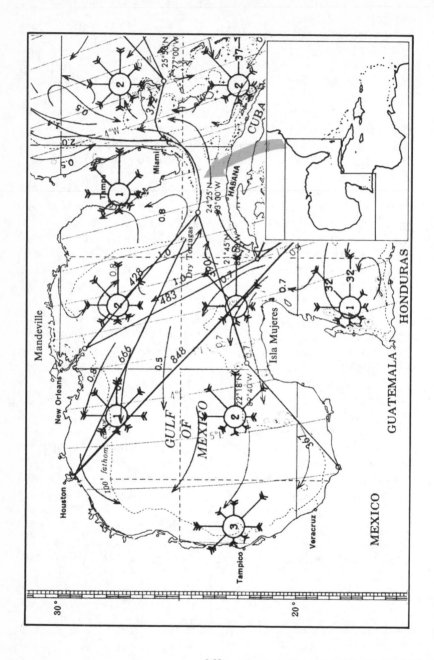

thicket of hostile current-arrows, and yet the seas were much smaller. This was strange. Usually, I told Daniel, the stronger and more contrary the current, the steeper are the waves. According to the chart arrows, here on the Campeche Bank the opposite was happening. *Kylie* was forging through leaf-green seas, surging down gentler gradients than a three-day gale would normally construct. The only way to account for the anomaly was to suppose that both wind and water were moving in the same direction.

'What d'you know?' I told Daniel. 'We have found the tongues of favourable current without having once used the thermometer.'

'It's just as well,' said Daniel, 'because you trashed it while stirring the porridge.'

I lit a pipe.

'Perhaps we'll get to Mexico for Christmas after all.'

Because of the will-o'-the-wisp currents, we did. During the final 24 hours of her passage, *Kylie* made good 137 miles across an area of the Campeche Bank where the chart showed an adverse current of 1.5 knots – a feat which raised questions about the chart data but which bucked us no end.

On Christmas morning the sun at last came out to cheer us further. The oakleaf-green water changed to the colour of lime leaves, topped by wave crests which chuckled and gleamed. I poured rum into my harmonica and blew fume-laden carols. Daniel sunbathed in the cockpit and asked questions about kangaroos. The coastline whizzed past so quickly that we almost overshot Isla Mujeres.

Opposite: Mandeville to Isla Mujeres. *This section of the US Pilot Chart for December 1988 gives general information for planning a passage. The thick, straight lines show courses and distances between waypoints. The arrow shafts protruding from the circles record the frequency and strength of the wind which may be expected in December from 8 sectors of the compass, while the figure inside each circle gives the percentage of time during which calms may be expected. The curved, unfeathered arrows show the direction of the Gulf currents, and figures alongside the arrows give the speed of the current in knots. Excellent though the chart is, the data must be used with caution. The information on currents, for example, cannot include the relatively small but crucially important warm eddies which may be flowing contrary to the current arrows at speeds of more than 2 knots.*

'Recognize it?'

'No,' said Daniel.

'But you said you'd been here before!'

'So I have,' he said, 'but it was by airplane.'

'So . . .?'

'Like they say, the land always looks *different* when you're seeing it from the sea, doesn't it?'

I sucked on my pipe.

Memories of cold porridge made me say yes.

18

Back to Basics

Pleasantly warm was the morning, delightfully blue was the sea and to top off the happiness we were drinking Earl Grey. But what had gone amiss with Nigel Calder? From the anguished look on his face, you would have thought that I had not put any sugar in.

'Is it bad?' I asked.

'I'm afraid so.' He tossed a spanner into his tool tray and wiped his brow. 'You've got a serious problem down below: I think the rotor has de-magnetised.'

Our boats were anchored off Cozumel, south of Isla Mujeres. I was fifty miles into the Caribbean again, but how much farther could I go into it without a functioning rotor? My face must have gone as blank as my satnav's, for Nigel was trying to enlighten me. As those who have read thus far without nodding off will have gathered, his task was not easy.

'The alternator's not charging the battery, and the alternator is inside the flywheel housing, so repairing it will mean a wholesale strip-down.'

I groaned.

I don't know what it is about me, but whenever I make approaches to an internal combustion engine we do not hit it off. Geographically I was in a new and delightful country but mechanically I was in a cesspit. The situation was familiar. I had been here before and every time I had not liked it. I knew vaguely how engines worked but when they did not work I was stumped. Those who in different contexts have been flummoxed by torque, toilets or T.S. Eliot will recognize the feeling, which loosely is called funk.

Of this feeling I had had plenty. Diagnosing the ailments of machinery was like entering Eliot's *The Waste Land* without pass notes. Working out what went on between, say, a self-purging silencer and a thermostatic expansion valve was as difficult as deducing liaisons between Madame Sosostris and Phlebas the Phoenician; but even when I had worked out what, if anything, either party was up to I was no better off. Analysis only deepened the poetico-mechanical mess, it did not clear it. The trusty steeds which galloped up and down inside everyone else's engine always in my engine turned out to be halt, lame and vicious. Whenever I tried to groom them the creatures nipped my knuckles, kicked my shins or further flattened my feet. In the end all my engines had tried to murder me or had committed suicide. So far I had sent two of them to the knacker's yard. Now it looked as if this one was going to be sent there too.

My failures may have had something to do with my soft nature. From time to time friends had told me off about this. I should have flogged the beast harder, they said when I showed them my first moribund motor, imminently on the brink – or so I thought – of departing this life among poppies in Norfolk. That engine had been revived by a youth who had acquired his engineering know-how in a factory which gutted turkeys. He looked like a Bisto Kid but he behaved like a fiend.

'Call yourself a sodding engine?' he'd growled, garotting the exhaust pipe. 'I'll twist your useless prick off!' After that he had lacerated the manifold with a pair of stillsons. When the engine still hadn't fired he had used an ancient Chinese torture, force-feeding it with fuel. He'd stuffed a rag into its mouth, beaten its belly with a spanner and cried, '*Go*, you wanking layabout!' Petrol had spurted from its holes and the creature had gone up in flames.

In spite of – or, as cold-hearted mechanics like Nigel might say – because of this treatment, it had spluttered back to life and run for weeks. Fired, as it were, by this, the Bisto Kid had sought advancement in Brixton.

'*Tall oaks*,' we'd said, tapping the sides of our noses, '*from little acorns grow . . .*'

Not expectedly, he had joined the National Front.

As for me, I had been no more successful with diesel than with petroleum engines. The second one had conked out in Boulogne, but a Frenchman had wooed it into purring compliance by murmuring endearments into its air filter, an appendage which is something like a nose. In Cagliari an Italian had sprayed its head with a scented gunk-remover and fingered its lower anatomy; the thing had gone into transports of bliss. Even Turkish camel-drivers were better with engines than I was. For a nation whose mechanics do not have names like Diesel, Rolls or Wankel, Turks can do marvels. Uttering cries to

Allah off Gallipoli, two of them had belaboured it with neolithic hammers. In Islam this was standard punishment for adulterers but *Kylie* had loved it, afterwards scampering up the Bosphorus like a ferret on heat.

But now my third engine had gone wrong and, despite subliminal urgings to go for a Rolls or, failing that, a Wankel, I felt like throwing in the towel.

'It looks like the end of the road,' I told Nigel. 'If it's no go the whirligigs, I can't go blundering on to Guatemala without electrics.'

Nigel coiled the wires of his multi-meter. 'Oh, you mustn't stop *now*! There are ways round every problem!'

'For people of our nationality, Nigel, hardship is *infra dig*. An Englishman abroad never feels comfy when short of electricity; there's no place like ohm.'

But as he rowed back to *Nada* he called again, 'There *is* a way! You'll see!'

I studied the sea and thought about the miles of jewelled waters lying south, a-spangle with reefs and islets. I hoped he might be right.

By the morning he had found a way forward – or, rather, backward. Grinning through the portcullis of his moustache, he exhorted me to return to the basics of cruising: cruising as it used to be practised in the days of kerosene, canvas and cramp. Returning to the USA wasn't on. Deprived of bedtime stories, his crew might mutiny. Therefore, *Kylie* must carry on cruising in company with *Nada*, using only sails for motive power and kerosene for lighting. When possible, *Kylie*'s battery would be transferred to *Nada* for recharging but because the vagaries of weather, the infancy of his cruising guide and the imperfect charting could separate our boats for days on end, the battery was to be used only for emergency starts of the motor and nothing else.

In other words: if I tagged along, he would help out when I got stuck. Still worrying, I agreed.

All problems have solutions, but all solutions generate problems. Shortly afterwards I needed to re-anchor *Kylie* farther off a clump of coral. It was not by any means a dire emergency, but it seemed more sensible to use the motor than the jib for the job. To save battery power I dug out the starting handle. After a flurry of fruitless swings I paused for breath. I set my teeth and attacked the engine for the third time. Wham! The handle recoiled and flung me to the cabin sole.

My screaming elbow suggested that cohabiting with coral could now be re-classified as a dire emergency, and so I pressed the starter button.

The engine fired at once, but its firing had cost the battery some precious amps. I motored to a safer spot, bandaged my elbow and teetered to the galley stove to make a pot of tea.

I have great affection for my galley stove, a 25-year-old Primus. There is a base – if not basic – pleasure in pricking its nipples. Certainly, I like measuring out exactly the right volume of alcohol into the pre-heating bowl beneath the burner. The measuring must be done to a nicety: too little alcohol, and the stove bursts into yellow flames which soot the deckhead; too much, and the spillage from the bowl incinerates the cabin woodwork.

The whang from the handle had crippled both my elbow and my judgement. I decanted too much alcohol into the bowl. In the resultant flare-up I burned the middle finger of my right hand. Cradling my elbow, I drank the tea, inspected my blistered finger and prised open the first-aid kit.

For some days after that, applying the back-to-basics philosophy was relatively painless. Under sail, I surfed through a 30-yard gap in the reef at Tulum, anchoring south of the Mayan fort and its 80-foot cliff. Swell broke heavily on the reef to the east, gnashing its teeth at *Nada* and *Kylie* anchored out of reach to leeward. But Tulum was no place for transferring batteries, for residual swell and the strength of the trade wind kept our boats bobbing and rolling all day. Likewise, winds and waves at other anchorages confirmed that *Kylie*'s dwindling battery power must indeed be kept for emergencies only. Luckily, with one exception the distances between the remaining anchorages on our journey to Belize and Guatemala could be covered in daylight, and so I would not need navigation lights until I made the passage from Bahia del Espiritu Santo to Xkalak, the southernmost harbour in Mexico.

The distance between the two places is seventy miles, a fourteen-hour trip in the prevailing wind, although the north-going current of up to three knots could add hours to the passage if the wind fell light. I wanted to arrive off Xkalak at dawn, so that a combination of star sights and/or harbour lights could tell me exactly where I was before the sun rose and the lights went off; this meant I would need to leave Bahia del Espiritu Santo during the afternoon of the previous day. By hugging the reef-bound shore, during daylight hours I hoped to evade the current altogether. However, during the night I would have to stand away from the reef and buck the current. I believed that the night passage would pose few problems. The easterly winds seemed steady in both strength and direction; I could therefore manoeuvre freely under sail alone. For a navigation light I would use another kerosene stand-by: a Primus lantern whose beams were visible for three miles.

Like the stove, the lantern has sentimental value, for its burbling warmth has cheered me through many a cold night in the North Sea. I inspected its verdigris-covered body and gave it a liberal dose of TLC to prepare it for the overnight passage but while dismantling the burner my bandaged finger brushed against the mantle, instantly reducing it to ashes. I rummaged the lamp locker for my last spare mantle. Gingerly I tied it onto its porcelain housing, reassembled the lantern and pumped it up for a trial run. I poked a flaming pipe-cleaner into its works. For half a minute the sight was disgusting, for the mantle writhed about like a slug on hot coal. But suddenly there came a faint pop, and the wizardry of combustion instantly transformed the charred carcase into a perfect lozenge of brilliant white light. As visual experiences go, the spectacle is miraculous. Every time it happens I feel that I am on the road to Damascus.

Telling it how pleased I was with its brilliant performance, I stowed the lantern away, cushioning it against chance shocks, for if the mantle crumbled I would have only wick-lamps and candles to light the cabin. Also – and more crucially – I would then be without a navigation light.

Confident that without engine or electrics I could manoeuvre in confined waters and be seen by other vessels at night, I turned next to the navigation department. For fourteen years I had relied on an unlighted compass, a sextant and a towed, non-electric log. The only electrical devices were the newly-purchased satnav and the depth-sounder, but neither of them was a basic necessity. Having sailed for years with only the sextant, I thought I could easily use it again to find my position off the coast of Yucatán if the need arose. As for not using the depthsounder; there was a hand leadline aboard and, in daylight at least, my eyes could easily pick out the areas of water which would take *Kylie*'s four-foot draught from those which would not.

My navigation aids seemed sufficient, yet I was uneasy. My largest-scale chart of this part of the Yucatán was the US 28015. Based on nineteenth-century British surveys with additions from 'other sources' to 1968, the chart does not record the coastal and submarine effects of recent hurricanes. More crucially, it is drawn to such a small scale that important detail is lacking or is imprecise. Towns such as Ubero, Puerto Chico and Gavilan are named, but no dot, circle or square marks their precise location. Although lights are shown, sometimes they too are not named. And the town of Xkalak, which has a port

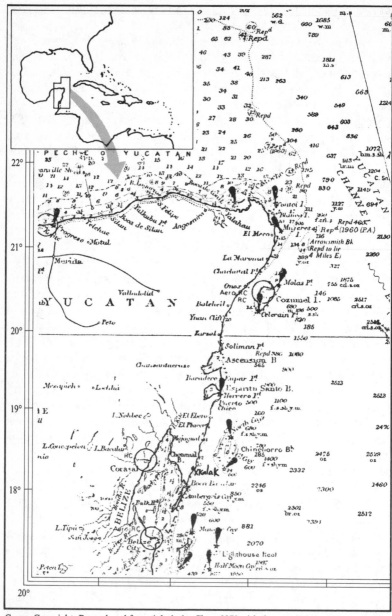

Crown Copyright. Reproduced from Admiralty Chart 3273 with the permission of the Controller of Her Majesty's Stationery Office.

captain and a naval post, is not shown at all. Only an unnamed lighthouse stands where *my* 'other sources' – bulletins of the Seven Seas Cruising Association – place the town.

Before setting out for Xkalak I practised another back-to-basics stratagem: I asked the locals for information.

The only informants I came across were three men in a pitpan. To get data for Nigel's cruising guide I had sailed away from *Nada* to survey the shallower parts of Bahia de la Ascension. In the lee of Punta Allen the water was murky. I handed sail and anchored. Armed with leadline, boathook and compass, I rowed out the dinghy and took soundings. It was a good job that I did. Without any change in the colour of the water above, the bottom shoaled from eight feet to four feet in twenty yards.

$L = Culebra\ C\ 195\ W.\ P.\ Allen\ 352\ L\ H\ 080.\ 60'\ E = <4'$, I wrote in my notebook aboard *Kylie*.

'*Cigarrillos?*'

The pitpan had come up out of the sun from astern and was lying alongside. Two men cradled paddles athwartships. From under a tattered sombrero, a third was trying to smile.

I threw them a line, bade them come aboard and gave them cigarettes. Two of them clattered their paddles into the pitpan and climbed into the cockpit. The third, no more than a boy, squatted on the after-hatch. When the cigarettes were drawing I pulled out the chart and asked questions: that light I was pointing to, was it at Xkalak? If making for Puerto Chico, where could I pass through the reef? How big a town was Ubero?

The men gazed at the chart in silence. The boy dozed off. Much ash fell from their cigarettes. At last a gnarled finger jabbed at the name Puerto Chico. I leaned forward to glean wisdom.

'Puerto Chico,' he said scathingly, 'does not exist!'

At one o'clock on a January afternoon two days later I weighed anchor under sail and set off for Xkalak from Bahia del Espiritu

---

Opposite: Yucatán. *On this 1903 passage chart, El Ebero is Ubero, Majagual is Majahual, Gavilan is not shown, and Xkalak appears only because I have written it in. The upside-down tear-drops represent light-stations. Isla Mujeres lies off the top right corner of Yucatán. Northward of Ambergris Cay the offshore reef is too close to the coast to be shown clearly.*

177

Santo. A ten-knot north-easterly dictated that I must tack twice before clearing the gap in the reef. Though the lightness of the wind suggested using the large genoa, instead I set its smaller sister, whose higher foot does not restrict my view of the water ahead – another basic requirement for single-handed sailing in coral seas, where safety more often lies in the helmsman's seeing what is beneath the water than in speeding across its surface towards a seamark above it.

Until sunset it was a lovely, trouble-free sail – and it was quite a speedy one, too. A quarter of a mile to seaward of the reef, *Kylie* sliced through the ten-foot swells at 5½ knots by the log. Bearings of Punta Herrero lighthouse showed that my boat was making the same speed over the ground: I was avoiding the current alright, so keeping the reef close aboard was clearly paying off. The differing colours of the water and the shape of the waves showed exactly where the current was running strongest. Far to the east the water was indigo and whitecaps; there, the current was flowing at two knots. Nearer to, the seas were ultramarine, less steep but still frothy; there, the current was about a knot. *Kylie*'s track was through water the colour of old geranium leaves. Here, in depths of eight to nine fathoms, the wavelets rarely broke, for here was no current.

A two-foot turtle sculled through skeins of weed, its shell a mottled brown and the weed a tawny yellow in the late sunshine. With the new moon a sliver in the western sky, at six o'clock I altered course towards the indigo seas to diverge from the lie of the reef. A 15-degree alteration of course, I told myself, would give me an ample margin for safety . . . but it didn't, not off that coast. An hour and a half later I saw the gleam of breakers on the starboard bow and imagined I heard their growls. I threw off the tiller lanyards, came hard on the wind, tacked, made a 160-degree alteration of course and hauled the foresail a-weather.

By the light of the cabin oil lamp I saw that alongside the Banco Chinchorro, thirty miles to the south, the chart stated:

> *The current sets strong into Firefly Bight*
> *and the whole eastern side of the reef.*

Five wreck symbols testified just how strong was the current. I let draw the foresail and edged back towards my former course, subtracting another ten degrees to counteract the on-shore set.

Doing this brought me face to face with another danger: offshore

178

shipping. At eight o'clock, with the dangers of the reef an unknown distance to starboard, the lights of a steamship came up ahead. He could not see me, for I was showing no light. I swung ninety degrees to the eastward, gave the same number of pump-strokes to the Primus lantern and thrust the flaming pipe-cleaner into the touch-hole. At once the universe imploded until it comprised only *Kylie* and me. Everything else – stars, steamship and all – was lost in the 200-candlepower glare from the lantern. One should never miss the chance of adding a bit of enlightenment, as the Inquisitor reminded Joan of Arc while torching the bonfire.

I clambered to the backstays and lashed the lantern in place, six feet above the hull. By sitting in the shadow of its tank, I could just make out the steamship's lights as she passed northward, a mile or so distant. Every detail of *Kylie* was brilliantly lit. From inside the cabin I could see the handrail on the coachroof through two thicknesses of coloured fibreglass which were normally opaque. The experience was thrilling. It was like looking at an X-ray of your fractured backbone while awaiting the surgeon.

The lantern stayed in the backstays until the first hour of the graveyard watch, by which time the cocoon of light had become a stifling shroud. I doused the lantern, the stars reappeared and I breathed more freely, but the fears were still fingering my spine. Apart from the stars, I could see nothing to tell me where I was – not a glimmer from all those ghostly, unmarked towns along the shore . . . *Puerto Chico does not exist!* Perhaps some seventeenth-century joker at the local town hall had twinned it with ancient Dunwich and both places had tumbled into the sea . . . But what about the other places, places which bore names of creatures from Old English sagas? If ogres like Grendel had slaughtered innocent boozers in beer halls, what on earth would monsters like Ubero and Majahual get up to when they came across liquor-drinkers like me?

Measured against the scale of the US chart, the names of the towns are a mile tall. It was inconceivable that they did not exist: except when they are doing Cuba, American cartographers do not purvey fiction.

I stitch-in a five-degree gusset towards the shore. Somewhere in the blackness a poet cackles '*Dread Majahual, on what reef dost thou roar?*'

At five o'clock, not having glimpsed shore lights and therefore unsure of my whereabouts, I work out the approximate altitude of

Arcturus. At a quarter past five I check the index error of the sextant and peer for the first signs of a horizon. At 0520 I think I discern a horizon and so I ready the sextant. Four minutes later a scarf of cloud muffles the Great Bear, and before I can capture Arcturus the cloud has veiled him from view. Where on earth am I? I stare at the chart and see again those five wrecks on Banco Chinchorro. I re-sharpen the pencil and re-plot the estimated position, but in the yellow light of the wick-lamp it is not easy, and my mind keeps murmuring a requiem about those wrecks: '*Saw ye the bones of galleons five in the jaws of the ghoul Ubero?*'

Half-past five. With the shore a faint blur in the west, I glimpse a light flashing once every five seconds on the starboard bow. The only charted light is unnamed, presumably but not certainly at Xkalak itself, and the chart states that it emits not one flash but two. Perhaps, it has been changed to a single flash since the chart was printed . . .? Perhaps the light I see is not at Xkalak at all but at one of those other places, even though they are supposed to be unlighted . . .?

'*Sir Gavilan.*' I murmur, '*is yon thy sword a-flashing in the glim . . .?*'

It must be, and it is. Some very basic figuring on the chart reveals that the light can come only – give or take five miles or so – from near where the G of Gavilan is printed, and the sighting of a straggle of pinky-white buildings and another lighthouse miles to the south in the sunrise confirms it. This other lighthouse can only be at Xkalak.

At eight in the morning, under genoa and full main, *Kylie* swoops through the reef, luffs up into the breeze and casts her anchor into a fathom of water north of the pier. Two hours later, having completed the basic routine of oiling the log and re-filling the lamps, I row ashore to check-in and take refreshment, the fears of the night almost forgotten.

Gourds are swinging in the breeze under the thatch of the *palapas*. In front of the naval post a rating is whitewashing rocks. A visiting chiropractor with a leathery face and a polka-dotted shirt is lying in wait at the bar. From a distance he looks like an effigy of Somerset Maugham. Beneath hooded eyelids, he inspects my bandaged hand and elbow.

'It's nothing,' say I, but I can see he doesn't believe me.

'Let me do some reflexology,' he says, 'and suss out your general condition . . .'

He presses diagnostically on a point between the thumb and index finger of my undamaged left hand. I yelp.

'Is it bad?' I ask him.

His eyelids flicker. Like Nigel's response to the self-same question, his facial expression would curdle milk.

'I'm afraid so,' he says. 'You're incubating an *awful* problem down below . . .'

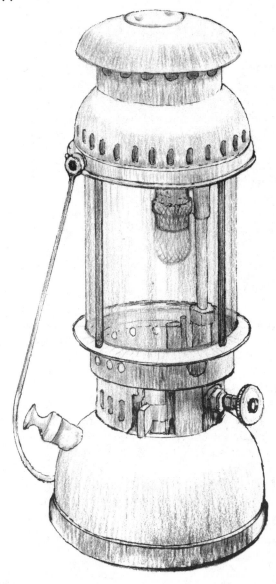

19

Captain Jorgé

I am getting to know every inch of this door. Years ago it had been
red, but much paint has flaked off and the wood has weathered grey.
Up from its bottom edge runs a crack the same width as *Kylie*'s chart
pencil. The crack is deep, but not deep enough. My cheek is flat on the
doorstep but I cannot see through the crack and into the room. Nor,
when I get to my knees, can I see through the keyhole. The keyhole is
on the left, two unbandaged finger-widths below the handle. When it is
shaken, the handle rattles.

It was rattling now, for I was becoming impatient.

Behind the door lay the office of the port captain of Xkalak. *Nada*
had anchored near *Kylie*, and Nigel and I were requiring his services.
We had knocked three times between ten o'clock and midday but the
door had not opened. At the third knock a young woman had emerged
from a nearby house and peered at us from beneath a lustrous bun of
black hair. If Mayan Indians went in for witchcraft she would have
been good at it. When I had asked a question she had inclined her
head, lowered an almond eyelid and prophesied that Captain Jorgé
would open up at 12.30. Fool that I am, I had believed her.

Now my watch was saying it was 12.45 and Paul was asking about
his dinner, but still the door had not opened.

I rattled the handle again.

'Nige, the kids need food. I'd better dinghy them back aboard.'

'Terrie, you can't; the port captain will want to check them out.'

Paul said: 'Nigel, I'm hungry.'

'Would you like a *chapata*, Paulie?' said Nigel.

'No.'

'He ate four *chapatas* already,' Terrie said; 'that's enough
carbohydrate for a week. What a three-year-old child needs is
protein; what he *really* needs is fish. How about some lovely fish,
Paul?'

'Yeah, Nigel,' said Paul; 'what I really need is fish.'

'Terrie,' said Nigel, 'you should seek employment in the Louisiana State Penitentiary.'

Just then there came scrunch from within the keyhole, the door swung open and there stood Captain Jorgé. We stood to attention.

His uniform was military style but in colour it was closer to the sandy seashore than to barrack-room khaki. The trouser creases were neat and clear but not knife-edged. His shoulder badges had once been in the shape of anchors, but laundering had eroded the flukes and bleached the shanks, so that now the badges looked like chalky worm-casts rather than anchors. The outlines were no more clearly visible than was the partly buried driftwood on his beaches.

Only if their anchors are well buried do captains sleep easy; the invisible anchor flukes were therefore a good omen. Already I knew that Captain Jorgé had slept late; now the omen was telling me that he had also slept well. I entered his office in what is called an optimistic frame of mind.

It did not last long.

From his rucksack Nigel pulled out the Calder passports, his ship's papers, two *zarpes* and a sheaf of crew lists.

In the north-west Caribbean the *zarpe* (**sarr/pay**) is a cruising permit. The Mexican *zarpe* runs to 120 words, set out in ten-point capitals. By rights, each boat needs only one *zarpe* to cover the whole length of coast from Isla Mujeres in the north to Xkalak in the south, but officials at intermediate ports had insisted that we needed extra *zarpes* and crew lists so as to cruise their local waters. It was chicanery, of course; they were trying to make a bit on the side.

Captain Jorgé was not a party to that sort of racket and it was hard to believe that he ever could be. With white hair, white moustache, and cheeks like ripe peaches, he looked as if he had just come down from a convocation of elderly angels.

'*Buenas tardes, mi amigo,*' he said, taking a bon-bon from his desk and holding it in front of Paul's nose. (Except when adding a dash of local colour, I will now stop rendering Spanish as Spanish: doing it every time a character speaks holds up the flow of the story.)

On Paul's behalf Terrie uttered a smiling 'No'. Sweets, she said, were bad for his teeth.

Captain Jorgé chuckled until his peaches bloomed with merriment. The child's mother was surely mistaken: sugar was one of God's blessings; sugar was heavenly energy. He launched into a history of his own taste in sweetmeats, from the time he had been Paul's age to the present day.

We pulled up chairs and sat down.

Some way into Captain Jorgé's eulogy of molasses, Paul contorted his mouth into a gaping leer, crossed his eyes and went rigid. To that mythical character called the dispassionate observer it would have resembled the rictus of death. Captain Jorgé stopped himself in mid-sentence and looked non-plussed. Nigel, who already knew about his son's talents in improvised drama, made a muted 'Hum!' and rustled the remaining copies of his crew list. When it is done by someone with Nigel's dexterity, even the rustling of a few papers can be impressive. He had arrived in Mexico with seven copies but after being subjected to a close scrutiny at Isla Mujeres and lots of heavy-handed stamping at Puerto Morelas and San Miguel, the numbers had dwindled to four.

In response to Nigel's rustle, Paul closed his mouth, uncrossed his eyes and regarded Pippin with an air of triumph.

'Huh! That didn't fool *me* one bit,' sniffed Pippin. Before she could start into a rival performance, Terrie eyed both children and said 'You two are heading for trouble.'

'To business!' cried Captain Jorgé, taking up the papers. 'I promise to read every one! Not a syllable shall I miss!'

He was – I have implied this already – a man of honour. We now discovered that he was also a literary critic. Separately, the two are not always easy to stomach; together they are sickening.

He studied the first sentence of the first document.

'The name of your boat is *Nada*?'

'Yes.'

'What a truly splendid name! *Na-a-a-d-a-h!*' The word came from his throat like oral sculpture, a column of aerial marble. 'I could wish that all mankind shared the same sense of humour. To call a 12-ton boat a "nothing" is the act of a true philosopher!' He enfolded the word-sculpture in mid-air and contemplated its beauty. '*De la em-bar-ca-ci-on Na-a-a-d-a-h!*' he said softly, stroking each syllable with his fingertips. His moustache trembled. He should have been in opera. 'My brother Francisco – whose soul is with God – had the same profundity of mind: he named each of his twelve children after the months of the year.'

Terrie and I slid our chairs to one side and tried to work out the implications of this while Captain Jorgé was reading the rest of the text. In all, it amounted to 112 words, and reading them took Captain

Jorgé four minutes. Nigel smiled through his beard and looked deeply philosophical. As he is the son of a dentist the feat was easy.

'What would he have named the last kid if there'd been thirteen?' said Terrie, lowering her head in case Jorgé could lip-read.

'Never mind about that,' said I. 'Apart from wet bottoms, what is the connection between boats and babies?'

'Excellent, Captain Calder!' said Jorgé, now at last at the end of the first copy and beaming. 'The substance is correct in both grammar and spelling. What is more, you do not confuse the Spanish genders.'

Nigel's toes perceptibly wiggled. They might have been expressing gratification but it could have been anguish. Lips I can read; with toes I am hopeless.

Captain Jorgé produced a rubber stamp and thumped it on the first crew list. Nigel and Terrie stood up. The interview, we thought, was over; soon Terrie could go fishing and Paul could be fed.

Half-way to being upright, I saw that Captain Jorgé had turned the page and had was studying the next copy.

'I hope,' he said, addressing Nigel, 'that this one will be up to the same standard. Any mistakes, and I shall have to ask you to do it again.'

We lowered ourselves back onto the chairs.

' "*Solemnemente*", for example,' went on Captain Jorgé, quoting from the document before him and at the same time shaking his head; 'you would be surprised at how many people cannot spell "*solemnemente*".'

We held our breaths, but only briefly. Nigel's grammar and spelling, continued Captain Jorgé, now accelerating his reading speed, seemed to be as impeccable in the second crew-list as they had been in the first. We looked at each other. Some of us supposed that carbon copies were exact replicas. Captain Jorgé shook his head. The world was filled with traps for the unwary: look what had happened, for example, in the Garden of Eden. With Tip-Ex and Liquid Paper around, one could never be too careful . . .

For all the time and stress which those carbon-copied crew-lists were supposed to have saved us, Nigel might just as well have gone back and done them all again.

'In ink . . .,' I whispered.

'. . . on vellum,' Terrie mouthed, 'and using a quill . . .'

Captain Jorgé's reading of the third copy gave rise to a homily on the difference of meaning between *la tripulación* (the crew) and *la tribulación* (severe suffering).

185

Deaf toad that I am, I said that to me it sounded like that there *was* no difference.

'Excellent!' cried Captain Jorgé again. 'Captain Hancock is correct; there is none! Consider, my friends, the following statements: "The boat is kept going by the crew, *la tripulación*" and "The boat is kept going by severe suffering, *la tribulación*". I ask you, Captain Calder, what is the difference? When voyaging across God's great ocean of life, do you not discover that the two are one and the same?'

'You bet he does,' muttered Terrie; 'especially when a Norther is blowing.'

I smirked. I like Terrie a lot.

This off-the-cuff semantical reference to suffering, went on Captain Jorgé, did not of course apply to *Nada*'s crew, though – by Saints Toméo and Francisco! – its youngest member was presently looking a trifle wan. Captain Jorgé's cheeks wrinkled with concern; he did not wish to press the point, but would Terrie like to re-think her attitude to bon-bons . . .? His late brother Francisco – for whom God had reserved indefinitely a place on high – swore by them. As antidotes to embarrassing dreams, ciguatera poisoning and yellow fever, bon-bons were infallible. Little October, Francisco's eighth child and prey to every ailment known to man and the Devil, had devoured them by the kilo . . .

'Eighth? October isn't the eighth,' said Terrie 'Whose calendar was he using?'

'Perhaps he was going by the month of its conception,' I said, 'and the birth was a bit late?'

'He's talking about human beings,' said Terrie, 'not elephants.'

Made ecstatic by the thought of more bon-bons, Captain Jorgé's eyes lifted skywards.

What saved ours from going up too was the reappearance of the Mayan witch, who slid through a curtained archway bearing glasses half-filled with an opaque liquid. The result was amazing. At her coming, Captain Jorgé thumped his stamp on the last copy of *Nada*'s crew list, thumped it more rapidly on all four of *Kylie*'s without reading even the first one, pushed back his chair and stood to attention.

'May fair winds always attend you!' he cried, raising a glass.

'And the same to you!' roared Nigel and I, springing to our feet.

'What is it?' said Terrie, sniffing the rim.

'Liquidized melon,' said Nigel tartly, 'with no added sugar.'

Captain Jorgé

'What's Spanish for "hypocrite"?' said I as we left.

'Same as the word for "diplomat", probably,' said Terrie.

We walked past the leading light which marked the reef passage, then along the jetty until we got to our dinghies.

Nigel stepped down into *Nada*'s and primed the outboard. Terrie tugged off the children's footwear so that it would not get wet.

'I'm *hungry*,' Paul said. 'I need a *big* fish.'

Out of her rucksack Terrie pulled a *chapata*. Paul looked confused.

I turned round and waved to Captain Jorgé.

From where I was standing he still looked like an angel. Behind him, the Mayan woman still looked like a witch.

Kylie's galley

20
Mud and Mangroves

The cruising-guide project was ambitious, Nigel had allowed himself only six months to survey hundreds of islands and reefs which stretch across 350 miles of the north-west Caribbean, from the head of the Yucatán to the thigh of Honduras. Forays up lakes and rivers and excursions to Mayan ruins meant that the Calders would be trying to cover 50,000 square miles. Some places were remote from motorised man, the marine surveys were out of date and one or two lagoons – so the charts implied – had never been systematically surveyed at all.

For this formidable task Nigel's tools were a small compass and a large boathook. The compass hung always on a cord around his neck. In certain light-conditions it winked and gleamed, and he fingered it like an amulet. Marked off in feet, the boathook was a portable depthsounder. Sometimes Nigel carried the boathook like a spear and sometimes like a staff. Either way, the sight was disturbing. With sunblock cream streaking his face he resembled a Carib on the warpath; without the cream he looked like a defrocked lollipop-man.

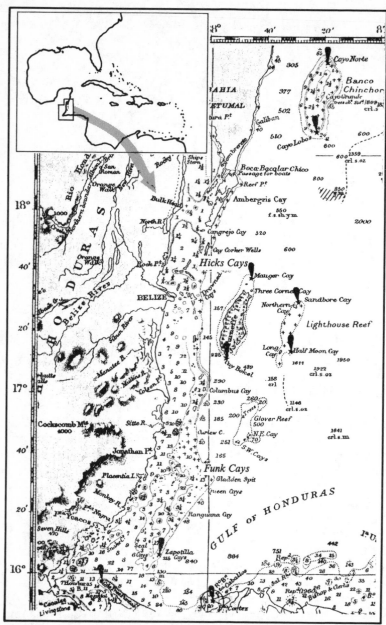

Crown Copyright. Reproduced from Admiralty Chart 762 with the permission of the Controller of Her Majesty's Stationery Office.

Six weeks had gone by and the survey was going well. While *Kylie* had sauntered southwards, *Nadà* had coursed seawards to the Banco Chinchorro and back to Xkalak. With Terrie at *Nada*'s helm, Nigel conning from the ratlines and the children swinging from the kicking-strap, the two boats had then picked their way through the northern Belizean cays: Ambergris, with its clapboard houses and coconut palms, Cay Corker with its solitary bar and its boatbuilder, sandy Cay Chapel, St George's Cay – where eighteenth-century cannon still peered seawards for Spanish attackers, and so on to Porto Stuck. I am attracted – disastrously, you will add – by tacky names, and so it will surprise no-one that at Porto Stuck I came unstuck.

People at Ambergis Cay had mentioned Porto Stuck and I had noticed Nigel copying their navigational sketches, but because the eternal fiddle had been screeching inside my better ear, at the time I had not taken much notice; I had assumed that when eventually I opened my chart, all – or rather, all the bits of Porto Stuck that mattered – would be revealed. I was wrong. Now I was looking at the chart it seemed that my chances of reaching Porto Stuck were zero.

There were two reasons for this. Firstly, the name Porto Stuck did not appear anywhere on the chart. Secondly, though I often boasted that *Kylie* had many talents, I could not believe that the ability to sail across land was one of them. But according to the chart that is just what she was doing. The land in question was Hicks Cay, and it was charted as being covered by dense mangroves. I re-checked my bearings and sighed with puzzlement; according to the bearings I was half-way into Hicks Cay. Cartographically speaking, *Kylie* was doing four knots through a jungle.

Later, I learned what I should have gleaned while the violinist had been playing his toccata: since the chart was printed, a hurricane had

---

Opposite: Banco Chinchorro to Gulf of Honduras. *Gabilan (Gavilan) has managed to creep onto this 1913 chart but Xkalak is still being left off. At 17° 38′N, one of the Hicks Cays awaits the hurricane which will carve Porto Stuck, while down south in Guatemala, Livingston (named after an American doctor) has been been given a superfluous 'e' by an Admiralty cartographer who is confusing him with the famous Scottish missionary. The Funk Cays have been labelled because they will come into a later chapter.*

re-sculpted parts of the Belizean landscape, including Hicks Cay. Where the mangrove jungle once grew, Caribbean water was now flowing copiously through a wide channel over a bottom of dark green weed and white sand. A passing bargehand had named the channel Porto Stuck. I hope they hanged the blighter. A sailor should not make dry jokes; he will seem shallow-minded.

From doing four knots, suddenly *Kylie* slithered to a halt. I let fly the sheets and felt irked. Until then I had gone by the generalised wisdom that darker water meant deeper water. Now I was discovering that the opposite could be true. During the years since Porto Stuck was formed, laden barges had scoured the weed from the navigable channel and this had exposed the white sand. I had thought that the lighter-coloured water was shallower, not deeper, and so had veered away from it. As a result, *Kylie* had run onto a weedy knoll and was pinned there by the current.

Kedging off took ages, for the current was strong. I rowed out two anchors, took the anchor warps to winches and heaved till the warps were thrumming in the current, but *Kylie* did not budge. I re-set the sails and sheeted them in until the wind pressure heeled her to an angle of ten degrees. The heeling reduced her draught by only an inch but I hoped an inch would be enough. Again I went to the winches and tried to crank them but the handles would not move. I braced my back against the cockpit coaming, bent both legs, set my heels against the winch handle and pushed. The handle moved; the pawls clicked. Little by little, *Kylie* was dragged clear. It took forty minutes to edge back into deeper water and another twenty to recover my breath.

'. . . *so much*,' sniffed my logbook, '*for antediluvian charts and Porto Stuck.*'

But to both boats such mishaps came often. In the muddy waters near Belize City *Nada* and *Kylie* sometimes ran aground three times a day. *Kylie*'s groundings usually happened because I was not looking where I was going – perhaps a beer can needed opening or a pelican wanted me to watch its aerobatics – but *Nada*'s groundings occurred because Nigel is a born sceptic. He refused to take twenty-year-old depth-soundings for granted and, what with finding Porto Stuck where a jungle was allegedly flourishing, who would blame him? He was determined to give his cruising-guide readers accurate data, and to get it he had to venture into tight corners and shallow waters.

He was doing that now. We had anchored at Robinson's Point, where we were sheltered from the trade wind by – Belizeans are so logical – Robinson's Island. In the early hours of the morning a new wind had blown strongly from the west, making Robinson's Island a lee shore. At half-eight we had eyed our descending barometers and yelled that we were going to search out a better anchorage at Ramsay's Cay, half a mile southward. Nigel had depressed the power switch of his new windlass, Terrie had started the engine, and in five minutes *Nada* had weighed anchor and Nigel was perched in her rigging.

Because she was drawing 20 fewer inches of water than *Nada*, *Kylie* went first. Being less than three hours old, the sun was not at the best height for reading the depths by eye, but in the approach to Ramsay's Cay the light would be coming helpfully from behind me. Under reefed main and working jib my boat sped south-eastwards towards a shoal. I toggled the tiller and went to the foredeck. Across my path ahead stretched a large patch of coral. Light brown in colour, the shoal was less than three feet deep but to the west and east of it lay two channels. The eastern channel was wide, bluey-green and clear but if I used that channel *Kylie* would then have to hook round the southern edge of the shoal and beat up into the lee of Ramsay's Cay. The western channel was lighter in colour and narrower, and it was hemmed with shallows of sand. At its narrowest the channel was pale green. Give or take three inches, I supposed it to be six feet deep. To *Kylie* the western channel would pose no pilotage problems. Also, by steering through it, I would get into the lee of Ramsay's Cay quicker and would not have to beat into the wind.

I returned to the cockpit and steered for the narrower channel.

From his perch in *Nada*'s rigging Nigel watched *Kylie* skim through the narrows, luff up and cast anchor. Then he gave a hand signal to Terrie in the cockpit. *Nada*'s bow sprouted a white moustache and she headed to follow.

The air was so still and quiet in the lee of Ramsay's Cay that a pelican was asleep on the water. I saw Nigel cup a hand to his mouth and heard him call something which could only have been 'Slow!' *Nada*'s moustache wilted and drooped.

'Stop!' called Nigel. Seconds later the moustache vanished. The pelican opened its eyes, looked around sourly and took off.

Still doing about a knot, *Nada*'s bow glided into paler green water. Then, like a woman examining her lipstick in a mirror, she bared more red paint and leaned towards the light. It was elegantly done, but the leaning told me that instead of making a smooth entrance the boat had run aground.

Nigel jumped into his dinghy, prodded around with his boathook for a few minutes and then returned aboard. White water boiled up the rudder stock as the propeller went full astern. *Nada* slid gently backwards and her mast came fully upright; she was afloat again.

Before laying *Kylie*'s second anchor I waited to see what Nigel would do next. Would he go back and hook round the shoal to try the eastern channel or would he try this shallower one again? I saw him climb the rigging higher than before, stand on the lower spreaders and point towards the shallower channel. Terrie engaged gear and opened the throttle, and the white moustache, which before had been no bigger than Walt Disney's, speedily reappeared and grew to the size of – excuse my Anglophilia – Lord Kitchener's. *Nada* blasted through the pale green shallows at four knots. I lowered the Danforth anchor into the dinghy and marvelled at Nigel's coolness.

Three hours later the barometer fell sharply and the wind veered to north-west. The wind-shift was worrying; no doubt about it, another Norther was coming through. We went on deck and took stock. Our boats were still sheltered by Ramsay's Cay but before long the wind might veer north-east and then the boats would be in danger again. We must find a better anchorage before nightfall, somewhere *Kylie* and *Nada* could lie safely whatever the wind did.

'Let's go to the Drowned Cays,' said Nigel. 'We can get into a bogue and anchor among the mangroves.'

The Drowned Cays lay 11 miles north of Ramsay's Cay and the sky was now heavy with cloud. In the dark water near Belize City, pilotage by eyeballing underwater mudbanks in poor light would be almost impossible. We would have to rely on whatever channel-markers we could find.

Find some we did, but not all of them. Again under reefed main and working jib, *Kylie* bustled northwards, heeling 20 degrees, spray rattling on the dodger, tea kettle steaming on the Primus and her skipper slopping Earl Grey down his jacket. Ahead and to starboard, *Nada* drove through the waves with her mast stolidly vertical, making four knots under engine. Below decks, Paul comforted his one-eyed teddy, Pippin practised writing her p's and q's and Terrie put final touches to her sketch of Cay Corker.

To reach our haven in the Drowned Cays we had to pass through three channels, locally called bogues. The first bogue was the trickiest, being narrower than the others and twisty too, but its entrance was marked by a tripod beacon, and its snake-like course by withies or stakes. This time *Nada* went first, slowly forging through the thick water. Spilling wind, *Kylie* followed. The withies were hard to spot. Some protruded only inches from the water, and we had to guess the whereabouts of others from a chance ripple above their splintered stumps.

After ten minutes of what to me looked like guesswork but certainly was not, Nigel piloted *Nada* out of the first bogue and entered the second. This one looked wider, straighter and easier. Irritated by all the wind-spilling I was having to do, I sheeted in, *Kylie* drew abreast of *Nada*.

'The next course is 153°, right?' I called.

'Yes, but only when the stake dead ahead is half a mile nearer,' shouted Nigel from his rigging.

'What stake are you talking about?' yelled I, standing on the coachroof for a better view.

'Careful!' shouted Nigel. 'You're close to the putty!'

Ever so slightly, *Kylie*'s mast leaned to windward.

'Nice of you to tell me,' I called back, 'just when I'm on it.'

Nada drew abeam and Terrie put the propeller into slow astern.

'Want a hand?'

'No, thanks; you're almost there. You go ahead and anchor, and put the kettle on.'

'You sure?'

'Yes.'

'Okay . . . See you in a mo'.'

'See you.'

Regretfully – for it would have been pleasant to be making into the anchorage under sail – I bundled the jib into its bag and started the engine. The propeller churned, and soon the sea around me looked like cocoa. More easily this time, *Kylie* slid off the mud into deeper water, and minutes later she was nosing into the final bogue of the day.

Rounding a slight bend, soon I saw *Nada* ahead. All around us the gusty wind was bending the uppermost branches of the mangroves, but the surface of the bogue was mirror smooth. Nigel was right; this was a good haven.

Surprisingly, though, *Nada* had not yet anchored.

I drew abeam of her and put my engine into slow astern.

'Want a hand?'

'No, thanks. We'll be afloat in a tick.'

'Right-ho! I'll anchor over there and – er – put my kettle on.'

Prodding around with his boathook for the umpteenth time that day, Nigel said: 'Yes, you do that.'

So I did.

21

The Blank on the Map

The Norther roared down the shores of Yucatán and Belize, through the Gulf of Honduras and onward to the Mosquito Coast. At our gloomy bogue in the Drowned Cays we watched the storm wrack being sucked southwards, revealing a clear blue sky.

'Someone is hoovering heaven,' said I.

Pippin glanced skywards and then she stroked my shoulder.

'Peeder,' she said, 'you're funny.'

'Look!' I said, pulling Capetown's hat over my ears. 'The sun has got his hat on and he's coming out to play. Let's join him!'

So *Nada* and *Kylie* put on their headgear too, scampering from the dark mangroves onto a sparkling sea. The farther south they ventured, the wider spread their playground and the brighter it glittered. From being close to the reef, the mainland south of Yucatán suddenly retreated westwards. At Xkalak the barrier reef had been less than a mile from the shore but off Belize city it was 15 miles distant. When in a few weeks our boats neared Guatemala, the distance between the barrier reef and the mainland would have grown to 25 miles.

Tracking eastward from the mainland across this widening seabed on a wheeled vehicle would have been like riding a fairground switchback; sometimes dropping into deep channels, then soaring up into slighter gullies and weedy shallows, or angling less steeply up sandy gradients before finally levelling off on to white plains which were tussocked with coral. We could not explore the seabed as intimately or extensively as that, though many times Terrie donned her snorkel and tried to. Just sailing the sea's surface kept us blissful, for all around in the sunshine danced islands: islands by the dozen and islets by the score. Few were more than a mile long; most were much smaller, some being no bigger than a football pitch. Cleared of its mangroves or its palm trees, an average-sized island would have been large enough to accommodate an Albert Hall.

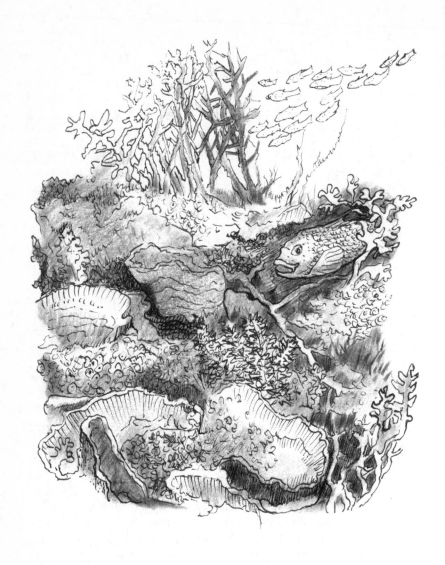

Coral clump

But supposing such buildings were buildable, they would not be fillable. Including a platoon or two of British soldiers on furlough, a sprinkling of time-travellers and a motley of yachties and other tourists, the total number of people on the more populous Belizean islands such as Ambergris and Corker would not have filled a fair-sized cinema, let alone an Albert Hall. Indeed, if all us visitors had suddenly packed our bags and gone elsewhere – had sodded off, as it were, to Bognor Regis – most islands would have lain empty. Even with hundreds of spaced-out visitors to-ing and fro-ing the area, many islands still had nobody sitting under their palm trees; on some days we sailed forty miles and surveyed half a dozen islands without spotting another sail or meeting a single soul.

It did not bother us. Sailing the waters between the barrier reef and the mainland was the nearest to heaven that we would ever get. Day after day the trade wind filled our sails and the furrows followed free. Heading south, *Kylie* was often logging six knots, on a fine reach all the way. Apart from the fair and constant wind, what made the sailing marvellous was that the barrier reef to seaward killed the Caribbean swells. Slicing through seas which were often no higher than a footstool, she scattered lots of spray but she mostly kept her decks dry.

We pressed on southwards, passing Robinson's Point again, until we were a mile from Bluefield Range. Here, the coral clumps were denser, so we heaved-to and looked around.

'I can see the stake on the northern tip of the reef,' called Nigel from his ratlines. 'Crank your motor and follow me.'

'No; I want to sail in.'

'Hum!'

'Not through the northern entrance though, because it's dead to windward and it looks a bit too narrow for safe tacking. I'll go south of the reef and the island, and get in through the other pass.'

'On my chart, that passage looks narrower.'

'Yes, but the wind'll be freer.'

Terrie started *Nada*'s engine and aimed for the channel marker. I changed-down *Kylie*'s foresail from genoa to working jib and directed my course away from it.

The island is half a mile from tip to tip, and it lies in the middle of a reef which is a mile longer. *Nada* was dog-legging through a channel which was a 100 yards wide at its narrowest. On the chart, the channel I wanted to use looked only about fifty yards wide. Not for the first time, I hoped the cartographers had been over-cautious.

Mangrove trees clustered at the sea's edge as I sailed the length of the island, some leaning forward on tiptoe to get a better view. In the Drowned Cays the mangroves had seemed doleful and incurious, but there the air had been heavy with scud. Here in Bluefield Range the mangroves looked happier. They were not freaking-out madly like the palm trees at Xkalak had been doing when I sailed past them, but at least they appeared to be friendly . . .

Nudged on by by the sunshine, I edged *Kylie* closer to the shore and called a greeting. Not a leaf stirred.

Disappointing, that; but I would go on trying. A change of environment can often alter human nature, but it does not seem to work with trees. Even if it is watered with Guinness, a palm tree is just as zany in Ireland as in Xkalak, and a mangrove stays mainly morose whatever it drinks. Mangroves must have terrible psychological problems. No matter how excited other trees get, mangroves never manage to let themselves go.

Suddenly the mangroves ended and I came upon a cluster of shacks on stilts. They were a piteous sight. Frail of leg, sagging at the shoulders and propping each other up, they squatted above the wavelets like elderly women having a pee. I edged towards deeper water and politely looked away.

South of the shacks, with the coconut palms of a distant cay almost in line with the tip of another island in the Bluefield Range, I found the beginnings of the channel. It led north-east, slightly free of close-hauled, shoaling quite steeply from 40 feet to 12, then more gently to 7, I eased the sheets and climbed to the spreaders. Three feet below the keel, the sandy bottom was strewn with stones and small coral. On either side, between ten and fifty yards distant and only a yard under the surface, coral hunks were browning in the afternoon sunshine. Ahead, the channel maintained its blue colour and swung twenty degrees to leeward, but the blue was narrower, and it ran close to a mangroved shore. When *Kylie* entered the lee of the mangroves she would run out of wind.

I sheeted in, and the boat moved forward quicker. The channel became leaner, and the coral hunks fell astern faster, stirring drowsily in the quarter-wave. Forty degrees on the port bow, the women were still peeing. Close to starboard, the mangroves were pretending not to look. However, they were sweating. This did not surprise me for, as I've said already, mangroves have deep problems.

Making three-plus knots, *Kylie* glided into the wind shadow of the nearby trees, which were now innocently inspecting their toes. When the first mangrove drew abaft the cockpit the foresail fell limp, and seconds afterwards the mainsail did likewise. The channel was now at its narrowest.

Squeezed by the coral, *Kylie* edged closer to the island and deeper into the wind shadow. Her speed fell slowly, but it fell. Now I rested only my fingers on the tiller, not whole hands: altering the rudder angle more than a degree or two would bring her forward motion to an earlier stop. I stared ahead and aloft, searching for wind. A hundred yards abeam to port, ruffled water told me that enough wind was blowing to keep my boat moving if I chose to head that way, but I could see that the ruffled water was only two feet deep: to go for that wind patch would be to impale *Kylie* on spikes.

Speed now about a knot, sails still limp. Half a mile ahead, *Nada* was already anchored and Nigel was launching his dinghy. Between us lay more ruffled water, acres of it. One hem of the ruffles stretched across my course, but it lay a hundred yards ahead. There, definitely, lay deep water, but *Kylie* could not carry enough headway to reach it. Another hem was much nearer; only thirty yards distant, but it lay on the port bow. *Kylie* might be able to carry her way thus far, but those ruffles were glazed heavily by the rays of the sun and so unseen coral could lie beneath.

Flatfootedly but softly, I crept to the bows and stared into the glazed water. Was it deep or was it shallow? I went on staring, trying to read what lay beneath the glitter, and then I returned to the cockpit and stared instead at *Nada*'s mainmast dead ahead. I shifted my body slightly left, until *Nada*'s mast was in line with one of *Kylie*'s foredeck stanchions. My fingers found the inboard end of the tiller and gently pressed it three inches to starboard.

For seconds nothing happened. I considered whether or not to push the tiller another inch to starboard, but *Kylie* was now doing less than half a knot, so I did not. On the ninth second I saw that *Nada*'s mast was shifting out of line. I stopped counting seconds and, raising my free hand to my forehead, I eased upwards Capetown's hat.

Kylie's bow nuzzled into the ruffles and soon the first whispers of wind were drying my sweat.

Though its islands were entirely covered with mangroves, we lingered at Bluefield Range, for the anchorage delighted us in other ways.

From sunrise to sunset frigate birds patrolled the sky or swooped and glided above their nests, and white-headed pelicans fished the lagoon. With awnings spread, our boats lay quietly, protected by a circlet of reef and islands. Deep in the lagoon grazed a shy manatee.

I totted up my logbook figures. *Kylie* had sailed 588 miles since leaving Isla Mujeres, but *Nada* had covered more than twice the distance. Nigel had surveyed about half the length of the coastline and its off-lying reefs and islands, and Terrie had sketched a dossier of navigational features. I was helping with the survey, but not much. Armed with his compass and boathook, Nigel puttered around the creeks and anchorages, taking ten soundings and bearings in the time it took me to take just one. And it was not only because his dinghy was equipped with an outboard motor: he worked faster than I did. His note-making was more comprehensive and accurate, too. Where I might take two bearings to fix the position of a reef, Nigel took three; when I returned aboard with news that a doctor resided two blocks west of the port captain's office, Nigel would discover that the doctor was also multi-lingual and that his neighbour was a dentist.

Kylie's shortage of mechanical and electrical power also limited my usefulness as a surveyor, but it did not often restrict my cruising. I was able to accompany *Nada* into most of the creeks and lagoons on her itinerary but sometimes it took me longer to get there. If the wind fell light and the sun was getting low, I sometimes cranked the engine, but for days on end I used only the sails. At the risk of sounding plummy, I would say that the sailing experience left me feeling fruitfully enriched.

And even the lack of a functioning alternator was easier to bear than I had imagined it would be. The only time I needed electricity was an hour after bedtime, to read. The light from the wick lamp was cosy, but holding up my 2 lb 10 oz *Complete Works of Shakespeare* close enough to the wick to be able to read Act I of *The Tempest* while lying in – of all aptly-named places – the Drowned Cays, had been exhausting. By the time I had got to *Full fathom five thy father lies* both hands had gone dead and I had felt knackered.

Since then, at bedtime I had been switching on the deckhead strip-light, but by the time we had got to Water Cay the battery was running low and I had not yet started Act IV.

I anchored in the lee of the island on six fathoms of short-link chain, fifty yards from *Nada*. Terrie was on deck, and she was looking my way, a happy circumstance which meant that I would be obliged to show off by doing a dive. If it had been only Nigel who was watching, he would have had to make do with an off-the-peg dive: head-first stuff, but piking neatly of course. Terrie, however, merited a backward somersault.

I did a scintillating somersault and swam over to *Nada* to receive my plaudits.

'You doved,' giggled Pippin, 'like a jumping frog.'

'That was a *very* unkind thing to say!' cried Terrie.

'Inaccurate, too,' said Nigel, who had sneaked on deck while I was not looking: 'he's not plump enough for a frog, and he's so old he can't jump. It was more like the death flop of a suicidal newt.'

'Talking of death,' I said, 'you seem to be neglecting your duties again: my battery is on its last legs. Is there any chance of giving it another kiss of life?'

'Come alongside,' Nigel said, 'and we'll use my jump leads.'

'Definitely not. The last time we tried it the wind and current pinned me under your bowsprit and I gouged my starboard capping. This time let's do the job differently: I'll dinghy the battery across to *Nada* and you can trickle-charge it all night.'

'What about your book at bedtime?'

'I'll manage without it,' I said loftily; 'I'll make something up.'

But back aboard *Kylie*, with no moon to gaze at I found the task difficult. I'd got no new stories to tell . . . Come to think of it though, perhaps there hardly ever had been such things as *new* stories: even Shakespeare pinched his plots. As my mother said, creativity is nothing more than re-knitting old wool . . .

Half a mile eastward, black swells were driving sullenly forward. Emboldened by the wind but cowed by it too, the swells had travelled the breadth of the Caribbees: fifteen hundred miles, from the Gibbs Seamount to Beata Ridge, over the Colombian Basin, peaking steeply on Rosalind and again on Thunder Knoll before breaking against the continental battlements. Some broke on Banco Chinchorro, (where lay, you remember, *the bones of galleons five*), and some on Lighthouse Reef (twenty miles long if an inch), or Glover's (six leagues from its thumb to little finger). Some had broken and crashed already, but not all of them. Now, on the reef edge outside Water Cay, the remaining waves – all of the all that was left of them – volleyed and thundered, follied and thundered, follied and blundered . . .

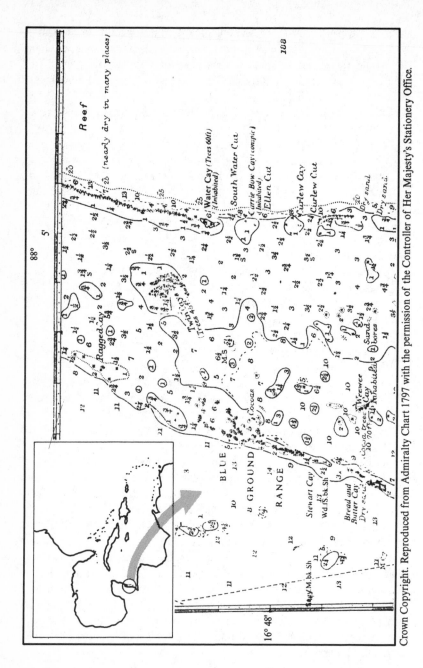

They kept it up all night of course, but I slept. The sound of the breakers was loud, even to me, but it wasn't a noise to stop you sleeping; there was rhythm to it, and a sort of music.

Next day, *Nada* returned to Belize city to collect mail. I rowed to Water Cay to collect data. A man cutting grass with a machete told me that the entrance to the Great Sittee River, twenty miles to the west, was buoyed, and that boats drawing six feet could cross the bar and enter the river.

'The Sittee entrance is deep enough for *Nada*,' I told Nigel when he returned; 'you only need to follow the buoys.'

We made out of Water Cay and dog-legged to more islands, beautiful palm-waving islands which bore unusual names and interesting inhabitants, islands such as Carrie Bow Cay and Weewee Cay, where another man swung a machete above our heads and told us to watch out for boa constrictors. 'Six feet long, some are. They drop theirselfs from the trees,' he said, 'and entwine theirselfs round your neck.'

Then we went back to the mangroves, to the Blue Ground Range and the Pelican Cays, surveying Baker's Rendezvous and Tarpum Cay as we went, and two days later sailed westward to the Great Sittee River.

Off the light-tower at Sittee Point, Nigel brought *Nada*'s bows onto a compass course of 217° and headed for the river entrance. Following astern, I trained my binoculars. The river was dark with jungle mud and the banks were dense with mangroves. I searched for the buoys but could not see them. Nigel was a mile ahead, doing three knots. If he can see those buoys, I thought, they must be very small ones.

Opposite: Blue Ground Range and the barrier reef. *Largely the labour of the ubiquitous Barnett, this shows a typical area of the Belizean barrier reef, the longest in the northern hemisphere. Off Curlew Cay the sea bed lies 188 fathoms (1128ft) below the Caribbean, but three miles westward it suddenly soars upward in a sheer cliff of coral rock to spread a sandy table with an array of variegated coral patches and islands. Westward of the Blue Ground Range it descends into a trench of weed, fine sand and broken shells (Wd.fS.bk.Sh) or soft grey mud and broken shells (so.gy.M.bk.Sh), then rises gradually towards the mainland, four miles farther west.*

But when I got closer I saw that there were no buoys at all. By the time *Kylie* came up astern and backed her foresail, *Nada* was hard aground. For thirty minutes the propeller churned cocoa, and then she slid off.

Nigel jumped into his dinghy and rowed over to *Kylie*. I cranked the engine and, with Nigel at the tiller, we tried again to drive across the muddy bar, this time in a boat which was drawing only four feet four inches.

In minutes, *Kylie* too was aground.

Nigel laid out *Kylie*'s kedge anchor with his dinghy, then borrowed her boathook and criss-crossed the river entrance, poling every ten yards. I backed the anchor warp to a winch and slowly wound *Kylie* off the mud.

'Where's the channel?' I called, swilling mud off the foredeck.

'There isn't one,' said Nigel, puttering alongside. 'The greatest depth is three feet nine inches.'

'Him and his six-foot channel!' cried I. '*And* him and his six-foot snakes!'

So we bore away southwards, and four miles down the coast came to the entrance of the Sapodilla Lagoon. We handed sail and peered ahead. The prospect did not look enticing. Although the water here was less opaque, the lagoon entrance was the same width as the Sittee River, and its banks were dismal with mangroves. Even more off-puttingly, on the chart the lagoon had no depth to it: not a single fathom, not even a vulgar fraction of a fathom. The lagoon was a blank on the map.

We cranked our engines and went for it.

Surprisingly, we found 14 feet of water in the entrance. The double-figure readings glowed on *Nada*'s depthsounder for half a mile, and did not fall to single figures until we drew abeam of an islet. North of the islet we cast anchors and grinned. The lagoon was not a scenic spot, and certainly it was not a view to be put into travel brochures; nevertheless, we were grinning. Our boats were entirely surrounded by mangroves of boringly uniform height and of boringly uniform colour. When the wind dropped, there would be legions of mosquitoes swarming the air. With the screens in place, the cabins would be stuffy and humid, and our clammy bodies would stick to the sheets.

'Good place to be if a hurricane comes along!' called Nigel.

As I said, we were grinning.

We would have gone on grinning longer if we had stayed there.

22

Tempest at Funk Camp

If asked about it, which I rarely am, I would say that when the trade wind falls so light that your tobacco smoke is coiling around your backstays, you can assume a gale is on its way.

Two hours after noon the next day, while *Kylie* was making easting under full main and large genoa, the wind speed suddenly fell from 12 knots to fewer than 2. I knocked the ash from my pipe, handed sail and – reluctantly as always – I cranked the engine, for without its help I would not be able reach my anchorage before nightfall.

The anchoring place was to be at Rendezvous Cay, an islet 17 miles south-east of the Sapodilla Lagoon and four miles inside the barrier reef. Although the name Rendezvous Cay sounds enticing, in fact in anything more than average weather it is not a good anchorage, for it lies in an area where deep gullies rise suddenly into sandy plateaux which are peppered with coral. It would not be the easiest place in which to anchor nor would it be certainly secure, but because the weather was fair and the barometer was behaving normally we had decided to anchor there. As likely as not the sand would be only inches deep and below the sand would lie rock. The anchor flukes would easily penetrate the sand but it was by no means certain that they would be able to bite on the rock. Two times in seven they would slide across the plateau until they caught on a knobble of rock, but if they failed to do this they would skitter off the plateau and dangle picturesquely in the chasm below.

The anchorage turned out to be much as we had imagined it would be. Perhaps the layer of sand was a little thicker than we feared it might be, but not by much. Arriving off Rendezvous Cay and finding the wind still no more than a whisper, we set our anchors with great care.

Nigel went below decks to put his kettle on. On *Kylie*, I poured myself two fingers of rum and afterwards I crossed them.

Soon after I had swallowed the rum the tell-tales in the rigging flickered and a sudden wind clouted me sideways. *Kylie* reeled, then turned her head and tried to run away. The anchor caught, slithered, caught again and held. *Kylie*'s bows jerked into the wind. I ran to the foredeck and paid out more cable. Again she angled away from the wind, but not so far this time and more briefly. Still tethered by the anchor, she rounded up smartly, quivering like a whippet. The anchor was holding firm, but for how long it would keep holding firm was not a matter on which even the old Third Mate would have placed bets.

By now the wind was blowing at 25 knots, rattling halyards and tugging at the dinghy on the coachroof, and grey clouds were racing in from the north. In *Nada*'s bows, Nigel had one foot on the chain, feeling for anchor-drag. Two boat-lengths astern, coral heads dodged and weaved among brawling waves.

Nigel looked in my direction and shouted something but I could not understand what it was. I waved my walkie-talkie above my head and shouted 'Radio!'

All fingers and thumbs, I twiddled its knobs.

'Peter, do you hear me?'

'Yes.'

'We'd better get out. I'm heading for the Funk Cays.'

'Okay, I'll come too.'

From the chart (see page 190), it seemed that anchoring off the Funk Cays would multiply our chances of riding out the blow safely. Two in number and surrounded by coral, the islands lay on their customary tables of sand. In this respect each Funk Cay was no different from what Rendezvous was, but the advantages of anchoring at the Funk Cays would be that, firstly, their sand tables were much larger; secondly, their surrounding coral was more extensive; and lastly and most importantly, between the cays lay a deep and muddy channel. If we could anchor in this channel the extensive Funk Cay coral would offer better protection from wind of gale-force 8, which was the force it was now showing every likelihood of getting itself up to. It would not be all-round protection such as we had enjoyed at the Sapodilla Lagoon but it would be better than anything that Rendezvous could offer. The problem was, anchoring in deeper water meant using a much longer scope of cable. This would lengthen the radius of the boats' swinging-circles and thereby increase their chances of hitting the coral heads which bordered the deep but rather narrow channel.

We started our engines, weighed anchor, and motored three-quarters of a mile to the Funk Cays. In a 25-to-30-knot wind, the passage was not easy, but somehow we made it.

Having a much more powerful engine, *Nada* got there first. By this time it was 5.30 and the sky was heavily clouded and so the light was weak. Still in the full force of the wind, *Kylie* was reeling like a drunken duck. Between the islands, near a spot known as Funk Camp, Nigel edged his boat into the channel, positioned her bows as near to the windward coral as seemed prudent, and let go his anchor. He waved a hand and beckoned me onward.

I swallowed a quick rum and did the same with *Kylie*.

By 7.30 it was fully dark and the wind was indisputably at gale force. Before sunset both of us had laid a second anchor and had brought a third anchor, a hurricane hook, on deck in case our other anchors failed or their cables parted. *Nada*'s hurricane hook was a bronze, half-hundredweight Luke anchor and *Kylie*'s was a 35-pound Bruce.

The chances of anchor breakage were low. Their scantlings were A1 at Lloyd's and their flukes were biting into mud. Provided that the mud was not oozy and the wind did not box the compass, if we paid out a long enough scope of cable – four times the depth of water if there was swinging-room – the anchors would hold firm. However, the possibility of the cable parting was always in my mind. Back in Louisiana I had ranged 30 fathoms of *Kylie*'s five-sixteenths-diameter chain cable on the dockside and had discovered that one of its links had fractured. The cable had been only two years old and its galvanizing had still been intact, but the link had fractured and the fracture had opened up more than an eighth of an inch. Even though I had thrown away the whole 30 fathoms of it and had purchased a fresh lot, since then I had been niggled by the thought that the same thing might happen again.

The chances of a rope parting were higher, especially so at Funk Camp. Nylon rope is wonderfully springy but it readily abrades. *Kylie*'s main anchor is a 25-pound CQR, and she was attached to it by 10 fathoms of chain which was shackled to 30 fathoms of eight-plait nylon rope but only 15 fathoms of the rope were presently in use. The heavy catenary of chain and the springy nature of the nylon meant that the shocks of violent wind-and-wave action were dampened before they could jerk at the anchor or the boat. If the gale had blown up while we had been lying in Sapodilla Lagoon I would have paid out every last inch of the 30 fathoms of nylon, but at Funk Camp I dared not do this.

Before sunset I had climbed the mast and confirmed the reason why. The wind was coming from the north at 30 knots. In every direction I could see that distant waves were breaking on reefs so violently that their spume was filling the air. The horizon had vanished; to discern where cloud ended and sea began was impossible. The maelstrom looked forbidding but not frightening, for *Kylie* was lying in the lee of a cay, protected from the waves. She was not near the breakers, and distance softened the danger.

What did alarm me, though, were nearer things. Between ten and twenty feet astern of me the olive-green water was smudged with ominous colours. In some places it was a milky brown, in others a burnt sienna or the bluey grey of Welsh slate. But whatever its colour, each smudge was certainly coral, the smallest piece of which could saw through a rope in a matter of seconds.

Halfway up the mast, the thought struck me that already it might have done so.

I went to the foredeck and heaved on the warp of the second anchor, a pint-sized Danforth. When used on mud, the Danforth sometimes dug itself in so deeply that I could weigh it only by winching it up on a trip-line attached to its crown. I had laid the Danforth at a 30-degree angle on the port bow, shackling 30 fathoms of three-strand nylon rope to its 9-fathom length of chain. Earlier on, after I had laid and set the anchors, their two ropes had been at similar tensions. Now, however, the rope attached to the Danforth hung down vertically in the water. From the way the rope was hanging, it looked as though I had come to its rescue a bit late.

I hauled on the rope. Thirty feet of it came back up through the fairlead before I felt any resistance. I hauled taut and pulled hard. Invisible, ten fathoms deep, the little Danforth did not budge. Good, I thought; *Kylie* is still attached to two anchors. I let the rope run back overboard and went below to light the lamps.

There passed a weary night. By ten o'clock the wind had backed to north-north-west and was blowing at up to 35 knots. Every half hour or so I went forward to check that all was well. Twenty yards to starboard in the darkness, *Nada* glowed whitely, groaning like a ghost in chains. At two in the morning the wind shifted to the north-west. The pitching rhythm altered, becoming deeper and longer. Straight away Nigel and I came out of our cabins and went to our foredecks to check. The wind shift meant that our boats were not now well protected: Funk Camp was becoming a rough house.

The wind blew at gale force throughout the night but at dawn it fell to 30 knots and by the time I was scooping up a panful of seawater for my porridge it had fallen to a steady 25 miles an hour. Coral heads were still smudging the water astern. Their colours seemed to have run: they had become smudgier but, thank heavens, they had moved no nearer. I stirred the oatmeal into the water and prepared a leisurely breakfast: *Kylie* was still safe; her anchors had not shifted.

Aboard *Nada*, though, Nigel was not at leisure. He too had hauled on the warp of his Danforth to test how well it was holding. Twenty-five fathoms of his best-quality three-strand nylon had come up though his fairlead without the rope tautening. His twenty-sixth fathom came up and, unfortunately, it was his last. The rope had frayed through. He had lost his Danforth anchor, and now the coral was only ten feet from *Nada*'s stern.

C. S. Forester and Captain Marryat had urged sailors in peril to be men of steel or, alternatively, of flint. Obediently I produced my lighter, flicked it and inhaled. From the safety of *Kylie*'s cockpit I exuded courageous thoughts to Nigel and Terrie. Their response was instructive. Nigel started the engine and Terrie took the tiller, gingerly edging *Nada* into the wind and away from the coral, while Nigel lugged his hurricane hook over the port lifelines and hung it off with a stopper. As *Nada*'s bow came nearer to where he had dropped his first anchor, the anchor chain began to angle astern. Nigel waited until a few more fathoms of chain had been dragged forward along the seabed 60 feet below, then he raised an arm and pointed westward, to port. Terrie leaned slightly forward, opening the throttle, at the same time moving the tiller to starboard. Though hampered by the dragging chain, *Nada*'s head was forced to port. When *Nada* could go no farther westward, Nigel cut through the stopper. The hurricane hook splashed into the water and Nigel skipped sideways. Two hundredweight of seven-sixteenths chain roared past his ankles and clattered over the bows. Then *Nada*'s propeller went astern and Nigel paid out cable as she responded. After the two cables had come taut and were angled equally on each bow, Terrie stopped the engine, Nigel secured the cable of the hurricane hook and peered over *Nada*'s stern.

The coral smudges were still visible but they were a whole boat's length farther off.

Like everything the Calders did, the job had been well done. I puffed my pipe and sighed with pleasure: except for the time when Wallis

Simpson ran off with Edward VIII, I have always had a soft spot for Anglo-American twosomes.

The anchors stayed put for five days. Mostly we kept to our cabins, gated by the weather. Rarely falling below 20 knots and most of the time blowing at 25, the Nor'wester kept the boats pitching awkwardly. For some crew members it was a trying time. Crayons rolled off cabin tables and one-eyed teddy bears crossly requested shore-leave. It was refused. Strong wind, driving rain and poor light meant that piloting through the coral towards mainland Belize would be loony: even two-eyed teddies with satnavs could not do it. Apart from these considerations, Nigel had no intention of leaving Funk Camp without his missing anchor. Whenever a lull came, he jumped into his dinghy and trawled the seabed with a grapnel. After two days of fruitless trawling the outboard motor had consumed two tankfuls of fuel and his back pain was playing up something chronic. He secured the dinghy and went below. It was the only time I have ever seen him give up.

By the afternoon of the fourth day the wind was down to a steady 20 knots but rain was still falling. Terrie came on deck and shouted to me to pick up my radio.

'How'd you like roast beef for dinner? Come across and join us!'

I slipped a bookmark into Shakespeare and inflated the dinghy.

Two hours later I was wiping the gravy from my plate and Nigel was closing the hatch and saying that, since the rain was still coming down, why didn't I stay longer aboard *Nada*?

'Thanks,' I said, 'I will.'

Clutching her nightie, Pippin scampered from the heads, pursued by a flying bear. I switched on a bunk light. Its beams highlighted her cheeks.

'Dell me a sdory, Peeder.'

'Wait!' cried Paul, still having his teeth brushed. Nigel stretched out on the berth opposite me, easing his back.

'Long ago, on a stormy night such as this,' I began, when the children had nestled alongside, 'a girl and her father were cast adrift on the wild and windy sea by her wicked uncle . . .'

'Whad their names?'

'Miranda and Prospero.'

'That better?' Terrie asked, hoisting one of Nigel's UK size-9 feet onto her lap and massaging its toes.

'M'm . . .,' said Nigel, closing his eyes.

'. . . and their dinghy came ashore on an island like the one we explored last week, but instead of red-footed booby birds and fishermen with plaited hair, who d'you suppose lived there?'

'Who?'

'An evil witch and her son, a monster named Caliban!'

'Whad Miranda do den?'

'Well, Prospero was a magician, and he'd brought some powerful weapons with him: his magic staff – nowhere near as big as Nigel's boathook nor as knobbly as his knees but pretty powerful all the same – and, of course, his books . . .'

Caliban

'Are books weapons?' said Paul.

'Boathooks can be weapons, so books can be, too,' said Pippin.

'But monsters can eat books,' said Paul firmly. 'Be me a monster, Peeder!'

I retreated to the galley, hung a mildewed jacket about my shoulders, stuck spaghetti into my hair, smeared tomato ketchup on my face and dropped onto all fours.

''*Ban, 'ban, Ca-Caliban!*' I growled, one eyebrow up to my hairline, the other intersecting my nose, eyes akimbo and jaw hanging loose.

'Monster!' shrieked Paul and Pippin, fleeing to the forecabin and slamming the door.

'Don't you want to hear the rest of the story?' I called through the lattice.

'You still a monster or you a Peeder again?'

'Whatever you say!'

'Be a Peeder!'

I wiped the ketchup from my face and tidied my hair.

'Okay, I'm Peter again.'

The door opened and I crept in.

23

The Stream Stops

The dark clouds lumbered southwards, trailing jagged grey peninsulas which looked like the Maine coast. The wind swung back to the east and gently the trades returned. I sharpened my 4B chart-pencil, weighed anchor and steered for Placentia, (see chart on page 190) making three knots under ghoster, watching the Funk Cays sink astern. *Nada* burbled past under engine, for the mainland was miles away, the sun was declining rapidly and the teddy was mutinous.

I waited till *Nada* had dwindled to a speck, then I poured rum and searched for a new moon. Five minutes after sunset I spotted it among wisps of cloud, no easier to see than is a nail clipping on mottled lino.

I turned over a coin and wished. The sky turned romantically pink. Then I readied the anchor by tilting it on its bow roller, pushing a toggle through the loop of the lanyard and securing the trip-line to a stanchion. By the time I had finished doing this the sky colours had smudged and daylight was ebbing fast. Now the sky was tarnished silver, the sea was pewter and ahead of me Placentia Cay was suddenly as dark as iron.

Before the light had quite gone, *Kylie* ghosted through the narrow channel between the cay and the mainland. Couples, most of them apparently headless, walked the strand to starboard, their tee-shirts glowing white.

Clear of the narrows, I luffed up into the wind and the boat slowed. I leaned against the boom, backing the mainsail. When *Kylie* was making sternway I pulled the trip-line, and the anchor chain clattered over the bows.

In the lamplight on the strand, a man and woman were kissing.

I rowed ashore and entered the lamplight. At a waterside table the couple had stopped kissing and were eating melon. A fair-haired girl behind the bar turned away from a dark-haired young man and clicked her tongue. She had blue eyes, a retroussé nose and a square jaw.

'Hi!' she said: 'What'll it be?'

'Tequila sunrise, please,' I said.

Ten feet away, the dark-haired young man pushed a slim blue box along the counter towards the girl.

The girl placed my drink before me and I handed her a ten-dollar note. On the way to the till she looked towards the young man and mouthed 'No'.

'Shirlene . . .!' said the man.

The girl turned her body away from him and pressed keys. The till whirred open. The man picked up the dark blue box and left.

Two tequilas later, she said: 'He made out they were real diamonds from Cartier's, but how'd a steward on a ten-cent charter boat get real diamonds? They weren't genuine, they were paste. He must've gotten them by mail order from Sears.'

The couple had finished their melon and were kissing again.

'It's the right time of year for it, though,' I said.

'What?'

'February is the right month for romance,' I said.

'Not for me and him it isn't; the season still has two months to run,' she said, going off to take orders.

I carried my drink to a table and sat down. The couple had stopped kissing and were holding hands.

I angled my chair away and stared into the water.

February 14th was not only a date for making love-matches: it also brought partings. I had never forgotten the month, the day or the hour she died, but since leaving England I had found it hard to remember the year. When the black limousines had come to our door, had Pip been 43 years old, or was it 42 . . .?

The couple laughed. In a corner of my eye I saw them kissing again and so I downed my drink and left.

Rowing back to *Kylie*, I passed close to a white-hulled ketch. Her cabin lights were dim but two figures were sitting on the coachroof.

'Peter!' called Nigel. 'Come aboard!'

'No, thanks,' I said. 'Not tonight, thanks.'

On long voyages a navigator watches time closely but simultaneously he neglects it [said my notebook before sleep came]. *The instant the sun kisses the horizon the man stops the watch. He bothers greatly about minutes and seconds but not about the years. Do years matter? On February 14 we remember that it is Valentine's Day but we don't remember the year he died. Even so, we kiss.*

216

We remained two days at or near Placentia. *Nada* took *Kylie*'s battery aboard and re-charged it while motoring to Big Creek and back. Meanwhile, I cleaned charts, counted my Tomsps and took stock.

Kylie was now 35 miles from the Guatemalan frontier and only 50 from Livingston, the port at the entrance to the Rio Dulce. Here, mountains as high as Snowdon and Ben Nevis were looming in the west. At sunset I raised my head above the coaming and saw the Cockscomb Range was edged with blood, and later, below decks, I ate cheese.

That night rain fell, beating like jungle drums on the coachroof, and I dreamt that men were chasing me with machetes.

Going farther south might plunge me into worse nightmares, for the rainfall was heavier and the mountains were bigger. The Cockscomb Range would give way to the higher peaks of Guatemala, and the Rio Dulce flowed through steeper country than did the Great Sittee. Instead of entering the sea through mangroved swampland, the Rio Dulce came out through a deep gorge.

In the bar at lunchtime, a man in a bush hat had said that going up the Rio Dulce was like putting your head into a dark tunnel which was crawling with snakes.

Although his voice had a jokey Australian twang and I had not eaten more cheese, that night I swallowed two Temazepams.

But Nigel and Terrie were keen to see the Rio Dulce. They planned to enter Guatemala from Punta Gorda, the last town in Belize before the frontier. After clearing into Livingston they would motor-sail up-river, leave *Nada* at a marina and explore the interior by bus. They hinted that I might go with them if I wished. I said that doing the boaty bits would be nice, but I was in two minds about doing the country by bus. I liked the idea of reclining in cockpits and watching the jungle go by, but bus journeys were usually a pain in the backside. I always ended up sitting on a hard seat next to either a fat woman who was feeding a baby and simultaneously nursing a chicken, or an old man with a gammy leg. However, I'd think about it; I'd see how the river trip went.

I reconnected the battery and set off south from Placentia. On the first day I was up at 5.30, had weighed by 7, and *Kylie* was making way soon afterwards, wearing a full main and large genoa.

Veined by suds from Big Creek, the sea was the colour of tombstone marble.

Between 9.30 and noon I changed headsails twice: firstly swapping

217

the genoa for the ghoster, and later, in a breeze off Monkey River, changing back to the genoa again, but in nine hours of broiling heat I worked south only as far as Moho Cays, eight miles short of Punta Gorda.

Next day, work started earlier and the sailing was better. I weighed at 6.36, was anchored off Punta Gorda soon after 9, had pumped up the dinghy and rowed ashore by 9.40, was back aboard at one o'clock with bread, fruit and vegetables, and by 1.15 had again hauled up, hand-over-hand, for the second time that day, 72 pounds of chain and 25 pounds of anchor.

I set the ghoster, steered 079° to follow *Nada*, spread the cockpit awning and sat under it to cool off. I did not stay cool for long. The wind, which until then had been south-easterly, at three o'clock backed north-east, making the ghoster unusable on the course I wanted to sail. I handed the ghoster, de-bagged and set the genoa, bagged the ghoster, stowed it in the forepeak, and in the following forty minutes tacked three times to clear shoals. Between plotting compass bearings, I adjusted the luffs, feet and leeches of the sails, tightened the kicking-strap, and kept one eye on the wave-forms to windward and the other on the colour of the water dead ahead. As a result of all these very ordinary shipboard activities, twenty-four minutes after sunset I was able to anchor – not without misgivings – in the lee of one of the Snake Cays. *On paper at least*, mused my notebook, *I am spending the night among serpents.*

I made a mug of tea but fell asleep before I could drink it.

The following day went badly. We needed to survey the banks lying between the Snake Cays and the mainland. Nigel had found differences between the actual positions of the cays and banks and their positions as shown on the chart, and he wanted to double-check.

After a lunch of salami aboard *Nada*, we set off again. Circumnavigating South Snake, Middle Snake and East Snake raised no problems: the water there was clear and deep but, heading back westward towards the mainland, we found the water becoming greener, muddier and shallower.

Our troubles began with *Nada* going aground.

Standing two miles north of me, bearing east-north-east and supposedly in deep water, at four o'clock she abruptly leaned to windward. I headed towards her to offer help, but twenty minutes later, with the east point of Stuart Cay bearing 024°, *Kylie* ran aground too.

I let go the sheets and went below to start the engine. Battery power being still as precious as ever, I slotted the handle onto the flywheel spindle and cranked the engine. Three swings started it. I replaced the engine cover, returned to the cockpit, hardened sheets and went full astern for three minutes, but *Kylie* showed no signs of budging. I eased the sheets, took up on the topping lift and handed sail.

Nada, I noticed, was still aground.

Unlashing the dinghy took three minutes; inflating it took five; launching, two. By the time I had poled around to find deeper water, half an hour had gone and the sun was low. In ninety minutes it would be dark.

I unlashed the Danforth and lowered it into the dinghy, together with two fathoms of chain and thirty of rope. Rowing out the anchor fifty yards on the starboard bow to where the deeper water lay took perhaps four minutes, and returning took only two, but hauling the rope in by hand took longer. By the time I had heaved taut I had to take a breather. I glanced to the north-east. *Nada* was now afloat, heading towards me, her hull tinged pink by the sun's afterglow. The sea and sky, though, were darkening: soon *Nada*'s hull would be a smoky grey.

I ran the engine full ahead, at the same time winching on the anchor warp. *Nada* crept closer, but *Kylie* did not shift.

I heard *Nada*'s anchor rattle over the bows. Soon Nigel was alongside in his dinghy, bearing a longer warp. Saying hardly a word, we shackled a snatch block to the forestay deckplate (a quarter-inch-thick channel bar), laid the rope in its throat and clicked shut the block. Nigel dinghied back to *Nada*, heaved taut the rope, made it fast to his stern cleats and depressed the power switch of his windlass.

Nada's anchor chain wound in slowly but steadily. When the line between the boats had stretched tight, *Kylie*'s propeller resumed its pushing, and at last she came off the mud.

I stopped the engine, cast off *Nada*'s warp, rowed out and set the main anchor, tidied the sails, bucketed the decks, coiled down the surplus kedge warp, decanted kerosene into the belly of the anchor light, cleaned its glass with paper, trimmed and lighted the wick, and hung the light in the rigging.

'*This is Ray-dee-oh Bel-ee-ze*,' cried a Walkman, '*bringing you the news across the nation!*'

Across the nation's coastal water, *Nada*'s anchor light winked.

Hurrying again – for it was already late in the day – *Kylie* turned her stern on the saddleback of Gorda Hill and headed a few degrees east of south for Livingston. The wind was free, the air clear, the breeze firm. Even more delightfully, no mudbanks or coral lay ahead: for 16 miles the course would be free of underwater dangers. I set the wind-vane, stretched the cockpit awning and played 'Bobby McGhee' on my mouth organ, but only briefly. The ballad's burden fitted neither the climate nor my mood. 'Bobby McGhee' was about about hitching lifts on rainy days and the sadness of losing your girl. It was somebody else's tune, not mine. I was sailing into Caribbean sunshine, not thumbing my way north from Baton Rouge . . . Louisiana had become a distant country; soon Belize would be too.

I took bearings and plotted them: Guatemala ('area 42,353 sq. mi.; max. alt. 13,182 ft.') was drawing closer, though only up-ended chunks of it were presently visible. They were offcuts of mountains, mostly with their heads muffled by clouds. Some were sitting on low green cushions and hunching their shoulders against the rain. Despite the impending rain and the stories about snakes, Guatemala looked attractive.

But (you will have come across this rhetorical device already) so what? It wasn't so much *where* you went, it was *how* you went that mattered. Certainly, it was mattering now. The wind was NE 4; the barometer was 985 and falling, but Livingston (or Mandeville or Xkalak or wherever) lay only nine miles ahead, the sun was shining on me, and *Kylie* was making five knots; but most importantly of all she was doing it (at last we come to the point) under *sail*.

No doubt about it, she *was* going well . . . Not as fast as some other boats, perhaps, but fast enough for me; and safely, too.

Ahead, *Nada* had folded one of her wings and was about to buzz – rather lopsidedly – into a cleft in the mountains.

I picked up the binoculars, trying to spot the landfall buoy before sunset.

I did not find it.

The wind fell away, *Kylie*'s speed slipped back from five knots to three, and by the time she got to the river bar off Livingston the shore lights were coming on.

Flowing against the wind, the Rio Dulce entrance was a popple of breakers. The crests were no more than three feet high but their whiteness masked the sea buoy, which was only about six feet tall and was also mainly white.

The dead-straight entrance channel is a mile long and has a maximum six-foot depth but it is relatively narrow. Stray a few yards either side of the channel, and boats of *Nada*'s draught will be bumping hard on sand or shale. Boats of lesser draught will stay afloat for a few more yards, but not many. To enter Livingston safely – indeed, to enter it at all – the prudent mariner is advised to position himself 200 yards to starboard of the sea buoy and then go steadily ahead, keeping a steep bluff lined up with a low-lying edge of the river bank.

At a quarter to six in the evening, with all the hills and mountains now curtained by cloud, I backed the jib and lay hove-to. I could see neither the buoy nor the low-lying bank, but the higher land was offering me a multitude of steep declivities. The trouble was, any three of them could have been called bluffs.

I scratched my head. This was worse than perming the pools.

'Just call me Stanley, please,' sighed I to a hesitant seagull; 'I'm going in.'

I put the helm to windward and trimmed sheets.

Soon afterwards, Stanley found Livingston.

'You came across the bar three hundred yards west of the buoy,' said Nigel.

'I followed a fishing boat in.'

'But it was drawing only three feet! You should have called me on your radio; I could've talked you into the deeper water.'

'Yes, I should've. Didn't think about it. Seldom do.'

'How much water had you?'

'Four-six, then five. She didn't bump once.'

'Hum! You were lucky; if the wind had been coming off the land, there would've been less water.'

'Yes.'

We had cleared immigration and customs and were setting off up-river. Nigel had unrolled his foresail and *Nada* was stemming the current. I heaved short the anchor, set the mainsail, weighed, and followed him.

Stealthily we entered the gorge. Few other people were in sight. A breeze was riffling the leaves but the air seemed still and reverential. Walls soared narrowly towards heaven and the light slanted down as if from high windows. It was as though we were creeping into a cathedral before the start of a service. Vegetation bannered the walls and was emblazoned here and there by white birds. Creepers roped the banners in case the wind lifted them, and lianas hung like ropes from the sky. I felt that if I pulled them, bells would toll.

221

LIVINGSTON AND THE RIO DULCE BAR

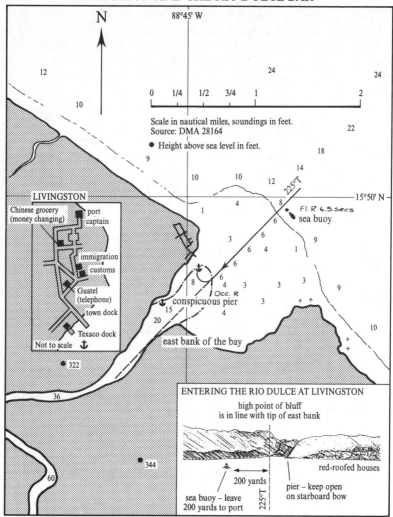

Livingston and the Rio Dulce Bar. *Though based on a chart published by the US Defense Mapping Agency, the details on this chart are by Nigel Calder and the sketch is by Terrie. Soundings of six feet and less were taken with the boathook from Nada's dinghy. The scrawls near the sea buoy and the conspicuous pier are my additions, describing their light-characteristics.*

Ahead of us cormorants took off, whirring like clocks. Behind them, pelicans lumbered steadily forward, their faces as blank as those of lorry drivers on long trips.

We overtook a dugout canoe being paddled by an Indian man and carrying a woman and a dog. The canoe was no different from the ones which Columbus had described five centuries previously, but when we lifted our cameras the Mayan faces turned away in case we stole their spirits.

The river opened out and the walls fell back, allowing us to anchor in the lee of an island. For a while I breathed more freely, but that night rain fell in torrents and imprisoned me below deck.

Before dawn the rain lessened. Prompted by a slight discomfort, I pulled aside my sheet, went on deck, stood against the guardrail and waited . . .

The rain was cold, but still I waited . . .

Having calmly (so my children say) departed from Suffolk, where the average annual rainfall is 26 inches, and arrived, still apparently hale and hearty, nearly six years and 20,000 sea-miles later at a coast where five times as much water fell on to people's heads, ran down their legs, and – if they were males who were standing around naked like I was – trickled off a shorter member, why was I angry? And why, having never before studied systematically the comings and goings – let alone the whys and wherefores – of water, was I now suddenly engrossed in its movements?

Thoughts of water plopping from tendrils, filtering through crannies sloshing down gullets, gurgling down tubes, coursing through chasms before gushing forth urgently, copiously, unstintedly and – were any of it my own – ecstatically, were filling my mind to overflowing.

Even so, I could not pee.

'Bugger!' I cried loudly, (for *that* word had at least got Bognor going), but nothing happened.

Still with only rainwater coming from it, I rushed ashore, intermittently holding my dick.

The journey was long, the stops many. Though offered by the jugful, lemonade was refused.

The doctor examined me in a wholly professional manner but his utterances seemed childish: a little fellow down below was playing up, but these pink sweeties would send him to beddy-byes, while these white ones flushed his chimbleys . . .

Fishing the Rio Duke

'Sooner rather than later,' he added while receipting the bill, 'you will need a re-section.'

Back at a marina, I double-checked *Kylie*'s seacocks and paid two month's berthage in advance.

'England in March will be freezing, won't it?'

'Send me a card with a picture of Southwold . . .'

'. . . bring me back a *bifurcated* bracket, not a plain one. It's 00173–299–030/4 in the catalog . . .'

'Have a good flight, old fart! Your plane leaves at nine . . .'

'We're *definitely* doing the Bay Islands in April if Hubert takes his finger out and fixes the fridge . . .'

However, seconds before the bus left, Pippin cried 'Peeder!' and kissed me.

I hoped it was a sailor's farewell, not a last goodbye.

Children are but children, but they know things.

Acknowledgements

All sailors owe thanks to those who have helped them on their way, but lone sailors who are also writers owe more thanks than most. Some of the people who assisted me have already been named, but I wish additionally to thank:

Don and Ginger Miller, who first welcomed me to Louisiana, and Norman and Pauline Frisbie, who beat me there at Scrabble. David Wright spent many hours on the drawings, Russell Bower and John Leach made helpful comments about the manuscript, and Peter Coles and his colleagues at Waterline Books piloted it into print.

H. L. Cooper of the Trinity House Lighthouse Service sent me useful information about Sombrero; William Wilson let me browse through the archives of Imray, Laurie, Norie and Wilson Ltd.; and Brian Duncan Thynne helped me to do the same at the National Maritime Museum. At the Johnson Space Center in Houston Lucy Lytwynsky and Steve Sokol researched Hurricane Hugo; and in Scotland Charles Wheeler fleshed out my lean knowledge of the Turks and Caicos Islands.

They gave me much time and care, and I am very grateful.

Appendix 1
Kylie

Kylie is a Contessa 26 class sloop, designed by David Sadler. The glassfibre hull and deck were built by Jeremy Rogers at Lymington in 1971, with additional stringers and layers of glassfibre as specified by her first owner, R. Playdon. Mr Playdon fitted out and equipped *Kylie* as a long-distance cruiser, with the intention of sailing to Australia. Her layout, equipment and scantlings differ from the normal production model in several notable respects. The Proctor E50 mast is fitted with mast-steps, and parallel twin forestays lead from a triangular plate at the masthead to a stainless steel channel-bar in the bows. The blade of the teak rudder, which hangs on one-inch diameter bronze pintles, is strengthened by six stainless steel rods. For at least 80 per cent of her passage-making, she is steered not by me but by a very reliable Quartermaster wind-vane steering gear.

The cockpit is reduced in its volume by a wooden engine-cover, or bridge deck, at its forward end, but it remains comfortable. Above the bridge deck, Inch-thick washboards behind stainless steel flanges protect the companionway from the weather. Instead of the usual six winches on standard Contessas, *Kylie* has only three: two in the cockpit and one on the mast.

During the period covered by this book, the boat was carrying the following ground tackle:

> 35-pound Bruce anchor attached to 10 fathoms of ⁵⁄₁₆-inch chain and 30 fathoms of eight-plait nylon warp
>
> 25-pound CQR anchor, 9 fathoms ⁵⁄₁₆-inch chain and 25 fathoms eight-plait nylon warp
>
> 12-pound Danforth anchor, 2½ fathoms ¼-inch chain and 30 fathoms braidline
>
> 10-pound fisherman anchor, 2½ fathoms ⁵⁄₁₆-inch chain
>
> 10-pound folding grapnel anchor, 2½ fathoms ¼-inch chain
>
> 50 fathoms braidline on a reel and two 12-fathom lengths of three-strand polyester for use with any anchor.

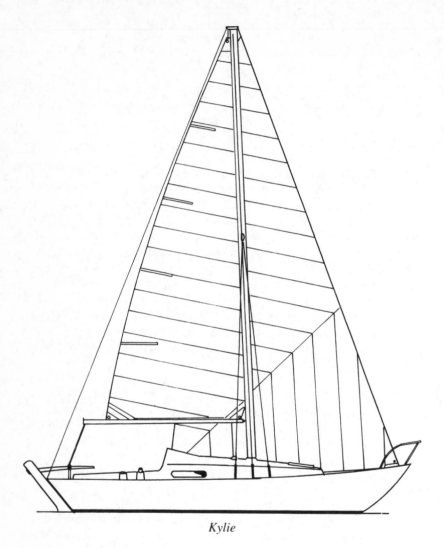

Kylie

Length Overall: 25 ft 8 in
Length on Waterline: 21 ft
Beam: 7 ft 6 in
Draught: 4 ft — 4 ft 4 in, depending on weight of stores
Displacement: 5,400 — 6,000 lbs
Ballast: 2,300 lbs
Sail Area: 304 sq ft

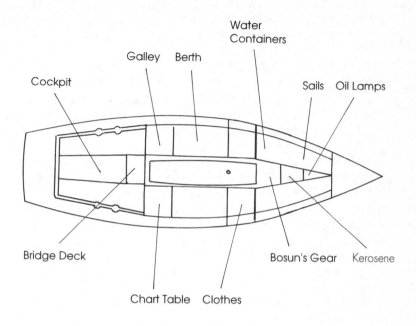

Water
Containers

Galley   Berth

Cockpit   Sails   Oil Lamps

Bridge Deck   Bosun's Gear   Kerosene

Chart Table   Clothes

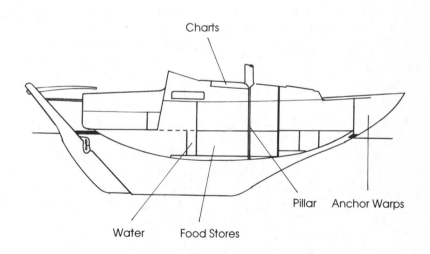

Charts

Pillar   Anchor Warps

Water   Food Stores

Kylie: interior layout

The working foresails are carried on deck in two large, sausage-shaped sailbags attached to the upper guardrail, one on each side forward of the mast. One bag might contain, say, a number one genoa and a storm jib, and in the other would be stowed a number two genoa and a working jib. Apart from the mainsail, which was never removed from the mainboom except when we appeared to be in the path of a tornado off Charleston, the rest of the sails – a ghoster, a spinnaker, a trysail, and a spare genoa and working jib – were carried below decks in what in other Contessas was the forecabin.

On standard boats the forecabin contains two berths and a sea toilet, but in *Kylie* the space is taken up by sailbags, three 5-gallon water-breakers, two 3-gallon kerosene containers and the many items of bo'sun's stores necessary to be carried on long passages.

The navigation equipment comprises a Bo'sun compass mounted beneath the tiller in the cockpit, a second Plastimo bulkhead compass, a sextant, and – after leaving Mandeville – a Navstar 2000S satnav. A towed, non-electric Walker log measures the distances run through the water, while the depths are measured by either a Seafarer depthsounder or a leadline.

The original two-stroke petrol engine was replaced in 1984 by a second-hand 5 HP diesel motor and two years later by another of the same model. Not entirely because of my own faults of character, all of them have been unreliable. When they worked, *Kylie* could make 5 knots flat out in smooth seas.

Though small, the cabin is very practical and comfortable. To starboard is a chart-table which will accommodate a standard British Admiralty chart folded down its middle, while to port is the galley with its gimballed two-burner Primus stove and its stowage for pans, mugs, plates and so on. The remainder of the cabin is taken up by two full-length berths, beneath which are stowed provisions. Above the foot of each berth is a clothes locker.

Following *Kylie*'s completion in 1971–2, Mr and Mrs Playdon set out in her for Australia. By the time they had reached the West Indies Mrs Playdon was in an advanced stage of pregnancy, and so they sold *Kylie* and continued their travels by air. John Campbell, her new owner, sailed her back to England through a severe storm, during which *Kylie* was pitchpoled (i.e. turned end-over-end) by a mountainous wave. After her arrival in the UK *Kylie* was purchased by Simon Hunter with the intention of competing in the 1976 OSTAR, the *Observer* Singlehanded Transatlantic Race. To obtain the necessary qualifying experience for OSTAR, Simon successfully completed the 1975 AZAB (Azores-and-Back) single-handed race.

Simon's experience in the OSTAR race itself was less happy. He attempted to sail to New York by the Southern Route, but many weeks of unusually light weather compelled him to abandon the race north of Bermuda, and not until his 73rd day at sea was he able to make port in the Azores.

After a brief period with a fourth owner, *Kylie* came into my possession in April 1977, by which time she had already sailed 30,000 miles.

Appendix 2
Bibliography

BARNETT, Captain E., R.N. *West India Pilot: Barbados to Cuba*, London, 1859

The West India Pilot, Vol. I. London, 1861

CALDER, NIGEL with HANCOCK, PETER *The Cruising Guide to the Northwest Caribbean*. Camden, Maine, USA, 1991

COLERIDGE, H. *Six Months in the West Indies in 1825*. London, 1825

FERMOR, PATRICK LEIGH *The Traveller's Tree*. London, 1950

JENKINS, Commander H. L., O.B.E., R.N., (Ed.) *Ocean Passages for the World*, 3rd Edition. Taunton, 1973

JONES, Commander ALUN, R.N. *West Indies Pilot, Vol. II* 11th edition. Taunton, 1969

JUNG, CARL *The Portable Jung*, Edited by CAMPBELL, J. New York, 1971

MCNEIL, KLARE (Ed.) *Antigua-Barbuda Marine Guide*. Antigua, 1986

POCOCK, TOM *The Young Nelson in The Americas*. London, 1980

PURDY, JOHN *The Colombian Navigator* Vol. II. (4th Edn, by FINDLAY, ALEX, G.). London, 1848

The Colombian Navigator Vol III. 2nd Edn. London, 1839

RAWSON, G. (Ed.) *Nelson's Letters*. London, 1960

STEPHENS, JOHN L. *Incidents of Travel in Central America, Chiapas & Yucatan*. New York, 1841

WINCHESTER, SIMON *Outposts*. London, 1986

Appendix 3
Glossary of Nautical Terms Used in This Book

A1 at Lloyd's: meeting the highest standards.

Abaft: towards the stern of the vessel in relation to some other position, e.g. **abaft the beam**.

Abeam: having a bearing or position at right-angles to the fore-and-aft line of the vessel.

Aboard: in or on a vessel. **Close aboard**: too close for safety

Able Seaman: man able to do all the tasks of a seaman, such as to reef the sails and steer a straight course in all conditions.

Aft: towards the stern.

A-lee: towards the sheltered side, away from the wind.

Aloft: above the deck, overhead.

Anchor: Bruce, CQR (a phoneticization of 'Secure'), **Danforth**, and **fisherman** are types of anchors. A **Luke** anchor is like a fisherman anchor but it dismantles into three pieces instead of two. A **mudhook** is a light, broad-fluked Danforth anchor.

Anti-fouling: paint which inhibits the growth of weed and other marine organisms.

Astern: in a rearward direction. **Full astern** and **slow astern** are, respectively, fast and slow propeller-movements in a rearward direction.

Athwart: transversely across the course or centreline of a vessel.

A-weather: towards the wind.

Awning: cover spread above the hull as protection from sun and rain.

Back, to: (1) to sheet the clew of a sail to windward. (2) to move in an anti-clockwise direction. A wind may back in direction from, say, south to south-east

Backsplice: method of finishing off a rope's end by tucking the strands.

Backstay: wire rope supporting the mast from aft.

Baggy-wrinkle: short rope-strands tied to a length of marline, fluffed out and wound around standing rigging to prevent sail chafe.

Barque: three-, four- or five-masted sailing vessel, square-rigged on all masts except the mizzen, which is fore-and-aft rigged. (See **Rig**).

Barratry: thievery and swindles perpetrated by ship's crews aboard their own vessels to defraud the owners and insurers.

Battle-cruiser: fast but lightly armoured battleship.

Beam: widest transverse dimension of a ship. A **beamy** vessel has proportionally greater width than others of similar length.

Bearing: angle in degrees or compass points between the direction of the True or Magnetic North Pole and the direction of an object. A **rising bearing** is taken as the object appears above the horizon.

Beat, to: to sail to windward in a series of zig-zag courses, with the wind on alternate bows.

Bells: sound signals marking the passage of time at sea, supposedly rung every half hour.

Below: below deck, in the cabin.

Bend: knot fastening one rope to another, a sheet to an eye, a line to a spar, etc. **To bend on** is to make such a knot.

Berth: (1) sleeping-place aboard; (2) place where ship may lie; also berthage.

Bilge: space beneath cabin sole. The **turn of the bilge** is the curve of the hull which forms the sides of this space.

Binnacle: housing for the compass.

Block: pulley with one or more sheaves. A **snatch-block** has a hinged side for the easier putting-in or release of the rope.

Bluewater: deepwater, oceanic, long-distance.

Boom or **mainboom**: horizontal spar for extending the foot of the mainsail.

Boot-topping: band of hull paint immediately above the waterline.

Bo'sun: person in charge of deck-working crew, taking orders from ship's officers.

Bottlescrew: screw for adjusting tension of standing rigging.

Bow or **bows**: forepart of a ship's hull.

Bowline: much-used sailor's knot which neither slips nor jams.

Bow roller: sheave mounted in the bows to accommodate the run of the anchor cable.

Bowsprit: spar projecting beyond bows, on which a foresail is set.

Box the compass, to: to know and be able to recite the 32 points (and their sub-divisions) of the compass both clockwise and backwards.

Break out, to: (of an anchor) to break free of the seabed.

Breaker: (1) small keg or barrel to hold fresh water. In *Kylie* a 5-gallon plastic container. (2) breaking wave.

Bridge: raised transverse structure on powered vessels, housing the main navigation stations, including principally the **wheelhouse**. The **flying bridge** on oil-tankers is a fore-and-aft walkway.

Bring up, to: to come to rest at anchor. A vessel may **bring up with** such-and-such a charted feature bearing so many degrees, on so many fathoms of chain, in whatever-it-is fathoms of water, at any old hour, and so on, until the captain's scribe runs out of prepositions.

Broach: (More properly: **to broach-to**). The tendency for the ship's head to fly up into the wind. In strong following winds this can cause the vessel to come broadside on to dangerous seas and result in a knockdown.

Buoy: floating sea-mark.

Burgee: broad, tapering, swallow-tailed flag.

Cable: (1) unit of measurement: 600 feet (approx, one-tenth of a nautical mile). (2) chain or rope attached to anchor. **To shorten cable** is to haul inboard some of the cable prior to weighing anchor.

Calenture: tropical disease affecting sailors. Sufferers become delirious and, believing the sea to be green fields, wish to leap into it.

Capping: strip of wood running along top of vessel's sides. In *Kylie*, two inches above the deck.

Cap shroud: transverse mast-support, running from each sidedeck to the mast-top, made of wire.

Capstan: cylindrical barrel revolving on vertical axis, used for hauling heavy weights.

Careen, to: to heave a ship right down onto its side so as to clean the hull or repair it. **Careenage**: steep, sandy beach where this is done.

Carry way, to: (See **Way**).

Cat o' nine tails: nine-tailed whip.

Centreboarder: relatively shallow-draught vessel having a pivoted board or plate on its centreline. When lowered, the board increases the lateral resistance of the hull, enabling the vessel to point better to windward.

Chainplate: 'V'-shaped steel deck-fitting to which shroud or stay is attached.

Chart: nautical map.

Cleat: fitting on which halyards, sheets, etc, may be secured.

Clew: lower rear corner of fore-and-aft sail.

Close hauled: sailing as nearly as possible into the wind (i.e. angling about 45 degrees from its direction).

Coachroof: roof of the cabin.

Coaming: sides of hatch, cabin or cockpit which project above the deck.

Cockpit: well near the stern to accommodate the helmsman and other crew.

Companionway: opening from cabin to cockpit.

Compass: The needle of the magnetic compass points to the North Magnetic Pole; the gyroscopic compass points to True North.

Constructive total loss: (An insurance term) the cost of repair will exceed the vessel's value, so the insurance payment is the smaller, latter amount.

Course: direction in which a vessel is proceeding, measured in degrees or compass-points from True North, Magnetic North, or Compass North.

Crown: part of anchor where the arms join the shank.

Cutter: single-masted vessel having a mainsail and two foresails.

Davit: small shipboard crane for lifting dinghies or lifeboats.

Day: A ship's day extends from one noon to the next.

Day's run: distance travelled from noon to noon.

Dead reckoning position: arithmetical account of ship's position, using only the course steered and the log-distance, and making no allowance for currents, tidal streams and the wind.

Deckhead: underside of deck, equivalent to a ceiling in a room.

Deckplate: steel eye-plate bolted to the deck, to which blocks and other equipment may be attached by shackles.

Depthsounder: electronic instrument for measuring the depth of water.

Derrick: ship's crane for handling cargo.

Dinghy: small open boat, driven by outboard motor, oars or sail. *Kylie*'s dinghy is a rubber doughnut inflated by a foot pump.

Dodger: canvas screen attached to guardrails in way of the cockpit to protect crew from the weather.

Donkeyman: petty officer with engine-room duties.

Draught: depth of water a vessel **draws**, i.e. the depth at which she becomes afloat; the distance from the waterline to the keel.

Draw, to let: to adjust the sheets until the sail fills with wind and drives the vessel forward.

Drift: (See **Set and Drift**).

Ease, to: to slacken.

Fairlead: metal fitting at bow or stern to lead ropes to their deck cleats.

Fake down, to: to coil down a rope or wire so that it will run out without tangles or kinks.

Fathom: unit of measurement (6 feet or 1.8256 metres), now regrettably obsolete, for measuring depths of water or lengths of rope. For practical and philosophical reasons, still used aboard *Kylie*.

Fix: determination of vessel's geographical position by reference to charted features or celestial objects, including man-made satellites. A running fix is a coastwise construct made with reference to a single charted feature.

Fluke: pointed part of anchor which digs into the seabed.

Foc'sle: under-deck space in the bows, traditionally the accommodation for deckhands.

Folkboat: popular class of cruiser-racer designed in late 1930s. The design of *Kylie*'s Contessa 26 class is closely related.

Foot: lower edge of sail.

Fore-and-Aft: from head to stern, the whole length of the vessel. A **fore-and-aft** rig such as *Kylie*'s is one in which the leading edges of the principal sails are set on the centreline. (See **Rig**).

Foredeck: deck forward of the mast.

Foremast: in vessels with masts of similar height, the one nearest the front.

Forepeak: under-deck compartment in bows of the vessel.

Foresail: any sail forward of the mast.

Forestay: wire rope running from the upper part of the mast to a deckplate in the bows. Acts with backstays to brace the mast in a fore-and-aft direction, and foresails are hanked onto it.

Frigate: fast, medium-sized warships, known in Nelson's day as 'the eyes of the fleet'.

Frigate bird: large, dark, tropical bird, which obtains much of its food by raiding other birds and causing them to disgorge.

Galley: ship's kitchen.

Gather way, to: (See **Way**).

Genoa: large foresail, the clew of which overlaps the mainsail. *Kylie* carries two genoas, number one being the larger.

Ghoster: very large, light-weather foresail.

Gimbal, to: to suspend something so that it stays horizontal.

Gooseneck: pivoting joint connecting the boom to the mast.

Grapnel: small, four-pronged anchor.

Great Circle: any circle (e.g. the equator) which girdles the earth and has its centre in the middle of the earth. The shortest distance between two ports will be the arc of the Great Circle on which the ports lie.

Guardrail: in *Kylie*, a knee-high rope running fore-and-aft along each side of the boat to prevent people falling overboard.

Gulf Stream: wide oceanic river of warm water which emerges from the Gulf of Mexico and flows northward up the Atlantic coast of Florida before fanning out and dispersing in the North Atlantic.

Gybe, to: to cause the mainsail to swing across the stern by allowing the wind to catch the sail on the opposite side. The stronger is the wind, the more necessary is it that the gybe shall be carefully controlled, otherwise much damage may occur.

Halyard: line which raises or lowers a sail.

Hammock: derived from the Carib *hamorca*, a rope bed which was slung between trees. *Kylie*'s smaller hammocks accommodate bread, fruit and vegetables.

Hand: (1) member of crew; (2) **to hand a sail** is to take it down.

Hand-lead: (See **Lead**).

Hank: clip attaching the luff of a foresail to the forestay.

Hatch: opening in the deck. *Kylie* has a **forehatch** and an **after-hatch**.

Haul-out: the transporting of a boat in a cradle to a shoreside place for repair or cleaning.

Heads: ship's lavatory.

Heave-to, to: to set the sails and rudder so that the vessel lies almost stationary.

Helm: alternative term for wheel or tiller, used for steering the vessel. To up-helm is to move the tiller in the opposite direction to the wind.

Hitch, to: to fasten a rope to an object such as a rail or spar.

Horse: transverse steel bar abaft the cockpit, to which the sheet of the mainsail is attached.

241

Hull: body of a vessel.

Inboard: towards the centreline of the vessel.

Index error: instrumental error caused by a mirror of the sextant not being perpendicular to the plane of the instrument.

Jib: triangular headsail set on the forestay. *Kylie* carries a **working jib** and a smaller, heavier **storm jib**.

Kedge: secondary, smaller anchor, often used for hauling a vessel off a bank after she has grounded.

Keel: lowest length of the hull.

Ketch: two-masted, fore-and-aft rigged vessel, having the after (or mizzen) mast mounted forward of the sternpost. A **double-ended ketch** is one which has a bow and stern of similar pointed shape.

Kicking-strap: tether attached to underside of mainboom so as to flatten the sail flat when the boom swings outboard.

Knockdown: action of a vessel being rolled 90° on to her side by wind and waves.

Knot: speed of one nautical mile (generally taken as 6080 feet) per hour.

Lanyard: short line.

Lead, Hand-lead or **Lead-line**: lead weight attached to 20-fathom line, used for discovering the depth of water.

League: ancient measurement of distance. It varied from country to country, but is generally taken as being 3 nautical miles.

Lee: side of the ship which is away from the wind. But although a vessel which is **in the lee of the land** is sheltered from the wind, a vessel which is being blown onto **a lee shore** is in great danger.

Leech: rear edge of triangular sail.

Lee-cloth: canvas side-piece attached to a sleeping berth and braced to the deckhead by lanyards to prevent the occupant from being thrown out by the vessel's motion.

Leeward: in a down-wind direction.

Leeway: distance a vessel is pushed sideways from her intended course by wind or tide.

Log: (1) instrument (sometimes referred to as **Walker's log** or **patent log**) for measuring the distance a vessel has progressed through the water. In *Kylie* it comprises a 'clock', to which is attached a **rotator** towed astern on a **logline**. (2) short for **logbook**.

Longboat: large boat carried aboard sailing vessels of the 18th and 19th centuries.

Loom: (1) inboard part of an oar; (2) vague first appearance of land, or of light from a light-station.

Low Water: lowest point to which a tide falls; the time at which this happens.

Luff: leading edge of triangular sail. **To luff up** is to bring the vessel's head to a lesser angle to the wind.

Mainsail or **Main**: principal sail. In a sloop such as *Kylie*, the sail on the after side of the mast. A **full main** is an unreefed mainsail.

Marcq St Hilaire: French naval officer who introduced a method of fixing a vessel's position by constructing intercepting lines derived from astronomical observations.

Marline: light line.

Mate: officer in merchant navy. The average mid-20th-century merchant ship carried three mates.

Messmate: companion who eats at the same table.

Mice the Splainbrace: Spoonerism of **Splice the Mainbrace** (*q.v.*).

Monkey island: deck above the wheelhouse on which was mounted the standard (principal) magnetic compass.

Mile: a nautical mile is the distance subtended by one minute of latitude at the earth's centre, generally taken as 6080 feet (1852 metres).

Moor, to: to lie a vessel securely alongside a quay, or between buoys or piles, or attached to anchors fore and aft.

Morse, to: dot-and-dash method of communication.

Navel pipe: deck pipe through which anchor cable emerges from its stowage place below decks.

Navigation light: under sail in *Kylie*, a tricolour (red, green and white) electric light at the masthead, or a 200-candlepower paraffin lantern hung in the backstays.

Nicholson 30: 30-ft cruiser-racer designed by Charles Nicholson.

Paddle: steering paddle of the 'Quartermaster' wind-vane steering gear.

Painter: line for securing small boat to its parent boat or to the shore.

Papers: official documents stating the dimensions, origin, ownership, flag, etc., of a vessel.

Parcel, to: to bind canvas or similar material round a rope to prevent chafe or to make it watertight.

Pawls: pivoting metal wedges which engage with the teeth of a winch.

Pennant: triangular flag.

Pilot: short for **pilot book**.

Pilotage: art of coastal navigation, used particularly when land and underwater dangers are close by.

Pitch, to: to see-saw in the waves.

Pitchpole, to: to be rolled end-over-end by a wave.

Pitpan: flat-bottomed canoe.

Plot, to: to set down (usually in pencil) on a chart.

Point: division of the compass card, amounting to $11\frac{1}{4}°$. Relative bearings or directions may be given using either points or degrees, as in, for example: **four points (45°)** to the wind, or **two points (22½°)** on the starboard bow. The compass card has 32 points, each of which may be sub-divided further as in, for example; **north-east ¾ east, north-east by east**, and **north by west**.

Point, to: generally, to sail close to the wind.

Pole: spar to extend the foresail clew outboard.

Port: left-hand side of vessel as viewed when facing forward.

Position: geographical location. A **position line** is commonly a terrestrial or astronomical bearing on which a vessel must somewhere be lying. A vessel's **Estimated Position** is its **Dead Reckoning Position** (q.v.) after adjustment for the effects of wind, current and tidal streams.

Prop-shaft: propeller shaft.

Pulpit: metal safety-frame in the bows, acting as end-support for the guardrails.

Quarter: afterpart of a vessel on each side of its centreline.

Ratlines: steps formed by rope or by wooden battens lashed between pairs of shrouds to enable crew to ascend the mast.

Reach: point of sailing with the wind abeam. Generally the fastest point of sailing.

Red Duster: colloquial name for the **Red Ensign**, flown by all British-registered vessels which do not have authority to fly the White or Blue ensigns.

Reef, to: to reduce the area of sail exposed to the wind by tying-down one or more of its sections, using the reef points. In *Kylie*, the mainsail has 3 sets of reef points, and may be **single-reefed**, **double-reefed** or **deep-reefed**. As the wind decreases, the reefs are **shaken out**.

Reeve, to: to pass the end of a rope through a block, a sheave or an eye.

Rig: general term, referring to different arrangements of masts and sails, as in, for example: **square rig, fore-and-aft rig, sloop rig**, etc.
The sails of a square-rigged vessel such as a barque are set transversely.

Rigger: person who makes and services a vessel's rigging.

Rigging: wire ropes supporting the mast (**standing rigging**), and ropes and lines for setting and trimming the sails (**running rigging**).

Right-of-Way Rules: International Regulations for the Prevention of Collisions at Sea, frequently memorised in verse form.

Rotator: component of the **Log** (q.v.). Shaped like a pointed torpedo and having angled fins to make it revolve when towed through the water.

Round Turn: whole turn made around an object using a line or rope.

Rudder stock: part of the rudder between the blade and the head.

Rummage, to: to search for smuggled goods.

Run down, to: to collide end-on with another vessel and overwhelm it.

Sail: **To make sail** is to set and trim the sails. A vessel is **under sail** when her sails are drawing and she is in motion, and **under all plain sail** when she is wearing her standard 'working' rig, i.e. not the spinnaker, ghoster, etc.

Sail car: nylon slide attached to the luff of the mainsail and running up and down a track on the afterside of the mast.

Salute: nautical salutes include the dipping of ensigns and the firing of guns. In the 18th century a **nine-gun salute** was fired as a mark of respect to an admiral.

Satnav: navigation system which depends on radio transmissions from space satellites.

Scantlings: dimensions and weight of the components used in building a vessel.

Schooner: two-masted, fore-and-aft rigged vessel, having a mainmast which is the same height as or slightly taller than the foremast.

Scull, to: to drive a boat forward by moving an oar from side to side over the stern.

Sea: wave produced by wind in the immediate vicinity.

Seacock: valve in an underwater outlet pipe to stop water from entering.

Self-drainers: large-diameter pipes allowing any water in the cockpit to flow outboard quickly.

Semaphore: system of visual signalling in which the position of the extended arms conveys the letters of the alphabet.

Set and drift: direction and distance a vessel is pushed by a tide or current. An undetected **on-shore set** has caused many a wreck.

Sextant: hand-held navigational instrument for measuring angles, most commonly the angle between the sun or a star and the horizon, to obtain a **sun-sight** or a **star-sight**.

Sheave: revolving wheel which accommodates a rope running through a block or spar.

Sheepshank: knot used for temporarily shortening a rope.

Sheerstrake: upper plank of a wooden-hulled vessel and, by inference, the same section of the hull in a vessel made of other materials.

Sheet: line attached to the clew of a sail for trimming the sail to the wind. This is done by **sheeting in, hardening the sheet** or **easing the sheet**.

Shroud: wire rope running from the deck to the upper part of the mast, supporting it in a lateral direction. **Upper shrouds** or **cap shrouds** run to the masthead, and **lower shrouds** to a point about halfway up the mast.

Slack water: period when there is little or no tidal flow, occurring for about twenty minutes each side of high and low water.

Slip, slippage: (1) launchway for boats; (2) percentage difference between the actual distance run through the water and the distance as recorded by the patent log.

Sloop: single-masted vessel having only one foresail.

Soldier's wind: (See **Wind**).

Sole: floor of cabin or cockpit.

Soundings: depths of water as shown on the chart. A vessel is in **soundings** when she is able to measure the depth of water beneath her, or is within the 100-fathom contour.

Spinnaker: three-cornered, full-bellied sail set forward of the mast but not attached to the forestay, used when the apparent wind is from abeam or abaft the beam.

Splice the mainbrace, to: traditional Royal Naval term for serving an additional tot of rum to the crew as a reward or celebration.

Sprayhood: screen at the forward end of the cockpit to protect the crew from foul weather.

Spreader: strut extending sideways from the mast to widen the angle between a shroud and its attachment to the masthead.

Stainless: **316 stainless** is the American classification of a top-quality marine grade of stainless steel.

Stanchion: metal pillar to carry the guardropes, or, when used below decks, to strengthen the hull.

Starboard: right-hand side of a vessel as viewed when facing forward.

Steamship: used loosely to mean any mechanically-propelled vessel.

Stern: rear end of a vessel.

Sternway, making: going backwards.

Stopper: short length of rope used to hold another rope, wire or chain temporarily until it is made fast.

Swage: compressed metal moulding securing the end of a wire back onto itself to form an eye.

Swell: longer than a sea, the result of wind blowing over long distances for hours, a swell may be running in a direction different from the locally-produced seas. If the swells and seas are high and are coming from widely different directions, even large vessels are endangered.

Swinging-circle: circle described by an anchored vessel if she swings through 360°.

Tack, to: (1) to bring a vessel's bows through the wind until it is blowing effectively on the other side of the sail. (2) to work upwind in such a manner, going alternately from **port tack** to **starboard tack**.

Tell-tales: ribbons of light fabric, hung in the rigging as wind-indicators.

Tide: rise and fall in the sea level caused by gravitational forces exerted by the moon and sun. The **tidal stream** is the horizontal movement of the water as it **ebbs** and **floods**. **Tidal range** is the distance between the level of the tide at high water and the next successive low water, or vice versa. **Spring tides** occur twice a lunar month and have the largest tidal range.

Tiller: horizontal bar secured to the rudder head, by which a vessel is steered.

Toggle: wooden pin passed though a loop of rope and thereby held in position.

Topping lift: rope supporting outer end of the mainboom.

Trade wind: (See **Wind**).

Trinity House: guild of mariners established by Henry VIII in 1517. Since Elizabethan times the Elder Brethren have been responsible for English and Welsh (and latterly some overseas) buoys and light-stations, and for the licensing of pilots.

Trip-line: line secured to crown of an anchor to haul it free if it is entrapped by an obstruction or has become too deeply embedded to weigh by normal means.

Veer, to: (1) to move in a clockwise direction. A wind may veer in direction from, say, south-east to south. (2) to pay out rope or chain cable.

Warp: rope attached to an anchor, or rope used to move a vessel around a dock or harbour.

Washboard: stout board which slots into grooves in the companionway to prevent water from entering the cabin.

Watch: division of the ship's day, most commonly of four hours' duration; or the collective term for the on-duty crew during each of these periods. The **middle** or **graveyard watch** runs from midnight till 4 a.m., and the **morning watch** extends from 4 till 8 a.m. **Watch-and-watch** is a regime whereby the watch members are on duty at four-hour intervals, day and night.

Way: generally, the movement of a vessel through the water, as in terms such as **carrying way, under way, getting way on, losing way** and **making way. To give way** is to pull on an oar, and also means, of course, to allow precedence.

Weather: used adjectivally to describe anything lying to windward.

Weatherfax: electronic print-out of a weather map.

Weigh, to: to raise the anchor from the bottom.

Westing: progress westward.

Wheelhouse: main part of the bridge on a merchant ship, housing the helmsman and the officer-of-the-watch.

Whitecap: small breaking wave-crest.

Winch: mechanism comprising a drum mounted on an axle. The drum is turned manually to produce increased power when taking in ropes, most usually sheets and halyards.

Wind: Wind-speed is given either in knots or in units of the Beaufort Scale, force 4 being an average breeze of 11 to 16 knots. The **trade wind** is a broad belt of steady, constant wind straddling latitude 20° on each side of the equator. **To bring the wind forward of the beam** is to alter course until the apparent wind comes from any point ahead. A vessel is sailing **free** when the sheets are eased. A **soldier's wind** is one which is blowing from abeam.

Windlass: winch having a drum to accommodate the anchor chain.

Wind-vane: aboard *Kylie*, the plywood vane which actuates the self-steering gear.

Windward: towards the wind.

Yaw, to: to wander from the desired course through the action of wind and sea.